The St. Croix

MINNESOTA
HISTORICAL
SOCIETY
PRESS

1979

The St. Croix
Midwest Border River

BY JAMES TAYLOR DUNN

Illustrated by Gerald Hazzard

∞ The paper used in this publication meets the minimum requirements of the American National Standard for Information Sciences — Permanence for Printed Library Materials, ANSI Z39.48-1984.

Reprint edition published 1979 by the
MINNESOTA HISTORICAL SOCIETY PRESS

Reprinted by arrangement with Henry Holt and Company,
Incorporated.

Originally published by Holt, Rinehart and Winston as part of the "Rivers of America" series, edited by Carl Carmer, as planned and started by Constance Lindsay Skinner; associate editor Jean Crawford; art editor Ben Feder; designed by Ernst Reichl.

Grateful thanks to the University of Michigan Press for permission to quote a stanza of "Swede from Minnesota" from Earl C. Beck's *Lore of the Lumber Camps;* to the State Historical Society of Wisconsin for permission to reprint part of "John Till, Plaster Doctor of Somerset," by James Taylor Dunn, from the Summer, 1956, issue of *Wisconsin Magazine of History;* and to the Minnesota Historical Society, for permission to quote parts of "Mail for Pioneers" and "The Minnesota State Prison During the Stillwater Era," by James Taylor Dunn, from the June, 1959, and December, 1960, issues of *Minnesota History.*

Printed in the United States of America
Library of Congress Catalog Card Number: 79-52970
International Standard Book Number: 0-87351-141-7
10   9   8   7   6   5   4   3

For my wife,

MÁRIA BACH of Esch-sur-Alzette, Luxembourg

A Word to the Reader—1979

WHAT was the present in 1965, when *The St. Croix* was first published, has with the passage of time become the past. During the intervening years, some statements made when the book was written in 1964 have become outdated. For example, the then widely opposed Northern States Power plant to be built south of Stillwater became a reality in 1968; the preservation of the St. Croix as a wild and scenic river was then only a hoped-for possibility; the story of the Minnesota State Prison needs amplification; the Marine millsite, birthplace of industry in Minnesota, is today protected from commercial exploitation; and new parks on both sides of the border river have been opened and old ones enlarged. Updating the more important changes, adding to the maps, correcting the index and some of the errors are the reasons for this reprint edition and for this introduction.

Among those "River Rats and Village Folk" of 1964, the Lord brothers, Glenn Hankins, Ray Orner, and Reil Prevost can today be met on the streets of Solon Springs. Nick Limpach, now in his mid-90s, continues a part of the local scene. Einar Nelson now lives in Grantsburg, having given up guiding fishermen. The passing years, on the other hand, have removed from their several communities other old-timers mentioned in this book: Harry Baker, Charlie Brown, Stanley Folsom, Frank Goldschmidt, Frank Lucius, Edgar L. Roney, Frank Waterbury — all now rest quietly in shaded local cemeteries. Gone too, from the Stillwater area, are three post-1964 river *aficionados* who so enthusiastically dedicated themselves to the preservation of the St. Croix; the work and friendship of Ray Humphries, Mary Jane Leonard, and Robert A. Uppgren will long be remembered.

Time has also altered certain public attitudes. Words such as "red men," "savages," or "aborigines," prevalent then, are no longer used when referring to the Indians of the North American continent. The second chapter in this book has been retitled "Indians Along the St. Croix." Statistics concerning the Indians are also obsolete. The paragraph on page 22 which gives 1964 facts and figures about Indian settlements in Wisconsin's Polk and Burnett counties requires updating. According to the Bureau of Indian Affairs in Ashland, Wisconsin, there are currently two Indian settlements in Burnett County — one at Sand Lake of 447 acres and another at Danbury consisting of 129 acres. One Indian settlement at Round Lake in Polk County comprises 148 acres. The Bureau had no current census information about these three settlements.

Errors seem to be an inevitable part of any publishing venture. Bergen Evans in *A Dictionary of Contemporary American Usage* distinguished between error and mistake, defining the former as an "unintentional wandering or deviation from accuracy." So, in the words of Abraham Lincoln in an 1862 letter to Horace Greeley, "I shall try to correct errors where shown to be errors."

In addition to a few typographical oversights in the book — Charles E. Mears's name, for example, appeared as "Means," and "Sodabeck," which should be spelled Soderbeck — there are three "unintentional wanderings from accuracy" which were quickly pointed out. The first came from a good friend and colleague, the late Bertha L. Heilbron, a thorough researcher, exacting scholar, and stickler for accuracy. Within a week of publication she called attention to two erroneous statements about the artist Henry Lewis, who traveled the lower reaches of the St. Croix River. On page 72, the beginning of the last paragraph should read: "When Henry Lewis, an American panorama painter, traveled in the St. Croix Valley with some members of David Dale Owen's geological survey in 1847. . . ." Owen himself did not accompany Lewis on this trip. And commencing at the ninth line from the bottom of page 213 the following should be substituted: "The artist and panorama painter, Henry Lewis, recorded that the fishing was excellent when he traveled the St. Croix area during the summer of 1847. Among the fish found in enormous quantities in the 'little lakes' were pike and trout. 'While we were busy sketching,' Lewis wrote, 'our guide caught 185 such fish with a hook in two hours.'" Although he did not ascend the St. Croix on the steamboat *Cora*, he did sketch and later paint the paddle-wheeler as it lay docked at the St. Croix Falls lumber mill landing.

The second "deviation from accuracy," called to my attention by a member of the McKusick family residing in a western state, was a historical error frequently made by many writers. Therefore, in the name of truth, lines seven through ten from the top of page 100 should be corrected to read: "John McKusick, a native of Cornish, Maine, called the place Stillwater after the placid lake at its front door. The new village prospered as a lumbering town."

A third error is the location of the Stillwater cemetery where Gold T. Curtis was buried (page 231). On that August Sunday in 1862 the funeral cortege wound its way not to Fairview Cemetery, which was yet to be established, but north up Fourth Street to Stillwater's original "Burying Ground" then located at the crest of the hill beyond Laurel Street between Second and Fourth.

Ongoing historical research necessitates the updating of another part of this book. In 1964 the Minnesota Historical Society was negotiating to acquire the site of an important North West Company wintering fur post (pages 35 and 281) located on the banks of the Snake River a mile west of present-day Pine City. The property has since been purchased and a replica of the original palisaded fort, based on extensive research and careful archaeological excavations, now monitors the waters of this St. Croix tributary. In 1970, Connor's Fur Post, as it was first named, opened to the public. Since that time, new information has contradicted a previously accepted historical theory — that Thomas Connor, believed to have been a North West employee, kept a journal recording in detail the construction of the original post in 1804. It now seems certain that Connor never learned to write and was probably an *engagé* of the competing XY Company. With this discovery, announced by Douglas A. Birk and Bruce M. White in the issue of *Minnesota History* for Spring, 1979, the next step is to ascertain the journal's real author.

Much recent evidence points to John Sayer, chief of the company's Fond du Lac Department. It is hoped that the true authorship will be determined by expert analysis of handwriting samples. In the meantime, Connor's name has been removed, and the reconstructed wintering post has been rebaptized the North West Company Fur Post. There seasonal guides man the post during summer months, working as the voyageurs of the North West Company did during that long winter on the Snake River in 1804.

Interest in history has effected a happy change in the story of the Marine millsite (page 77). In 1970 a group of Marine residents lobbied effectively to preserve the site, and the following year funds for its purchase were appropriated by the legislature. A final half-acre of land was donated in 1972 by the Alice M. O'Brien Foundation, and today the historic old mill, administered by the Minnesota Historical Society, is in the *National Register of Historic Places*.

The story of Minnesota's State Prison at Stillwater has also kept pace with the permutations of time. By 1978 the inmate population was reduced from the 1,450 men of Warden Wolfer's day to 1,075 (page 127). The more-than-1,000-acre farm, except for 90 acres adjacent to the prison, was given to the Minnesota Department of Natural Resources in 1973 when agriculture was abandoned as an occupation for inmates. Cordage is no longer manufactured; today the principal industries are farm machinery manufacture, school bus repair, and subcontracted work for private businesses.

The present warden, Frank W. Wood, states with some pride that the maximum-security prison, despite its limited 65-year-old architecture, is among the best in the country. And the prison's facilities are being improved. Construction began in 1978 on a high-security structure located just west of the present building. Designed to be energy efficient, the new house of correction is scheduled to open in 1981; it has four levels built into the ground with eight 50-man units opening onto a common yard that is surrounded by a man-made cliff.

Among the many letters received after *The St. Croix* was first published was one which happily offered no corrections; it did, however, provide a description of Ed Hart, the well-known timber cruiser of the upper valley, which is too good to omit. On page 254, under the discussion of the ballad of "Mickey Free," whose exploits were Ed Hart's, the following deserves to be added: "According to one old-timer in the region, Ed was a 'runty little feller with wispy gray whiskers and a soft spoken feller until he grew angry — then he was a little hellion on red wheels.'"

The most far-reaching changes since this volume first appeared have occurred in the preservation and protection of the St. Croix for public use. In 1964 federal study teams were traveling the river's upper region, renewing the hope that, in spite of previous setbacks, the St. Croix and the Namekagon rivers might be placed among America's protected wild rivers. The St. Croix-Namekagon waterway — from the Gordon Dam to Taylors Falls and from Lake Namekagon in Wisconsin's Bayfield County to the junction with the St. Croix — was selected as one of eight original components for "possible preservation in their natural condition" (pages 7 and 281).

From the inception of the project, then United States Senators Walter F. Mondale of Minnesota and Gaylord A. Nelson of Wisconsin, expertly dodging the flak of frequent hostility, were its chief proponents and sponsors in Washington. Thanks to their championship, to the unstinting and selfless work of dedicated midwesterners, and to the helpful co-operation of the Northern States Power Company, owner of large tracts of river frontage, the dream became a reality four years later. On October 2, 1968, President Lyndon B. Johnson signed Senate bill 119 into law. The Wild and Scenic Rivers Act preserved "in free-flowing condition" 200 miles of the upper St. Croix and Namekagon and protected them from uncontrolled development.

Since 1968 much has been accomplished under the administration of the National Park Service toward achieving that protection. Zoning ordinances have been instituted; needed controls and restrictions have been established along the St. Croix National Riverway; and in 1972 the 27-mile stretch of lower river from Taylors Falls south to the northern limits of Stillwater was made a part of the Wild and Scenic Rivers System. The park service has also opened three visitor information ranger stations. Two of these function only during summer months; one is located on the Minnesota side of State Highway 70 near its St. Croix crossing four miles west of

Grantsburg, and the other is near Trego, just northeast of Spooner, Wisconsin. The park service's headquarters, open all year under Superintendent Gustaf P. Hultman, is in St. Croix Falls.

New parks have been established on both sides of the river and old ones have been enlarged. Since 1964 the Minnesota Department of Natural Resources has developed two. Afton State Park, now comprising some 200 acres along the western heights of Lake St. Croix, is presently devoted to skiing and hiking, but there are plans to expand it. The newest addition to the Minnesota parks of the area is Wild River State Park, 6,583 acres located some two miles north of Almelund and bordering a 20-mile stretch above and below the mouth of the Sunrise River. The new park, which opened in 1978, boasts a handsome visitors' center and 25 miles of challenging horseback, snowmobile, hiking, and cross-country ski trails, plus more than 70 semimodern campsites and a primitive group camp.

Three older parks on the Minnesota side of the St. Croix have undergone change since this book first appeared. Thirty miles north of Afton, William O'Brien State Park (page 208) has been enlarged to more than five times its original size and today covers 1,343 acres on both sides of State Highway 95 just north of historic Marine on St. Croix. Farther north in the valley, Banning State Park (page 187) is now a reality. Established by the legislature in 1963, the 5,877-acre area lies along the St. Croix's turbulent tributary, the Kettle River, at Hell's Gate Rapids just north of Sandstone in Minnesota's Pine County. First opened in 1967, the park has grown by 389 acres. Finally, the Minnesota side of the Interstate Park at Taylors Falls (page 207) has been augmented by 131 acres.

Two new parks have appeared on the Wisconsin side of the St. Croix Valley since 1965. Willow River State Park, 2,600 acres northeast of Hudson in St. Croix County, boasts three lakes, deep gorges, high overlooks, and breathtaking panoramas. Opened in 1971, this park provides camping, swimming, boating, hiking, and skiing facilities. Farther south, hugging the shore line of Lake St. Croix across from Minnesota's Afton park, is Kinnickinnic State Park. The 1,000-plus acre facility was established by the Wisconsin legislature in 1972 and is expected to open officially in the early 1980s.

Wisconsin, too, has added land to two of the recreation areas described in these pages. Interstate, Wisconsin's first state park, now contains over 1,200 acres. And the Crex Meadows Wildlife Area (page 208) north of Grantsburg now totals 27,040. The area's present manager, James O. Evrard, recently pointed out that maintaining the Crex in prairie condition is one of the primary objectives and that controlled use of fire has proved the best tool for doing so. He also reported that prairie chickens have been successfully reintroduced into the area.

Not all the changes along the river, however, mitigate on behalf of conservationists and nature lovers. During 1964 what came to be called the Battle of the Power Plant gained national attention (page 150), as a lively new organization, Save Our St. Croix (SOS), joined the venerable St. Croix River Association in a futile struggle with the Northern States Power Company. The two groups hoped to preserve the Lake St. Croix region from air and water pollution, from overdevelopment, and from the hazards of heavy barge traffic. Although the battle was a prolonged one, the power company won — as power companies usually do everywhere, whether they be on the Hudson River or along the St. Croix. Today coal-laden barges ply the waters of Lake St. Croix; the power plant is there too, with its 785-foot chimney and pyramidlike coal piles — obtruding on the scenic beauty of the lake's wooded shore line and quiet waters.

On the upper river, however, canoeists who take the water route from Solon Springs to Taylors Falls will find it little altered from those days in May, 1964, when Don Holmquist and I explored its clear reaches. That trip is described in this book's final chapter, "Down the Two Valleys." Save that I am now counted among the so-called retired and Don has left piano tuning for stone sculpture, everything is just about the same with four major exceptions — three of them man-made, the fourth a catastrophe of nature.

First, a once-popular Wisconsin resort and restaurant at Riverside, bordering State Highway 35 near the Minnesota boundary (page 276), has been replaced by a National Park Service picnic area. The second exception is highly visible a short distance above the junction of the Yellow River and the St. Croix close to Danbury. The half-dozen two-room shacks built for the Indians by WPA workers in 1934 (pages 22-23 and 276) have been razed, and in their place the Bureau of Indian Affairs has constructed modern, comfortable houses. Only one of the old tenement buildings remains. The third alteration came about with the growing public use of the river. In 1964 there was only one private canoe-rental service along the St. Croix between Riverside and St. Croix Falls (page 283). Today there are five.

The final change on the upper river was a devastating one. Shortly after midday on July 4, 1977, tornadolike winds descended on the area between Fox Landing and Norway Point. The violent storm stranded numerous vacationers and reduced large tracts of magnificent conifers and deciduous trees to a tangled jungle from which it will take years to recover. The destruction caused by the winds is still much in evidence, especially at Einar Nelson's Landing above the Kettle River Rapids and along the Namekagon in the Trego region.

One final note — a minor one from page 290, the last in the text. The diminutive excursion boat *Miss Prescott* no longer plies the waters of Lake St. Croix; she sank in 1975. Others have since taken her place at the port of Stillwater. As for those remaining, less important mutations that are inevitable after the passage of almost fifteen years — their detection is left to future eagle-eyed readers.

Since 1965 a number of worth-while books which center on the St. Croix Valley should be added to the bibliographical essay, "St. Croix Sources" (page 293). They are: *Marine on St. Croix: From Lumber Village to Summer Haven* (1968) by James Taylor Dunn; *Looking Backward* (1970) by Edgar L. Roney; *In the Land of Kichi Saga* (1973) by Theodore A. Norelius; *Scandia — Then and Now* (1974) by Anna Engquist; *Westward to the St. Croix* (1978) by Harold Weatherhead. A well-written children's book, *A St. Croix Valley Story*, prepared by Independent School District 834 in Washington County, was published in 1972. Although *The Brothers* (1969) by John E. Hawkinson is ostensibly a genealogy, it is also an interesting introduction to the story of Swedes in the St. Croix region as seen through the experiences of ten brothers who came to the valley with the second wave of settlers. In 1970 the Minnesota Historical Society published *The Journals of Joseph N. Nicollet: A*

Scientist on the Mississippi Headwaters with Notes on Indian Life, *1836–37*, edited by Martha C. Bray and translated by André Fertey. Pages 141–153 of that book contain the first complete English translation of Nicollet's important "St. Croix Journal" which recorded his August, 1837, exploratory trip up the St. Croix. Two additional county histories have also been printed: *Washington: A History of the Minnesota County* (1977) edited by Willard E. Rosenfelt, and *An Early Look at Chisago County* (1976) compiled by the Chisago County Bicentennial Committee. It should be noted, too, that a scarce collector's item, *The Valley of the St. Croix: Picturesque and Descriptive* (1888), was handsomely reprinted in 1970 by the Croix-side Press, Stillwater.

The past fourteen years, however, have produced no known publications about the northern Wisconsin counties of Douglas, Burnett, Washburn, and Sawyer. Good reference material in more permanent book or pamphlet form continues to be needed for this neglected area, as well as for the towns of Osceola, St. Croix Falls, Danbury, Grantsburg, Solon Springs — all in Wisconsin — and for Taylors Falls and Pine City in Minnesota.

My thanks go to June Drenning Holmquist and to her assistants at the Minnesota Historical Society, Jean A. Brookins and Mary D. Cannon, for aid and counsel and for making possible this reprint edition of *The St. Croix*. Once again, I am grateful to my wife Mária for her continuing help. As the English author and critic Max Beerbohm once wrote in a letter, "It is only the good opinion of the few that keeps a book alive."

"Pine Needles"   JAMES TAYLOR DUNN
Marine on St. Croix
May, 1979

Contents

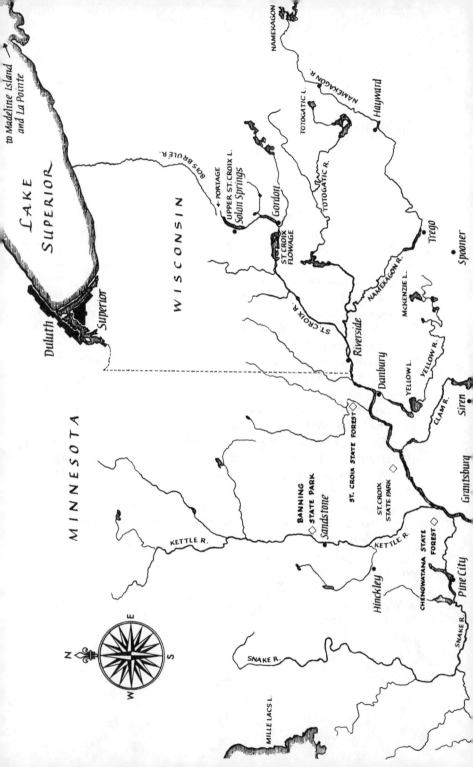

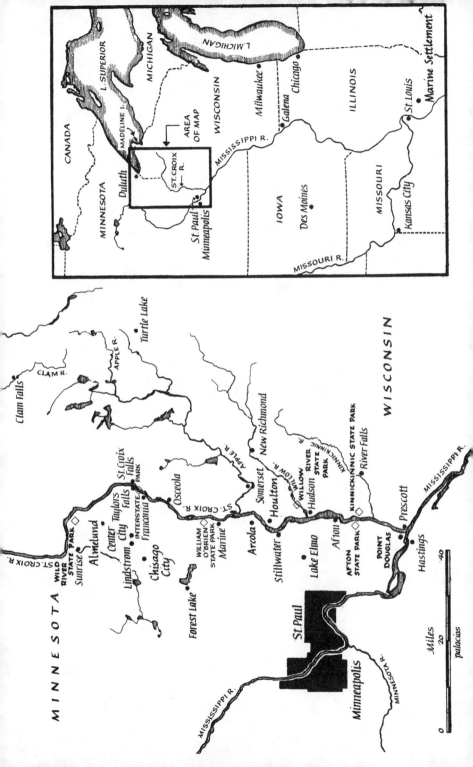

Chapter One

The River Has Two Valleys

THERE are two St. Croix Rivers in North America. Both are border streams, one between Maine and Canada, the other separating Wisconsin from Minnesota. Each in its heyday was an important highway for carrying logs and cut timber to market.

The first St. Croix is a winding, narrow Atlantic seaboard river which, before entering Passamaquoddy Bay and the ocean, runs southeasterly to form seventy-five miles of the International Boundary between the Pine Tree State and the Canadian province of New Brunswick.

The second St. Croix, the one that concerns us here, is all U.S. Its ultimate source, hidden among sandy hills near the village of Solon Springs in northwestern Wisconsin, is an icy, bubbling spring on the edge of a tangled cedar, black spruce, and tamarack swamp. This muskeg area extends over a ridge of land that divides waters flowing north into Lake Superior by way of the Brule River from those reaching the Gulf of Mexico. Within a dark, cool, moss-carpeted forest, the spring's seepage courses south to a large pond. From there a narrow stream, locally called St. Croix Creek, flows into Upper St. Croix Lake, that "handsome sheet of clear water" so often mentioned by the early explorers. At this point, the St. Croix River begins its journey through wilderness fastnesses toward the Gulf, traveling 165 miles and draining a region of 7,650 square miles, until it reaches the great Father of Waters—the Mississippi, at Prescott, Wisconsin. For 127 of these miles, the St. Croix has since 1848 formed the border between Wisconsin and Minnesota.

The Midwestern St. Croix might itself be called two separate rivers, so different in character is the upper valley from the fifty-mile stretch below the twin villages of Taylors Falls, Minnesota, and St. Croix Falls, Wisconsin. Minnesota's territorial governor Alexander Ramsey in 1852 referred to the lower region as "the opulent valley of the St. Croix"—pastoral, rich soiled, fine for the production of wheat, and an area of lush farmland. This is the wider river of more placid, slow-flowing waters, of jutting sand bars, and quiet, tree-shadowed sloughs. By contrast, the upper valley—north of the rocky, ridge-locked Dalles at Taylors Falls—once a dense forest of centuries-old white pines, is now a sandy country of second growth, occasionally burned by devastating forest fires, and generally unfit for farming except along the outer reaches of its feeder streams. Here is the narrow, unknown valley, here are the myriad tributaries, the winding, turbulent, often white-water rivers that rush headlong over boulder-strewn rapids.

The upper valley is a rugged, wild region, a lonely and beautiful one, a land of brooks and creeks and rivers. The Totogatic and Namekagon, the Yellow and Clam, the Kettle and Snake, all once busy lumbering streams, today join the main channel to become true water trails for modern canoeists and fishermen on trips of personal discovery and exploration. Much of the upper St. Croix below the Flowage Park dam at Gordon, Wisconsin, only a few miles from the river's source, bears hardly a mark of modern-day civilization. Only an occasional bridge spans the fast-moving waters; a few rude Indian homes and once in a while a summer cabin are tucked away in the forest. In certain portions it is primitive and quite inaccessible. This part of the St. Croix, and the tributary Namekagon River below the dam at Trego, Wisconsin, remain today much as they were a century ago. For this reason they have been selected as two of only twelve waterways in the United States for possible preservation in their natural condition, part of a nationwide plan to save unconfined, free-flowing rivers. Few streams more deserve such an accolade. With wild, unpolluted waters fast vanishing, and those remaining beset by the possible encroachment of power dams and factories, the warning has been sounded by Minnesota-born Supreme Court Justice William O. Douglas that some day "Americans are going to wake up to the fact that they need more than beer and television for recreation."

Historian Carl Carmer, in defending his personal vistas along New York State's great Hudson River, has also spoken out for all preservationists, everywhere: "All over the face of America—wherever rivers run," the popular author recently stated, "the people are asking that they be preserved. The people would lift up their eyes to river highlands undefaced by quarries. They would cleanse their minds and hearts by waters undefiled by sludge and pollution."

In contrast to the wilderness of the upper valley, the broad and pleasant river south of the Dalles courses through a land of many summer homes and year-round residences for commuters to the industries and offices of river towns and the Twin Cities. It is also a region of scenic grandeur which author-traveler Mrs. Elizabeth Ellet first eulogized in 1852 when she wrote, "The graceful curve of the line of shore, the alternate swelling and sinking of the wooded hills, the deep ravines occasionally opening between them—the dark shadows thrown by the heights of the water, with a narrow line of light near the shore marking the departure of the sun, and now and then a projecting headland further out, a dark and shaggy mass—were so beautiful, that one could not regret the scenery of the Mississippi."

Along this opulent lower valley the river widens and below Stillwater, Minnesota, spreads out to form a lake. Long, rolling hills frame the deeper waters held back by a jutting estuary at Point Douglas, Minnesota, where the St. Croix joins the Mississippi. Here is the biggest and busiest playground in the region for outboard motorboats, miniature houseboats and pontoons, for easy canoe-floating trips downriver from Taylors Falls, and, during high water, for high-powered craft on "sail aways" from yacht clubs along the Minnesota and Mississippi rivers. This is the heart of the chamber of commerce's "Friendly Valley," and an important Midwest playground familiar to many thousands of people who know nothing of the upper river. This is the stream of quiet weekdays and busy, noisy weekends, probably the most popular boating water between Lake Michigan and the West Coast except, perhaps, for the Mississippi at St. Louis. It is a fishing river, too, famous for its smallmouthed bass, sturgeon, and muskellunge. Here the morning mists smoke up lazily from the valley almost like steam from a drying blanket, and the setting sun reflects through haze over the brilliantly colored Wisconsin hills. The St. Croix is a river of many moods, many colors, much beauty.

The reason this river became two such diverse valleys goes back many hundreds of thousands of years, before there was any St. Croix or any rock-bound Dalles, to early postglacial times when melting masses of ice shaped two immense lakes. The first, Glacial Lake Grantsburg, extended over the land from Grantsburg, Wisconsin, westward into east-central Minnesota. The torrential runoff from this extensive body of impounded water forged southward from near St. Croix Falls to the Mississippi, gouging out the more fertile valley of the lower St. Croix.

Much later by the glacial time clock the upper valley was formed when a vast reservoir of water from Glacial Lake Duluth, the ancestor of Lake Superior, unable to drain eastward along a St. Lawrence Valley exit blocked by a massive ice pack, bulldozed a path south through the Brule River Valley and Upper St. Croix

Lake. This northern region became a land of pine barrens, of sandy and generally poor soil. When the powerful glacial waters reached a concentrated outcrop of hard igneous rock they drilled out a path to fashion the deep, narrow gorge and sheer rock walls today appropriately named the Dalles of the St. Croix. Below this point the newer stream then followed the existing bed of the lower valley, widening and deepening it. Also carved from the basalt lava flow at the Dalles, where Angle Rock seems to strangle the stream, were numerous weird configurations which modern publicists and prosy poets, with little inspiration, have labeled the Devil's Chair, the Devil's Icebox, the Maltese Cross, Old Man of the Dalles, and most inappropriate of all, the Devil's Pulpit. Another curiosity in this scenic area and along the cliff-lined section of Minnesota's Kettle River (some miles to the north near Hell's Gate and the ghost town of Banning) are the remarkable cistern-like potholes—stone wells up to sixty feet deep which were ground out by river eddies swirling and rotating rocks and gravel.

Man's accomplishments and failures along this northern stream (especially in the populous lower valley) are the theme of all that follows, although few names and fewer great deeds will be recognized by any but those living within its watershed—and perhaps not by all of them. Here are the stories of the adventurers who traveled the St. Croix, cut its forests, and settled the land. They built no capital city nor great university along its banks; no walled garrison shadowed its waters. No President fished its streams to bring everlasting glory to the region. Yet from the everyday events of their unheroic lives the people of the valley emerge to become a part of the American story. It has been said that wherever an American river runs there is always someone to love it and to feel the story of our country is intimately linked with his river.

Chapter Two

Indians Along the St. Croix

IN THE obscurity of unrecorded history a nation of Indians calling themselves Dakota, meaning "friend" or "ally," lived on much of the land which is the valley of the St. Croix River. These red men of stone age culture fished, hunted, and trapped along its waters. They harvested wild rice from the myriad northern lakes of their broad land and followed the trail of the buffalo across the prairies to the west.

During the 1500s another nation of Indians, the Chippewa or Ojibway, came out of the valley of the St. Lawrence River. Moving slowly westward across lower Canada and then along both shores of Lake Superior, they followed the trails of abundant food and wildlife. Forced from their eastern lands by the powerful Iroquois and needing more furs to trade with the whites, they traveled toward the setting sun, well supplied by civilization with steel scalping knives, firearms, and gunpowder. During the mid-1600s in what is now northeastern Minnesota, these invaders first found and fought the Dakota, who were not the fortunate possessors of such persuasive weapons. The Chippewa derisively called their Dakota enemies *Na-dou-esse*, meaning "Snake in the grass," which the French fur traders spelled *Nadouesioux* and contracted to Sioux. By this name the Dakota became known.

Several locations along the St. Croix have in recent years produced evidence of early occupancy by the Sioux and Chippewa. On the precipitous sandstone cliffs, bordering the west bank of the river three miles north of Stillwater, the Sioux carved and painted vermilion figures and images. It is said that this "Painted

Rock" was once greatly venerated by these Indians. But time and man and the friability of the rock have effaced all vestiges of their ancient art. Archaeological investigation in the caves and rock shelters of the Stillwater-Arcola area have also brought to light numerous aboriginal artifacts. During 1931, for example, careful investigation of a small cave three miles north of Stillwater, on what was then the property of Dr. Rodney B. Harvey, uncovered interesting pictographs and fragments of Indian pottery, fishhooks, awls, and bone beads. What appear to be Indian markings have also been found on the walls of Knapp's Cave near Cedar Bend, a few miles south of Osceola, Wisconsin. Indian burial mounds were once numerous throughout the lower valley; the most notable were those located close by Osceola and on the Minnesota side at present-day Copas just north of the village of Marine on St. Croix. Over the years, however, most of these have been leveled by farmers' plowshares.

For a time before the mid-1700s the Sioux and Chippewa lived in seeming harmony, or in a sort of suspended enmity, since the war between them was soon revived. In the decisive battle of Izatys or Kathio near the outlet of Minnesota's Mille Lacs Lake about 1745 the Chippewa drove the Sioux forever from their lake-studded, timbered homeland, including the valley of the St. Croix, and soon not a Siouan village remained east of the Mississippi or north of the Falls of St. Anthony at the location of present-day Minneapolis. Frequent forays into each other's territory, however, continued over the years.

Just when the first major Indian battle took place in the valley of the St. Croix River is not known. History and legend, almost indistinguishable one from the other, tell of a great massacre at Point Prescott, along the water's edge on the Wisconsin shore where Lake St. Croix narrows to join the Mississippi. The time of this onslaught of the Chippewa against their hereditary enemy has been handed down only in the uncertain form of oral tradition. Some historians place it vaguely in the seventeenth century; others are perhaps more nearly correct when they mention a date as late as 1755. Under the pretense of smoking the pipe of peace, a band of Chippewa warriors fell upon the assembled Sioux, and it is reported that the invaders garnered 335 scalps. Many more Sioux were thought to have perished as they tried to escape by canoe to the river's opposite shore.

Other occasional movements attained the dignity of campaigns, and some encounters could be called battles. One such contest took place toward the close of the eighteenth century among the rocky palisades rising high above the turbulent river at the Dalles of the St. Croix. A band of Fox Indians, from whom the Chippewa had long before wrested their Wisconsin River hunting grounds, persuaded warriors of the Sioux nation to accompany them up the Mississippi and St. Croix rivers to meet the Chippewa in a final, determined effort to regain a portion of their former country. Learning of the existence of this war party through scouts, Chippewa Chief Waub-o-jeeg (White Fisher) assembled three hundred of his braves and led them south from the Lake Superior region to encounter the enemy. When the chief missed a prearranged meeting with additional forces at the junction of the Snake and St. Croix rivers, he did not wait, but pushed on down the St. Croix. He met the foe early one morning in the middle of the east bank portage around the falls and rapids at the Dalles.

The Fox were so confident of victory that they asked their Sioux allies to stand by and watch the quick defeat of the Chippewa. After the battle had raged until nearly noon, the Fox began to weaken and would have been routed had not the Sioux abandoned their passive role and joined in the fray. The Chippewa, bravely resisting the renewed Sioux onslaught, were outnumbered. At the crucial moment, when they in turn faced certain annihilation, the Chippewa were reinforced by the arrival of the sixty warriors that Chief White Fisher was to have met at the Snake. The Fox and Sioux were savagely driven from the high crags into the roaring waters below, and many of the wounded sought shelter but found death in the crevices of the rock-walled gorge. The slaughter, it is said, was so great that for years afterward Indians called this area the "Valley of Bones." In triumph for the Chippewa, the bloodiest intertribal battle in the story of the St. Croix Valley ended.

The Chippewa and Sioux continued their relentless battles for many years, a tribal warfare of sporadic sorties and scalping raids that lasted until the middle of the nineteenth century. Through the hopeful efforts of explorers, missionaries, and government agents, truces between the traditional enemies were occasionally agreed upon until the actual or imagined wrongs of some hotheaded Indian would renew the slaughter. One such attempt at a compact was made during the Grand Conference of 1825, held by representatives of the federal government under a protective bower outside the walls of Fort Crawford, now Prairie du Chien, Wisconsin. To insure what the treaty signed on August 19 called "a firm and enduring peace," both the Sioux and Chippewa agreed to respect an imaginary line dividing their areas. The truce line was to extend diagonally through Indian lands from the Chippewa River near the present city of Eau Claire, Wisconsin, west to the Mississippi about where St. Cloud, Minnesota, now stands, and on to the Red River of the North. This figurative demarcation crossed the St. Croix "at a place called the Standing Cedar, about a day's paddle in a canoe above the lake at the mouth of that river." Today's traveler on the Minnesota-Wisconsin border stream is at the spot when he reaches an abrupt eastward turn in the river at Cedar Bend, some eight miles below the village of Osceola. The cedar trees are gone now, but the name remains.

The 1825 tribal agreement in no way deterred Indians from making desultory raids into each other's territory. And when, in 1835, a portion of the line was finally surveyed, the savages considerably complicated matters by pulling up many of the marker stakes. The boundary established by the council in 1825 accomplished nothing. "War, War, War, will be carried on between the Sioux & Chippeways," Lawrence Taliaferro, the Indian agent at nearby Fort Snelling, complained on December 30, 1828, "as long as there is a *Brave* of either nation in exhistence."

The St. Croix, always an important highway and favorite hunting ground for the nomadic Indians, witnessed no further unusual activity until one day during the third week of June, 1839, when the canoes of a sizable contingent of Chippewa sped southward, bound for the American Fur Company's trading post at what is

now Mendota, Minnesota. Approximately nine hundred Chippewa warriors from the Crow Wing area, Leech Lake, and the St.
Croix Valley arrived and set up their tents in the shadow of the
fort. They came to protest the change in the location for the payment of their annuities from nearby Falls of St. Croix to the distant, inaccessible Indian agency at La Pointe on Lake Superior's
Madeline Island—a difficult and arduous trip. Missionary Edmund F. Ely recorded in his diary that they wanted to be paid
nearer home. But since President Martin Van Buren's decision
could in no way be altered, this complaint was the least of Taliaferro's worries. He feared more serious trouble because over 850
Sioux were already camped about the Fort Snelling Indian agency
to receive the money promised them under the terms of a treaty
signed in 1837. When the welfare of both mutually hostile tribes
became his responsibility, Taliaferro was perhaps justified in saying that he had his hands full.

But on the neutral grounds of the federal military reservation at
the fort, and under the watchful eye of the soldiers, all was harmony, and many dances, games, feasts, and visits were enjoyed by
the traditional enemies. Even Agent Taliaferro was encouraged,
recording in his journal on June 28 that "The Chippewas met the
Sioux in Council. . . . The *Pipe* of peace went round & after 4
hours in conclave the Council broke up—both parties promising
to abstain for *one* year from war & longer if practicable."

A few days later, on July 2, the Chippewa killed and scalped a
Sioux hunter at Lake Calhoun, in present-day Minneapolis. When
the Sioux learned of the murder, the Chippewa had already left
the Fort Snelling area. One Chippewa group under the elder
Chief Hole-in-the-Day, refusing to go to La Pointe to collect the
annuities, headed for home up the Mississippi. Another contingent of about a hundred warriors, commanded by Hole-in-the-
Day's elder brother Song-uk-um-ig (Strong Ground), took the
St. Croix-Brule River route to the Indian agency on Lake Superior.

The infuriated Sioux immediately sought out Taliaferro and
asked his advice. Unfortunately, he told them to do as they
pleased, and their pleasure was the immediate formation of two

war parties. One Sioux expedition trapped and fought the Chippewa under Hole-in-the-Day at a point on the Rum River several miles above Anoka, Minnesota; the casualties numbered some ninety braves. The other Sioux group, which was composed of warriors from the Kaposia band (who lived where South St. Paul now stands), early on the morning of July 3, 1839, surprised Strong Ground's men camped in the deep, cliff-lined ravine at the north end of what is now Stillwater.

At dawn, from atop the steep bluffs surrounding three sides of the encampment, over a hundred ornamented, greased Sioux warriors poured a volley into the tents of the sleeping Chippewa below and precipitously descended on their unsuspecting enemies. Surprised though they were, the defenders fought bravely to cover the retreat of the women and children to the birchbark canoes at the St. Croix's shore. Although the Chippewa lost an estimated twenty-one braves in the fight, the number of Sioux killed is said to have been small.

A runner carried news of the battle to Fort Snelling, and a lieutenant from the fort was dispatched to the St. Croix with a few soldiers. He soon returned to tell the Indian agent that he refused to enter the ravine. Nor did he allow his men to go near the place because, as Taliaferro reported, of the "*excessive* stench from carcasses." Well could the agent call it a "momentous day," and write of the "lamentable state of things on the St. Croix." The arena of this bloody retaliatory fight to this day bears the name "Battle Hollow."

The last intertribal massacre in the valley took place on April 3, 1850, somewhere along the banks of the Apple River, a Wisconsin stream which serpentines from its source on the east-central edge of Polk County into the St. Croix a number of miles above Stillwater. At sunup on that day fifteen Chippewa women and children, accompanied by three old men, were engaged in collecting sap from the maple trees. (Another account says they were hauling a keg of whisky back to their camp.) Sioux braves fell upon the sugar camp, killing and scalping all the Chippewa except one nine-year-old boy who was taken prisoner. Crossing the St. Croix, the Sioux on the following day appeared on the streets of Stillwater, then a growing settlement of more than six hundred inhabitants, and celebrated their victory by treating the terrified residents to a scalp dance. They encircled the captured Chippewa boy, and as they danced round and round and sang to their own wild, abrupt music, they struck him full in the face with the reeking, gory trophies.

The *St. Paul Pioneer* of April 10 strongly condemned the Apple River incident, calling it "one of the most foul and dastardly acts of wholesale assassination that ever disgraced the annals of Indian ruffianism." A few days later, however, the rival St. Paul newspaper, *Minnesota Chronicle and Register*, appealed for reasoned understanding, stating that Indian warfare had always been one of extermination and that this belief was an important part of the red man's religion. "Each tribe believes that the gods created them to slaughter one another," the paper said. Moreover, the Chippewa were trespassing on ground where the Sioux were the only Indians having the right to hunt. "Let us," concluded the appeal, "deplore the darkness which surrounds these poor creatures." With this incident, tribal warfare along the river seems to have come to an end, although the aborigines remained very much in evidence as white settlers moved into the St. Croix Valley.

At the busy lumbering village of Marine Mills, according to Stillwater's *St. Croix Union* in January, 1855, the Sioux were "frightening our wives and children, plundering our premises, laying vicious hands on every thing their savage eyes crave, and not leaving unmolested the domestic sanctity of our potatoe holes." Only two months later about two hundred Sioux warriors paid a mass visit to Marine. They aroused a great deal of curiosity and excitement among the residents, many of whom had never before seen so many Indians at one time. The Sioux were returning from Goose Creek, just north of the Sunrise River, where they had robbed some Chippewa lodges, secured forty valuable furs, and killed and scalped four of the enemy. "They danced in great glee," reported the *Union*, "around a barrel of sour crackers . . . put out for them. . . . They made just [such] a noise as a flock of hungry geese would under the same circumstances. But Indians must be human. . . . They do a great many things that civilized humanity is guilty of doing. They get whisky sometimes and get drunk. Animals do not do that—they must have a human soul. They do not understand the civilization, the enlightenment of the present age; it confounds them, it overwhelms them, and they go and resolve anew deeds of plunder and murder."

For the next two years, Indians were frequently encountered around Marine and in the Swedish settlement to the northeast near Big Marine Lake. They continued to harass the white settlers, and would sometimes slaughter 1,200 deer a week, leaving more than half of the meat on the ground as food for wolves. The residents feared that, if this continued, the game would vanish. "It *is* hard," said the *Union* in December, 1856, commenting on the situation at Marine, "for the industrious and poor white settler to have his wood and stacks of hay burnt up, his traps and their booty stolen, and his game shot down, and much of it wasted." Periodic protest meetings were held, appeals were sent to Minnesota Governor Willis Gorman, and the irate settlers threatened to turn out with firearms and drive the Indians from the region. The only move the governor made, however, was to send a curt letter disclaiming all responsibility for what the Indians did. Then suddenly, without direct action from anyone, the red men were gone.

In 1857 a few marauding Chippewa reappeared to terrorize settlers in the area a short distance north of the Dalles where the Sunrise River empties its waters into the St. Croix. They apparently stole food and fired the haystacks on the Jemmy Burns farm. When word of this adventure reached St. Paul, Governor Samuel Medary ordered out the troops on what has come to be known as the "Sunrise Expedition." Genial, British-born Captain James Starkey was placed in command. Before his departure from St. Paul he encountered State Senator Henry M. Rice and his guest, Illinois Senator Stephen A. Douglas, on the steps of the capitol. Starkey later reported in his *Reminiscences* that Douglas advised him: "If you ask me what to do, sir, I would say, do your duty, or show the white feather."

Thirty men of the St. Paul Light Cavalry answered the patriotic call, delighted at the opportunity to display for the public's admiration their immaculate, new, blindingly red coats and white pants, flashing sabers, and polished army pistols. In the August 25 issue, a reporter on the *St. Paul Pioneer and Democrat* wondered if these brightly outfitted soldiers weren't perhaps "dressed rather gaily for a war party." As the company of forty horses set off, fully expecting to meet in battle a host of carefully picked Chippewa braves, they were cheered on by "quite a concourse of citizens." The same cynic wryly quipped: "They are likely to have a good time if they can manage to keep clear of the enemy."

It was August 28 when the troopers met the Indian forces on the fields of Sunrise Prairie, but it was a terrified enemy in full retreat, zigzagging through the stalks of standing corn. What was thought to be a "host" of Chippewa turned out to be six panic-stricken, cornered Indian hunters. One shouting, pistol-waving private was killed, more by error and out of fear than by intent. An Indian also fell and the other five quickly surrendered, to be led triumphantly back to the Ramsey County jail in St. Paul. Instead of returning as conquering heroes, however, Starkey and his crestfallen soldiers were met with ridicule and censure. At the court hearing six days later, four of the Chippewa were immediately released; only the one thought to be responsible for the soldier's death was held. He was shipped off to Chisago County to stand trial for murder, and because there was no jail at Taylors Falls, he was lodged in the sheriff's home. During the night the miscreant escaped with seeming ease, swam the swift waters at the St. Croix Dalles, and quickly disappeared into the tree-shrouded Wisconsin hills.

This end to the farcical Sunrise Expedition of 1857—the "Cornstalk War" as it was called—satisfied almost everyone, for it was the general opinion, which the press strongly echoed, that the whole affair was outrageous. "The expedition was uncalled for," editorialized the *Daily Minnesotian* of St. Paul. It "was badly managed; and tended to impair the security of the people from Indian depredations, instead of protecting them." Captain Starkey, later defending the military expedition which he led, said that the St. Paul Light Cavalry followed orders and above all "did not show the white feather."

Amid derisive laughter, the excitement of the "Cornstalk War" was soon forgotten. By the 1860s most of the Chippewa had left the river's lower valley, forced to move into the more remote reaches of the upper St. Croix as white farmers took over their land. Late in August, 1862, however, news of the bloody, harrowing Sioux Uprising in the valley of the Minnesota River reached St. Croix residents and made them fear for their own safety. Alarms spread of possible attacks, and it was rumored that the younger Hole-in-the-Day, head chief of the Chippewa along the Mississippi, would soon join with the Sioux to massacre valley residents. Excited citizens around Chisago Lake hurriedly constructed earthen breastworks and brought in a cannon from St. Paul to protect the residents of Center City. Under the command of former territorial prison warden Colonel Francis R. Delano, volunteer militia companies were formed at Stillwater, Marine Mills, Taylors Falls, and Sunrise City. At Sunrise City a company of soldiers constructed a temporary garrison with barracks, stables, and hospital. There the mounted rangers spent the winter and, according to valley historian William H. C. Folsom, presumably had "a very good time, but repelled no savage foes."

So jittery were the residents of Stillwater that on August 27 a farm couple living a few miles to the west imagined they heard Indians and started for the village "as if the devil himself were after them." As Ada Cornman reported the farce in a letter to Sam Bloomer, her soldier friend in the Union Army, "They came screaming that Indians were out there burning houses, and murdering everybody. . . . Martin Clancy came into town with his boots and pants in his hands. . . . He met Mrs. Greeley coming to town with a shawl over her head, and thought she was an Indian. He threw his pants at her and never got them again."

A week later the *Stillwater Messenger* strongly censured the people for becoming so hysterical. The newspaper was astonished that so much exertion was required on the part of "staid and sensible Citizens to convince the excited crowd that they were making mules of themselves, and to induce them to go home and put on their clothes."

Residents of Osceola were on tenterhooks, too. They asked the captain of the steamer *H. S. Allen* to sound his whistle loud and clear if he found any evidence along the river of imminent danger from the Indians. At two o'clock of an August morning, a long, shrill whistle startled the entire village out of its sleep. Some of the citizens immediately made ready "for manly resistance to the impending butchery, others to skedaddle," reported the *St. Croix Monitor* of Taylors Falls. Later it was discovered that the ruckus was caused by the passing steamer *Enterprise* whose captain innocently blew his boat's whistle as a well-meant, courteous greeting to the inhabitants of Osceola—even if it was 2 A.M.

On August 26, the day before the Stillwater scare, a Home Guard was organized for the protection of Taylors Falls, but rumor had it that the soldiers' guns were so rusted as to be unfit for duty. "There has hardly been a day since the first settlement of this place," the *Monitor* calmly advised its readers, "that Indians have not been within the town limits—the county . . . to the east and north is as much the abode of the Indian as the white man. As yet there is no trouble." Fannie Field of St. Croix Falls expressed her very real concern when she wrote a friend in Racine, Wisconsin: "We are much afraid that the Chippewas will join the Sioux and we then [will] be in danger. We rise every morning very thankful that we have not been scalped and our house burned. . . . I try to be cool and contented but I tremble every time I look at an Indian." The *Prescott Journal* also ridiculed the danger to residents of Pierce County, Wisconsin. Captain Sam Harriman of Somerset reported to the governor of Wisconsin that so far as he could judge, "the fear is mutual . . . while the whites are running in one direction the Indians are running in the other."

In spite of increasing fears of impending attack and massacre, all remained peaceful and quiet along the St. Croix. The Chippewa were completely bewildered by the many rumors and by the sudden warlike attitude of their white friends. They found it difficult, as the *Monitor* put it, to understand why all the elaborate preparations were necessary, in this valley at least, "to resist—nothing."

River residents, looking upon the Indians with contempt, continued to complain about the red men and to resent their closeness as neighbors. Questionable characters like Sylvander Partridge and Maurice M. Samuels, who thrived on the illegal sale of "Corn Cob" liquor to the Indians at the Falls, did not help matters. Partridge during the late 1840s set up a grogshop and bowling alley at Silver Grove near the upper end of St. Croix Falls village, which was immediately dubbed "Quailtown" and soon had a reputation for drunken midnight orgies of Indians, whites, and half-breeds. "The resort was noted for its riotous disorder," reported Folsom. "The quails in this 'Partridge' nest were evil birds."

In July, 1850, with the formation of the St. Croix Lumbermen's Union, an attempt was made to remove the "miserable traffic in whisky" among the Indians. It is not known how successful the effort was, but by 1854 Partridge, at least, had left the scene and was saloonkeeping in Stillwater. He soon skipped the country to avoid paying his debts. Firewater continued to flow freely at the Quailtown rendezvous and the exploitation of Indians by the local sporting class flourished. It was still very much in evidence in June, 1862, when Lute Taylor, the genial and hearty editor of the *Prescott Journal,* visited the place and spent the night—much to the consternation of his fellow excursionists. On board the *Enterprise* the following day Taylor, who was the valley's most colorful stutterer, would only say, "Great country this—nice people— beautiful scenery—Chippewa maiden 'b-b-big t-t-thing, m-m- mighty b-b-big t-t-thing!'" Before another ten years had passed, Quailtown was deserted and silent.

In 1854 when the northeastern Chippewa agreed to give up a vast tract of land bordering Lake Superior, reservations were created in both Minnesota and Wisconsin to receive the dispossessed, but the Indians of the St. Croix refused to desert their ancestral homes for the confinements of reservation life at Lac Court Oreilles near Hayward, Wisconsin. By their refusal they forfeited any chance of receiving land allotments; they became, in effect, the "Lost Tribe" of the St. Croix.

As late as January, 1867, Folsom, then a Minnesota state senator, informed Congressman Ignatius Donnelly at Washington that the government should compel all Chippewa of the Lost Tribe to live within their reservations. "Those Indians on the St. Croix," wrote Folsom, "have become an intolerable nuisance. . . . They have been suffered to remain looking upon our borders already too long." As more settlers came into the valley to cultivate their newly acquired land, the Indians were compelled to move still farther north into the wilder, sandy regions of the upper St. Croix where for years they have eked out a miserable existence, still plagued by Folsom's modern-day counterparts and their fatuous attitudes.

Today, in the immediate area of the St. Croix River watershed, some 227 Chippewa inhabit two of Wisconsin's valley counties— Polk and Burnett. In the region of Big Round Lake, Polk County, approximately twenty miles northeast of St. Croix Falls, there are 790 acres of tax-free, restricted land on which live about eighty-two members of the Lost Tribe. Burnett County directly to the north contains six Indian settlements totaling 145 Chippewa established on 907 acres. One of these settlements is along Clam Lake a few miles east of Siren. Four others are at Big Sand, Bashaw, and Gaslyn lakes, all within the drainage basin of the Clam River and near the village of Hertel.

The sixth Burnett County Indian settlement is located on 129 acres bordering the St. Croix a short distance above Danbury, Wisconsin. Here, part way up the sloping east bank of the river, paralleling Highway 35, is a bleak, shadeless row of some half-dozen houses constructed by the government in 1934. In each of these two-room, split log buildings live from eight to ten persons. One outside pump furnishes the only available drinking water, and the nearby St. Croix, into which seeps fetid drainage from dilapidated privies, is the colony's common bathhouse.

Attempts by the missionaries and the Bureau of Indian Affairs to turn the red men into farmers have proved less than successful. In 1946 John Lonestar, then the spokesman for his tribe, said that "They just don't take to farming—they'd rather hunt and trap like their ancestors." Two hopeful steps have been taken in recent years to restore some modicum of pride to the Chippewa in the St. Croix Valley. At Danbury the establishment of the St. Croix Improvement Association by the late Mrs. Elise East has given hope

to the Indians around the St. Croix and Yellow rivers. Gus Premo
has built a wild rice processing plant, and others like the Wayne
Staples and the Joe Holmes are constructing new homes. But it all
seems to move so slowly. "We want to tear all these hovels down,"
says Gus, pointing to the split log and other tar-paper and board
shacks along the river, "and build a pleasant, well planned little
village of larger houses, arranged in attractive design with trees
and sidewalks and a paved street." The work so far has been done
by the Indians with the help of a few dedicated whites. It is a step
in the right direction. The future may yet see Gus's dream replace
the present sun-parched, treeless village of the Lost Tribe.

Over in Hayward, along the banks of the Namekagon River
some fifty-five miles east of Danbury, a more spectacular movement is afoot, the work of one seemingly indefatigable man. The
results of his tireless energy are already beginning to show along
the St. Croix and its tributaries—in fact wherever in the valley
there are Indians in need of help. The spearhead behind this re-
vival of the Chippewa is Anthony Wise, banker's son, great-
grandson of an immigrant from the Grand Duchy of Luxembourg, World War II army officer in the European theater, real
estate dealer, father of six lively youngsters, and first citizen of
Hayward. He calls what he is doing the "Rebirth of a Nation."
"Relief is the worst form of human life," Tony Wise tells the Indians of Hayward and the nearby Lac Court Oreilles Reservation.
"It reduced a completely self-dependent nation of people down to
nothing. You are Indians. You always will be. It's in your blood.
You can't escape it. You shouldn't want to. So be Indians and be
proud of it." Through Wise's army-inspired, dynamic leadership,
the red man is beginning his fight against what Fred Morgan of
Hayward has called "three hundred years of degenerating, disrup-
tive destruction."

The Chippewa youngsters along the Namekagon are now learning how to speak their almost forgotten tongue. "You must know
your language," Tony Wise tells them, "your history, your songs,
your religion." And he is putting these words into action, too—he
sees that they are taught. He wants to be sure that the answer will
not be *Gawin ni nisido tazin*—"I don't understand"—when they

are asked, *Ojibwemina?*—"Can you speak Chippewa?" Many of these Indians are now taking new pride in the old ways.

According to those who have watched this "one-man Indian Agency" at work, it hasn't been all "daisy picking." It's been ruthless, unbending, around-the-clock labor, for in no way is it easy to fight against what has, since the advent of white men in the valley, been the curse and despair of these people—liquor. "It takes about a year to cure the Indian of the drink habit," Tony will tell you. In the meantime, employment has to be furnished and the Indians' lives have to be run for them until they get over the period of adjustment. Anthony Wise is providing that employment—in winter at his popular ski resort, Mount Telemark in nearby Cable. During the summer months, at Historyland along the banks of the Namekagon in Hayward, he has a logging camp, an Indian museum specifically organized by and for the red men, and a complete aboriginal village going full swing. Colorful Indian powwows are held twice a week and every midsummer there is a great ceremonial gathering of red men from half a dozen Midwestern states. By giving these Chippewa back a pride in their own way of doing things, Tony Wise may some day fulfill his dream, too—a hope for a whole new nation of Indians.

The story of the Chippewa on the land of the St. Croix Valley is not one in which either the red men or white can take pride, but with the Tony Wise Peace Corps in action, the future looks brighter than it has since the advent of the rum-carrying fur trader.

The Indians and their culture were virtually destroyed by the onslaught of white men. "At best," states Henry E. Fritz in his excellent book *The Movement of Indian Assimilation, 1860-1890,* "Indians were regarded as a nuisance, as members of a primitive race, and as a hindrance to progress. Generation would succeed generation before many . . . would admit that an injustice had been done the red man."

Chapter Three

"The Channel of Considerable Intercourse"

ABLE and enterprising Daniel Greysolon, Sieur du Luth, was the first white man to leave any record of a visit to the pine-clad valley of the St. Croix River. In 1679 this member of the lesser French nobility made his way into the Great Lakes region, and at the strategic Sioux village of Izatys on Mille Lacs Lake, he erected the royal arms and claimed a vast, unknown wilderness empire for Louis XIV, King of France. When Du Luth traveled the western waters of Lake Superior, the Indians there told him of twin streams joined by a carrying place and leading south to the mighty Mississippi. He learned that "eight leagues from the extremity of Lake Superior on the south side" was a rough, tumbling river flowing north into the lake which the Sioux called *Nemitsa-kouat*. To the Chippewa it became the *Newissakode* (Burnt Wood Point) and *Wiskada Sibi* (Burnt Pine River). The French named this narrow and turbulent stream the Bois Brulé, and we know it today as the Brule. Although it has been said that the Brule was named for Etienne Brulé, interpreter for explorer Samuel de Champlain, existing records are too vague and uncircumstantial to support that theory or the claim that he found and explored the Bois Brulé and St. Croix rivers in the early 1600s.

Linked to the headwaters of the St. Croix by a portage of about two miles, the Brule-St. Croix corridor was part of a well-traveled Indian canoe route and the shortest north-south passageway between Lake Superior and the lower reaches of the Mississippi. In

June, 1680, a year after his first trip into the Lake Superior country, Du Luth and his *voyageurs* traveled this water highway in their fragile birchbark canoes. Du Luth's claim as the first recorded explorer of the area rests on a letter he later wrote to the Marquis de Seignelay. "After having cut some trees and broken about a hundred beaver dams," Du Luth reported, "I reached the upper waters of the said river, and then I made a portage of half a league to reach a lake, the outlet of which fell into a very fine river, which took me down into the Mississippi."

In the meantime, late in February, 1680, an experienced *voyageur,* Michel Accault, Antoine Auguelle (sometimes called Picard du Gay), and Father Louis Hennepin were dispatched from Fort Crèvecoeur on the Illinois River by explorer René Robert Cavelier, Sieur de la Salle. The men had orders to reconnoiter the upper Mississippi region, but along the way they were captured by a Sioux war party. In the course of his wanderings with his captors during the next few months, the Flemish friar in July, 1680, discovered and named for his patron saint the Falls of St. Anthony.

In the same month, Sieur du Luth's canoes reached the confluence of the St. Croix and Mississippi rivers where he learned from Indians about the capture of white men to the south. He immediately left the "very fine river" St. Croix, started a search down the Mississippi, and several weeks later came upon the three captives, presumably near the mouth of the Wisconsin River. Demanding that the Indians release them, and forgetting his own plans for further exploration, Du Luth escorted Father Hennepin and his companions safely back to civilization.

During the next ten years, Du Luth spent a good share of his time in the Great Lakes country. In 1683 La Salle reported him again on the Brule-St. Croix route. Du Luth "ascended the river Nemitsakouat," reads the account, and after a short portage, went down the St. Croix where he "passed forty leagues of rapids." Possibly it was on this trip that the French explorer erected a wintering or fur trading post and called it Fort St. Croix, since such a name was printed on Jean-Baptiste Franquelin's map in 1688. The location of this earliest fort in interior Wisconsin could have been either on the carrying place between the two rivers, or somewhere along the upper lake where the St. Croix has its source—a body of water most early cartographers identified as Lac de la Providence, and which is now prosaically known as Upper St. Croix Lake.

In January, 1683, the year Du Luth traveled the St. Croix route for the second time, Louis Hennepin's small volume recounting his North American experiences reached the bookstalls of France. Entitled *Description de la Louisiane,* it became immediately popular and was soon translated into many languages. In this pocket-sized book appeared for the first time printed references to the St. Croix and Brule rivers, obviously furnished the author by Sieur du Luth, but in no way acknowledged. "There is another River," wrote the Recollect priest, "which falls . . . into the Meschasipi (Mississippi); thro' which one may go into the Upper Lake, by making a *Portage* from it into the River Nissipikouet (The Bois Brulé). . . . It is full of Rocks and rapid streams. We named it *The River of the Grave,* or *Mausolaeum,* because the Savages bury'd there one of their Men, who was bitten by a Rattle-Snake . . . and I put upon his Corps a white Covering; for which the Savages returned me their publick Thanks."

By calling this stream the Rivière du Tombeau, Father Hennepin gave the St. Croix a name which few seemed anxious to copy. On contemporary Italian, French, and Dutch maps, for example, the stream was invariably labeled Rivière de la Madeleine or Magdeleine. Who was responsible for that name is not known.

Although Franquelin's map of 1688 locates a Fort St. Croix on the upper reaches of the river, it was Nicolas Perrot, a French trader and explorer, who seems to have been the first man to apply the name to the stream itself. He referred to it as the St. Croix in a proclamation issued May 8, 1689, on Lake Pepin near present-day Stockholm, Wisconsin. In it Perrot claimed for France all of interior North America, including the country of the Nadouesioux and the "rivière de Sainte-Croix." French-born, Canadian-bred Pierre Charles le Sueur, a *voyageur,* was among those who signed the manifesto.

Members of one of Le Sueur's later exploring parties contributed two explanations of the river's present name. In 1700 one of his companions stated that the St. Croix was so called from a cross planted over the grave of a French trader or *voyageur* buried near the present villages of Prescott and Point Douglas. Today we can only speculate that this chronicler may have read and been influenced by Father Hennepin's account of the Indian burial at the mouth of the Rivière du Tombeau. A second member of Le Sueur's party explained the name by saying that the boat of a French trader named Sainte-Croix was once wrecked near the conflux of that river and the Mississippi. Credence is given to this version by Du Luth himself, who later mentioned a Sieur de la Croix, and by Bernard de la Harpe's manuscript of Le Sueur's third voyage which records that a *voyageur* of that name was at the time engaged in dealing with the Indians along the upper Mississippi.

Toward the end of the nineteenth century, eager publicists further confounded the confusion surrounding the origin of the river's name by advancing several new and unsubstantiated theories. Newspaper reporters picked up the idea that the St. Croix was called "Holy Cross" because of the large rock formation resembling a Maltese Cross familiar to tourists at the Dalles—an error which continues to be perpetuated. In its issue of July 25, 1917, the *Stillwater Messenger* stated that Jesuit missionaries (who are not known to have traveled the St. Croix) gazed over the broadening river at Afton, Minnesota, and in its waters saw the shape of a cross. Still another explanation, promulgated by the Reverend Alfred Brunson in an annual report of the Wisconsin Historical Society, also has no basis in fact. He claimed that French missionaries named the river because the reddish-brown waters (resembling blood) enter the Mississippi nearly at a right angle to form a slightly lopsided cross. Exactly how the river received its name will probably never be fully known, although the weight of present evidence favors the explanation given by Le Sueur's companions about the trader, Sainte-Croix.

From almost the earliest days, French exploration and travel into the northern Minnesota and Wisconsin border country was motivated principally by the demand of European high fashion for beaver pelts. As these hapless animals became scarce in eastern waters, the fur seekers looked for new sources of supply farther afield. Into the western rivers they moved, tempting the Indians to trap the animals and exchange the valuable skins for shining knives, guns, axes, French goods, trinkets, and liquor. Traders quickly learned how to cheat the Indian, and the beaver skin became the prize of a continent.

In 1693, Pierre Charles le Sueur, the Canadian *voyageur* who had signed the 1689 proclamation, was sent by the authorities of New France into the Lake Superior region as a successor to Du Luth for the expressed purpose of keeping open to French trade the St. Croix-Brule water route. Le Sueur constructed fur trading posts at Madeline Island in Lake Superior and on a Mississippi River island near today's Hastings. Although there are no records specifically describing his trips along the St. Croix, this explorer must have traveled that waterway in the fulfillment of his duties. The forts he established were among the numerous bastions that dotted a vast area stretching from Lake Michigan to the Red River of the North. Le Sueur was eminently successful in developing the French fur business, and he became for a time the undisputed master of the region. Then evangelizing missionaries, who decried the use of brandy as a bargaining agent with the Indians, persuaded the government at Paris to retrench. With King Louis XIV engaged in costly European wars, dealing with the Indians was prohibited, licenses were canceled, and the posts were leased.

The errors of such a program soon became evident. Unlicensed, free-lance traders, or *coureurs de bois*, continued to deal in furs and bilk the Indians. Pressed by British competition, the French tried to regain their former position in the extensive fur trade. In 1749 Paul Marin de la Malgue, having persuaded the governor general of New France to restore the licensing system, constructed a fort on the Mississippi close by the mouth of the St. Croix and called it La Jonquière. When the elder Marin was transferred to the Ohio River in 1752, his son Joseph succeeded him as a trader among the Sioux. In a diary kept during the winter of 1753-54, the younger Marin wrote frequently of his fur trading rivalry with Louis-Joseph la Vérendrye, a trader with the Chippewa. This youngest son of the great explorer Pierre was at that time commandant of the La Pointe post on Madeline Island, and he claimed the entire St. Croix River as his region. Although La Vérendrye in 1752 authorized a wintering post on the Rivière du Soleil Levant (the Sunrise), the southern limit of his territory was actually farther up the St. Croix at the Snake River. It is evident, therefore, that the French kept open the St. Croix-Brule trading route, one of the gateways to the American West, for a longer time than was heretofore thought.

The traffic in pelts continued on this north-south artery. The river remained a highway of the fur trade—the biggest business in North America—and whether they worked for the English or the French mattered little to the Indians, the traders, the wild and undisciplined *coureurs de bois*, and the *voyageurs*. Nor did most of them hesitate to change allegiance after 1760 brought an end to the French and Indian War and England began slowly to take possession of the French garrisons and trading posts.

Not until seven years after the end of the war, however, did the first and only known English explorer come into the valley. Early in July, 1767, fifty-seven-year-old Jonathan Carver with two fellow travelers, two interpreters, an Indian guide, and some canoe men, under orders from the audacious frontier soldier, Major Robert Rogers, ascended the Chippewa River from the Mississippi. Carver had spent the previous winter trading with the red men along the Minnesota River and was heading north to Lake Superior hoping, as had so many before him, to find the fabled Northwest Passage to the Pacific. By way of Lac Court Oreilles, he portaged west to the Namekagon River. "Having crossed a number of small lakes and carrying places that intervened," Carver reported that he "came to a head branch of the River St. Croix. This branch I descended to a fork, and then ascended to its source." He went down the Namekagon to the St. Croix and up that stream to its source in Lac de la Providence. Here the English explorer speared some "delicate and finely flavored" sturgeon and renamed the lake to honor this "exceeding fine" piscatorial delight. From there Carver took the usual two-mile portage to the Bois Brulé, which he christened Goddard's River in honor of one of his traveling companions. But the water in that

stream was so low he had to reverse the procedure of a predecessor on a similar voyage of exploration eighty-seven years earlier.
Whereas Du Luth found it necessary to tear down many beaver
dams to get up the Brulé, Carver had to rebuild these obstructions which, in his words, "had been broken down by hunters," so
there would be enough water to float his canoes to Lake Superior.
When Carver reached the Grand Portage at the northeast tip of
present-day Minnesota, the supplies he expected to get from
Major Rogers were not there, and he was forced to abandon his
plans for further exploration. "Here," the explorer wrote, "ends
this attempt to find out a Northwest Passage."

The lucrative fur trade, begun by the French, continued to increase throughout the upper Mississippi Valley. The years of English supremacy saw its greatest development into an organized
and ruthless business that was for many years the continent's most
important industry. Great Britain remained in control long after
the definitive peace treaty of 1783 which established independence for the United States. Under the aegis of the powerful North
West Company and a somewhat later rival offshoot, the XY Company, competition was feverish for pelts collected by the Indians,
and the English became masters of artful trade methods. The St.
Croix Valley continued an important travel route and a good trap-
ping ground. Several profitable collecting points for furs were also
established on such tributaries as the Yellow, the Snake, and the
Namekagon rivers, but not much is known when these posts
started nor how long they lasted.

Most of the information we have today about fur company activities along the St. Croix comes from the diaries and reminiscences of three men—George Nelson, Michel Curot, and Thomas
Connor—who spent the winters of 1802 to 1804 trading among
the Indians in the valley. The daily journals kept by two of these
men, Connor and the hapless Curot, are vivid and fascinating on-
the-spot records of fur trade in the valley.

Nelson was a sixteen-year-old apprentice clerk from the Montreal area when in the fall of 1802 he joined XY Company traders
under the leadership of William Smith and traveled into the

Folle Avoine country—the wild rice region of the upper St. Croix Valley. Leaving Lake Superior by way of the Brule, Nelson portaged to the source of the St. Croix where, according to the reminiscences he jotted down many years later, he "glided gently down its placid bosom, but little obstructed by rapids." The river must certainly have been at flood stage. "I do not remember," he continued, "if we were two or 3 days. But we arrived in the afternoon opposite the mouth of the 'Riviere Jaune', Yellow River, where we landed on [a] most beautiful island. The Indians, the moment they saw us gave a whoop. They were all drunk, the N[orth] W[est] Co. had a little before given liquor. They came rushing upon us like devils, dragged our Canoe to land, threw the lading ashore, ripped up the bale cloths, cut the cords & Sprinkled the goods about at a fine rate. Such a noise, yelling & chattering! 'Rum, Rum, what are you come to here without rum?'" they asked. Nelson's rivals well knew that the white man who went into the Indian country with the most whisky always came out with the greatest number of pelts.

The traders soon moved up the Yellow to a spot sixty yards from an encampment of the competing North West Company. There the XY men built a house, and from that location, during the winter of 1802-03, they trudged valley trails on fur-collecting trips to Indian camps along other tributary streams, principally the Chaudière (or Kettle River) and Coquille (now the Clam). Throughout their stay on the Yellow, the traders heard frequent rumors of possible Sioux forays into this hotly contested Chippewa country. For this reason they were glad to leave the area early in April and "escape from danger & be relieved of so much anxiety," as Nelson put it.

A few months later, in mid-August, another group of XY Company fur traders set out for the Yellow River country led by Michel Curot, a young, inexperienced French-Canadian whose abilities as a leader left much to be desired. Smith, the head trader during the previous year, was also a member of the party, but he had been demoted for inefficiency—an arrangement he accepted with bad grace. After traveling slowly along the established route from Lake Superior to the upper St. Croix, Curot and his men reached their wintering grounds on September 20. Again, the post was located in the heart of the wild rice region, not far from the North West Company's encampment on the Yellow River.

Soon after Curot arrived, the Chippewa began to take advantage of his indecisive, vacillating ways and his self-admitted "lack of resolution in the management of men." He was, the Indians soon discovered, a soft touch for extra rations of rum, and they cajoled, teased, and threatened him until he produced the wanted liquor. The Frenchman's own men, especially Smith, also gave him considerable trouble. "It is unfortunate for me," Curot wrote in the journal he had to keep for the company, "that my First Wintering I should have fallen among Men of whom I have only Complaints to Make. . . . I am not afraid of Smith, and I have not Much Time to bother with Him. I have promised, even taken an Oath, that I will not come back to this Post here with Men who only want Their own way, and that at every moment threaten to come to blows. . . . Too much Kindness with certain Men will never succeed in getting anything done."

Curot's life on the Rivière Jaune was made even more uncomfortable by continuing rumors that the Sioux were on the warpath in Chippewa country. When the nearby North West traders began making preparations to defend their garrison against attacks which never materialized, Curot and his men quickly sought protection in their rival's stronger fortification, where they remained until mid-May, 1804. With a not-too-successful winter's work finished, Curot headed north by way of the Brule to the great inland fur post of Grand Portage on Lake Superior. He went out of the valley with only ten packs of skins; his competitors were loaded down with thirty-seven.

During the early fall months of the same year, arrangements were under way at Montreal to merge the North West and XY companies and bring an end to the rivalry and competition of the previous six years. A final agreement on terms, however, was not reached until November, some time after the traders of both firms had established their winter posts along the headwaters of the St. Croix. There were XY men in the valley, as well as North West traders on the Namekagon and Rivière du Serpent (now the Snake).

Thomas Connor, a representative of the North West Company, began early in October to construct a post on the Snake in the area of Cross and Pokegama lakes not far from today's Pine City, Minnesota. On October 12, Connor reported that the weather had cleared and the "men perform'd a great Days Work. gave them each a Dram morning & Evening & promised to do the same till our Buildings are Compleated provided they exert themselves." On the fifteenth the store was finished and the provisions safely placed under lock and key, "a happy Circumstance in time of Danger," Connor added. By October 31, Connor's house was floored and completely plastered, and on November 5 his men were able to occupy their new quarters. Two weeks later a stockade surrounded the buildings and the gates could be "fixed & Shut." The English (some say Irish) Nor'wester then settled down to a long winter of busy trading with the Indians and coping with those he called the "XY Banditti." News of the merger of the North West and XY companies did not reach the Snake River post until New Year's Eve. "I receivd a letter," Connor recorded that day, "advising me of a Settlement having taken place between the 2 parties trading in the N.W. which puts a Stop to Opposition." But in spite of the plans for co-operation between the two companies, Connor, threading the back country, continued his efforts to get as many beaver pelts as possible away from his competitors. Trading activities at this post went on until April 27, 1805, when the men packed the winter's peltries in their canoes and started downriver and out of the St. Croix Valley. Connor himself returned later to live and operate a trading post for many years in this same area.

During the summer of 1963 Joseph Neubauer, an amateur archaeologist living near Pine City, discovered at a strategic point on the Harry Cummings farm along the south bank of the Snake River what appeared to be the remains of an old fortification. The Minnesota Historical Society and Dr. Leland R. Cooper, professor of sociology at St. Paul's Hamline University, have carefully excavated the site and both are of the opinion that this important find has at last established the exact site of Tom Connor's North West Company wintering post of 1804. Future plans include purchase of the property and reconstruction of the palisaded fort.

The British continued to hold control over the vast western region, including the valley of the St. Croix, because a languid, disinterested United States was slow to occupy the land. The American Revolution and the War of 1812 came and went before the new government bestirred itself. Traders employed by the English North West Company gathered furs on both sides of the Canadian-United States boundary even after 1816, the year in which Congress decreed that only United States citizens could be licensed to trade on American lands. When Major Stephen H. Long, an army engineer on an exploring trip from St. Louis to the Falls of St. Anthony, passed the mouth of the St. Croix in July, 1817, he commented that the river was still "the channel of considerable intercourse between the British traders and the Indians." It is doubtful that the traffic ceased until after law and order came to this northern region with the establishment in 1819 of the military post that became Fort Snelling, at the confluence of the Mississippi and Minnesota rivers.

The fur trade was still an important business in 1820 when Henry Rowe Schoolcraft, a twenty-seven-year-old mineralogist from New York, first heard of the St. Croix River. In that year, Schoolcraft accompanied Lewis Cass, governor of Michigan Territory, on a preliminary exploring journey to seek out the source of the Mississippi. Although the young man did not actually see the St. Croix on this trip, he published in 1821 a *Narrative Journal of Travels* in which he stated that "in its whole extent" the St. Croix was "not interrupted by a single fall or rapid."

Not until eleven years later when he returned to the Minnesota-Wisconsin country as an Indian agent attempting to end the continuing hostilities between the Sioux and Chippewa did Schoolcraft learn how wrong he had been. Leaving his headquarters at Sault Ste Marie on June 25, 1831, Schoolcraft spent seventy-two days traveling some 2,300 miles "visiting the Chippewa villages . . . between Lake Superior and the Mississippi." Entering the Mauvais (now the Bad) River which flows north into Lake Superior east of the Brule, Schoolcraft's impressive flotilla, with an American flag flying from each canoe, proceeded by way of numerous portages to the Namekagon. From there the party traveled down the St. Croix, reaching the fur trading post and Indian village on the Yellow on August 1. To visit other Indian settlements Schoolcraft then followed the route taken by Carver in 1767—via the Namekagon portage to Lac Court Oreilles and down the Chippewa River to the Mississippi. Schoolcraft's mission was successful in that the Indians agreed not to fight, in his words, during the "present fall and ensuing winter." He reported to the Office of Indian Affairs that the Chippewa on the St. Croix would "sit still and remain at peace." Lawrence Taliaferro, at Fort Snelling, was not impressed by the journey of his fellow Indian agent. "The trip of Mr. Schoolcraft has proven to be an abortion," Taliaferro recorded in his journal on September 1, 1831. "He has talents, but not for Indian feelings."

This trip was but a prelude to the important exploratory expedition undertaken by Schoolcraft in 1832. His official instructions for that excursion, approved at Washington by Lewis Cass, now Secretary of War, ordered Schoolcraft to curb Indian hostilities, investigate the fur trade, compile statistics concerning the aborigines, and vaccinate them against the dreaded smallpox. But for Schoolcraft, the basic reason was to trace the Father of Waters to its true source. As fellow adventurers, he chose the Reverend William T. Boutwell, a young Presbyterian missionary who later settled in the Stillwater area; Dr. Douglass Houghton, the competent physician of the 1831 expedition who also served as botanist and geologist; George Johnston, Schoolcraft's Irish-Chippewa brother-in-law and interpreter; and Lieutenant James Allen of Ohio who was in command of a military escort of ten men and was charged with preparing a map of the route.

Early in June, 1832, this first American expedition to ply the full length of the St. Croix left Sault Ste Marie for the interior country west and south of Lake Superior. After the expedition discovered and named Lake Itasca on July 13 as the *veritas caput,* the true headwaters of the Mississippi, the travelers reached Fort Snelling on July 24. Only two days later they started the homeward journey north by way of the St. Croix and Brule rivers.

In the diary he kept during this trip, Lieutenant Allen was the first to admit that his men were "totally unaccustomed to canoes." Even after a month and a half of travel through the wilderness to Lake Itasca, he confessed his inability to teach them "the whole science of canoe management." Schoolcraft knew this, too, and he customarily halted his twenty agile, experienced *voyageurs* so that the military escort could catch up. When Allen was delayed by a snagged canoe on the first leg of the St. Croix trip, even before reaching that river, Schoolcraft's French-Canadians paddled swiftly and steadily ahead, leaving the lieutenant and his men to follow as best they could. This left Allen without the usual Indian steersmen to pilot the fragile canoes, without the necessary services of a doctor, and with no interpreter to help him through the Chippewa country. Of the three other men to keep records during this trip, two expressed concern for the fate of Lieutenant Allen. The Reverend Mr. Boutwell felt he would "find much difficulty in coming through," and Dr. Houghton wrote in his diary on July 29, "we had many fears for him." This concern may or may not have been shared by Schoolcraft, although from his actions we assume that it was not.

It is interesting to note that en route to the falls of the St. Croix, Schoolcraft's party and then Lieutenant Allen's military contingent met up with Joseph R. Brown, the "intellectual lion" who later became one of Minnesota's leading pioneers and an important figure in the story of the St. Croix Valley. He and a group of Frenchmen with their Indian families were descending the river in four canoes. Brown had been engaged in trading with the Chippewa along the upper river and Schoolcraft, as an Indian agent, examined Brown's papers to see if he was legally licensed. He also searched the canoes for whisky, which the trader was known to have used in bartering for furs. "None of this article, or strong drink of any kind was discovered," reported Schoolcraft, who nonetheless revoked Brown's license and "permitted him to proceed out of the country." When Schoolcraft reached the head of the rapids a few miles above the Dalles, he found nine cabins of Brown's abandoned post which he ordered burned, since they were there contrary to government regulations.

A harrowing experience at the Dalles was the first of many discouragements encountered by Lieutenant Allen and his inexperienced soldiers. "I had the greatest difficulty," he wrote in his daily journal, "in getting through this rocky, rapid, and difficult pass, to the foot of the falls and portage, my canoes being frequently in the most imminent peril of being driven on the rocks, and dashed to pieces by the force of the current." But the most unnerving moment came when, after five hours of exhausting work pulling the canoes over beds of boulders and rocks, the party finally reached the end of a five-mile stretch of difficult rapids above the falls, to find Schoolcraft's campfire still warm and a note written by Dr. Houghton impaled on a stake. The message informed Allen that the expedition's leader had no intention of waiting for him anywhere on the route. Because the water was falling rapidly, Schoolcraft had determined to proceed "with all possible speed."

At this point, with the troops worn out and discouraged, the bark canoes leaking badly, and no pitch gum to mend them, Allen gave up all hope of overtaking Schoolcraft. The lieutenant seriously considered turning back, and in his record for that day strongly castigated Schoolcraft for his thoughtlessness in leaving the group in such a fix without any advance warning, "knowing, as he did, the unfitness of my men for the sole management of canoes on this difficult route."

But the military contingent did not turn back, preferring to struggle through rapid after rapid from the Snake to the Yellow to the Namekagon to the Eau Claire. Having no goods to barter, Allen was unable to secure Indian guides, but he did manage to obtain gum for mending the weakened canoes. Schoolcraft sent three Chippewa to help, but they refused to go more than a few miles, and the agent later claimed that they defected because the soldiers expected them to do too much work. It took Lieutenant Allen and his men ten days to reach the river's source at the handsome body of clear water which by then was no longer referred to as Lac de la Providence or Sturgeon Lake but simply carried the

name Upper St. Croix Lake. "On leaving Fort Snelling," Allen
said, "we expected to reach Lake Superior in eight." Two guides
and a canoe, sent back by Schoolcraft, met them as they descended the swift waters of the Brule, and were of much service,
the lieutenant admitted, in finally bringing the soldiers to Lake
Superior, a full five days behind the others.

When Allen and his men reached La Pointe on Madeline
Island, Dr. Houghton and Boutwell were waiting. "Lieut. Allen
arrived," the doctor reported, "his men nearly worn out & gave a
heart rending picture of his travels from the Mississippi." Boutwell, too, was "happy, indeed, to greet him once more." The
leader of the expedition, however, had left La Pointe for Sault Ste
Marie four days previously.

Schoolcraft's trip up the St. Croix was comparatively unevent-
ful, thanks to his expert guides and experienced canoe men. En
route, Dr. Houghton made notes on the area's geology and had
little difficulty vaccinating more than two hundred *Folle Avoine*
Chippewa against smallpox for which, he said, "they have a wonderful dread." It is presumed that the Reverend Mr. Boutwell
held Sunday services along the St. Croix on July 29, as was his
custom, addressing the Indians through the interpreter. Schoolcraft was, of course, assiduous in obtaining as much information
about the Indians and the fur trade as he could. The results, when
published in 1834, were hailed by the *New York American* as a
valuable addition to the knowledge of Indian life. The newspaper,
however, called Schoolcraft's treatment of Lieutenant Allen on
the St. Croix "unaccountable and inhumane" as well as "un-
Christianlike." Although it does not appear that Schoolcraft pur-
posely abandoned Allen to his own inadequate resources, the latter's acrimony can be easily understood.

As early as 1836, when the Territory of Wisconsin was formed,
men were anxiously eying the vast forests of the St. Croix Valley
and seeking ways, legal and illegal, to cut the virgin pine timber.
In the fall of that year genial Joseph N. Nicollet, French explorer
and scientist, reached St. Peter's (Mendota) on his return from
charting the source of the Mississippi. A cold spell set in which
threatened to freeze the river, and he resolved to spend the winter

at Fort Snelling as Major Taliaferro's welcome guest. "We were then only in the beginning of October," Nicollet reported, "and the Indian summer (which is beautiful in the valley of the Mississippi) soon brought around several weeks of mild weather, that reopened navigation." At this time the explorer made several trips into the St. Croix Valley, one of which was reported by Agent Taliaferro. On October 24, with two Fort Snelling officers and a boatload of soldiers, the scientist traveled the waters of the St. Croix for four days to continue "his observations of the Latitude & Longitude"—the first such specialized expedition along the river. The result of his explorations throughout the Midwest was an unusually accurate map published in 1843, entitled "Hydrographical Basin of the Upper Mississippi," which became, according to historian William Watts Folwell, the basis for "all the subsequent cartography of an immense region."

To continue his investigations the following year, Nicollet, in the company of traders William A. Aitken and Lyman M. Warren with his wife, the Reverend Mr. Boutwell, interpreter Jean-Baptiste Dubé, and a group of Lake Superior Indians left St. Peter's on August 2, 1837, for La Pointe by way of the St. Croix and Brule rivers. During their second day out they ate breakfast among the long, narrow islands above Stillwater near the angular, decorated sandstone cliffs—the Painted Rock of the ancient Dakota. *"Rivière très pitoresque,"* was Nicollet's appreciative comment.

A short, succinct, and hitherto unquoted diary kept by this French astronomer describes in some detail the physical features of both the St. Croix and Brule rivers, with special attention to the numerous and difficult rapids of the upper valley. The Namekagon River, he said, was "long and beautiful" and was the stream most frequented by the Chippewa. "Seven miles above the Namekagon," continued Nicollet, "is a portage that is used to avoid the difficult rapids on the St. Croix. Called *portage des femmes,* women's portage, it borders the river and is only a quarter of a mile long. At this same spot begins a direct route to the village of La Pointe, a trip which the savages make in from 2 to 2 and a half days. This land route is 2 to 3 days shorter than by water along the St. Croix and the Bois Brulé." At this point Mr. Boutwell, Mrs. Warren, and guides left the party to head directly north to Lake Superior and Madeline Island. The others continued the river route, visiting Chief Kabamappa's Chippewa village about twenty-one miles above Women's Portage. Another ten miles brought the party to the Eau Claire or Clearwater River, near the site of the present-day Wisconsin village of Gordon where two railroads now cross the St. Croix. On the afternoon of August 8 they entered Upper St. Croix Lake and made the portage to the Brule River.

Perhaps the most interesting portion of Nicollet's diary is his study of the sources of the St. Croix and Brule. "The opinion of the Savages and the *voyageurs*," the Frenchmen explained, "is that the Source of the St. Croix and Bois Brulé is the same little lake which can be seen from the portage. Schoolcraft repeats this opinion in his book, but it is too unusual to be believed without seeing it." Nicollet's careful survey of the area proved, at least to his satisfaction, that the Brule took its source from the little lake close by the portage, and that the St. Croix grew out of the nearby muskeg swamp. It was Nicollet's considered opinion that a common source did not then exist.

But ask Ray Orner, clerk at the Douglas County Forestry Department, or any of the Solon Springs men who have for years tramped the woods along the St. Croix-Brule headwaters in search of deer. They will show you the spruce-lined pond which Nicollet called the source of the Brule and tell you that out of this small body of water to the northeast of the portage flows St. Croix Creek into Upper St. Croix Lake. A few hundred yards farther north, at the edge of the muskeg swamp, they will also point out what the Reverend Mr. Boutwell called the "boiling spring." From here seepage heads south to the muskeg pond and, by way of the creek, to St. Croix Lake. Out of the same limpid spring also flows a larger and more steady stream heading north to the east fork of the Brule River. This small bubbling pool of cold, clear water, they will tell you, is therefore the ultimate source of the St. Croix and the Brule.

The long period of organized exploration in the St. Croix Valley ended with Nicollet's expedition. By mid-century the picturesque fur traders, *voyageurs,* and *coureurs de bois* were also to disappear from the scene when beaver pelts became more and more difficult to find. The St. Croix was then no longer, in Major Long's words, "the channel of considerable intercourse." Furs, nonetheless, were still being eagerly sought when explorer Nicollet ascended the St. Croix in 1837. The Chippewa and Sioux lived in the region through which he traveled. Only a short time before his trip the Chippewa had disposed of their lands and the Sioux were soon to follow suit.

Chapter Four

Opening the Land

IT WAS in early July, 1837, about a month before Joseph Nicollet left on his trip up the St. Croix, that Chippewa chiefs and braves, from what later became a part of eastern Minnesota and west-central Wisconsin, began converging on Fort Snelling. They were summoned there by messengers from the fort to meet in council with representatives of Uncle Sam. The white man's government needed more land, and with a new President, Martin Van Buren, inaugurated only four months earlier, it was at last ready to negotiate a treaty for the purchase of the Indians' broad acres. Up to this time, no part of the St. Croix Valley had been available to the whites.

Some thirty years earlier, during his expedition to the headwaters of the Mississippi, twenty-six-year-old Lieutenant Zebulon M. Pike of the United States Army negotiated with the Sioux Indians to acquire a location for a future military post. Pike chose two possible spots, and on September 23, 1805, he signed an agreement with the Indians for the acquisition of large tracts from St. Anthony Falls down to the confluence of the Mississippi and Minnesota rivers, where Fort Snelling was later built. He also included as a part of the same treaty nine square miles (or 51,840 acres) at "the mouth of the river St. Croix." The price for this property came to approximately one and a quarter cents per acre. Being military land, however, neither of these locations was open to settlement.

For some time settlers pouring into Wisconsin Territory had been pressuring the powers at Washington to remove the red men and so provide protection and security from the dangers of possible Indian attacks. Lumbermen—their eyes on the lucrative white pine timber of the upper St. Croix—were also demanding the extinction of the Indian titles and the opening of the land to settlement and exploitation. On the satisfactory outcome of the treaty negotiations with the red men, therefore, depended the eventual organization of the future state of Wisconsin and the territory of Minnesota.

To the 1837 treaty-signing conclave at Fort Snelling came chieftains and warriors with their wives and families. From distant Leech and Gull lakes in present-day Minnesota the delegated red men paddled swiftly southward. They arrived also from Lac Court Oreilles and the Flambeau in Wisconsin and from the regions of Lake Superior and Mille Lacs. Senior representative of the St. Croix band was Buffalo of the Bear Clan (Old Pizhickee, as scientist-explorer Schoolcraft called him) who once visited the District of Columbia and returned weighted down with a profusion of ornaments. In 1837 Chief Buffalo was the venerable and respected head of the Snake River Chippewa. Although Schoolcraft made no mention of the fact in his writings, the renowned hunter was also his wife's uncle.

From another Indian village farther to the north, where the upper St. Croix broadens to form a rice lake called Whitefish near today's Wisconsin settlement of Gordon, came Kabamappa (Wetmouth). This was the Indian whom Schoolcraft and his fellow travelers in 1832 called a "friendly and respectable Chief," and whose flourishing gardens of corn, potatoes, and pumpkins drew special comments from the entire exploring expedition.

Also from the valley of the upper river and its tributary the Snake (called the Kinábic by the Indians) traveled many others. Among them were Kabamappa's son Nodin (the Wind); there was the half-breed Sha-ko-pe (Little Six); Na-goun-abe (the Feather's End) who was at that time a warrior of the Wolf Totem or clan on the St. Croix; Sho-ne-yah (the Silver), then a warrior but later to become head man of the Snake River band; and another Snake chief, Pay-a-jig (the Lone Man). A thousand Indians pitched their tepees outside the walls of the fort.

Notables were also among the white men assembled at Fort Snelling. Henry Dodge, governor of Wisconsin Territory and one-time Indian fighter, was the United States commissioner. Cartographer Joseph Nicollet, too, was an interested spectator and witness, as were Henry H. Sibley, Hercules L. Dousman, Warren, Aitken, and other fur traders of the area anxious for the payments of Indian debts. Agent Taliaferro, who was responsible for the show at the fort, undoubtedly had his hands full feeding and caring for the Chippewa. He must also have been hard pressed to keep at a discreet distance some four hundred curious Sioux. "This unexpected convocation of Red Men," Taliaferro later wrote in his autobiography, "brought also a host of expectants in anticipation of some benefit from the Indians, interested fur traders and agents not a few." The Fort Snelling agent could find no time to make daily entries in his journal.

The council assembled to begin its deliberations on July 20, shielded from the summer's sun by a protective canopy of green boughs laid over a high framework which was erected some seventy yards from the agent's office. Governor Dodge opened the proceedings: "Chiefs, Head men, and Warriors of the Chippewa Nation," he began. "Your Great Father, the President of the United States, has sent me to see you in council to propose to you the purchase of a small part of your country, east of the Mississippi River. This country, as I am informed, is not valuable to you for its game, and not suited to the culture of corn, and other agricultural purposes. Your great Father wishes to purchase your Country on the Chippewa and St. Croix rivers for the advantage of its pine timber, with which it is said to abound."

"My Father," replied the elderly Buffalo at the conclusion of Dodge's speech, "I am taken by surprise by what you have said to us, and will speak but few words to you now. We are waiting for more of our people who are coming from the country which you wish to buy from us. We will think of what you have said to us, and when they come, will tell you our minds about it. . . . I have nothing more to say now."

The arrival of the remaining chiefs and warriors was patiently awaited by the whites. Meanwhile the Indians enjoyed the rations provided by Agent Taliaferro, grumbled about the supplies being furnished, especially the small whisky and tobacco allotments, and indulged in one of their favorite pastimes—oratory. "My Father," complained Pay-a-jig, "what has happened to you? Have you cut off your breasts, that you cannot suckle your children. If you did so, it would render them more pliant and ready to yield to your wishes." What the Indians wanted was four times the allotment of the white man's milk—whisky.

The oratory continued during the next five days, and not until the twenty-sixth were the final events put into motion, after the arrival of the expected chiefs from Lac Court Oreilles and Lake Superior. On that morning Governor Dodge again briefed the assembled Indians, as he had on the first day. He defined the limits of the vast purchase of Chippewa lands in the area east of the Mississippi River and north of that portion of the 1825 Sioux-Chippewa boundary line which extended from Sauk Rapids, through the Standing Cedar on the St. Croix, and then southeast to the Black River beyond Eau Claire.

On the following day Ma-ghe-ga-bo (the Trapper) of the Leech Lake Pillager band was the central figure and focus of attention, dressed in his full regalia—naked except for leggings, a red-flapped breech cloth, long hair falling over his shoulders, a crown of bald eagle feathers decorating his head, and medals dangling loosely on his chest. He spoke on behalf of his nation.

"My father," said Ma-ghe-ga-bo, pointing to a map in his hand, "this is the country which is the home of your children. I have covered it with a paper and so soon as I remove the paper the land shall be yours . . . My Father, in all the country we sell you, we wish to hold on to that which gives us life—the streams and lakes where we fish, and the trees from which we make sugar." This request was approved by Governor Dodge, and after a standing vote among the other chieftains, Ma-ghe-ga-bo ceremoniously lifted the paper from the map and grasped the commissioner's hand. All that remained was to come to a quick agreement on terms. The Indians were happy and anxious to hand over the timber rights to their land. Not until 1849 when they were forced off this land did the red men realize that they had also bartered away their earthly heritage.

In exchange for this immense tract of land which stretched from the Mille Lacs region of Minnesota across a good part of Wisconsin as far as Crandon, the United States agreed to the following: The government would pay $190,000 in cash over a period of twenty years, as well as $380,000 in goods, $60,000 for blacksmith shops, $20,000 for farmers, $40,000 in provisions, and $10,000 for tobacco. In addition, lump sums of $100,000 were allotted to the half-breeds, and $70,000 earmarked to pay back the Indian debts claimed by the fur traders. For the total sum of $870,000 this purchase was a steal—even in 1837. No wonder the Reverend Alfred Brunson, Methodist Missionary among the Chippewa in the vicinity of Fort Snelling, wryly commented, "The whites showed their skill in making a good bargain with the ignorant Indians."

While the commissioner's secretary, Verplanck Van Antwerp, was busy drawing up the treaty, a joyful three hundred Chippewa braves danced in the shadows of Fort Snelling's walls (the agent took care to lock the gates, just in case). They sang at length of great exploits at war and boasted of their deeds of bravery while the Sioux looked on with seeming indifference. After the Chippewa chiefs touched the quill as their part in the signing of the treaty, they prepared to return north to the country they no longer owned.

In the meantime, steps were being taken to inform the Sioux chieftains of a proposed visit to Washington, where in a separate treaty they, too, would sign away their lands east of the Mississippi and south of the 1825 Chippewa boundary line to Wisconsin's Black River. On August 18, 1837, Taliaferro temporarily resigned his office as Indian Agent to the commandant at Fort Snelling, Captain Martin Scott. He then took the small Sioux delegation by river steamer, picking up other chiefs at stops along the Mississippi as they traveled south to St. Louis. From there the twenty-six Sioux headed overland to Washington where they met the Great White Father, President Van Buren, and on September

29 signed a similar treaty with Secretary of War Joel R. Poinsett. For considerations totaling almost one million dollars, the Sioux ceded about a third the amount of land given up by the Chippewa. That same day, fur trader Sibley commented in a letter to Ramsay Crooks of the American Fur Company that "The whole treaty is but one series of iniquity & wrong. . . . This is the boasted parental regard for the poor Indian." Agent Taliaferro, however, was of the opinion that he had made a better bargain for the Sioux than Governor Dodge had for the Chippewa.

After the conclusion of these two treaties, there began an anxious period at Fort Snelling, waiting for news of their ratification by the United States Senate. Toward mid-June, 1838, the Indians were becoming eagerly restless for the money, goods, and provisions promised them. Steamboats arrived at the fort, the *Ariel* on the twentieth and the *Burlington* eight days later, yet no word from Washington. Anxious Indians flocked in from the St. Croix and other regions, but they got no news. "So much the worse for them & the United States," reported the Indian agent, and he predicted that there would be trouble if word did not come soon.

On June 30, Taliaferro appealed to Governor Dodge at Madison. "We are on thorns as to the fate of the Sioux & Chippewa treaties," he wrote, "as upon these hang the future peace & tranquility of this fair land." It was not until July 15 that the welcome news arrived. The paddle-wheeler *Palmyra*, which would later play an important role in the settling of the St. Croix Valley, unexpectedly reached the fort on that day. With it came a month-old copy of the *Washington Globe* confirming the ratification. "All sunny like a new day," rejoiced the agent, "countenances brightening with smiles of pleasure and real delight." The receipt of official documents at a later date was obviously an event of minor importance, for Taliaferro made no record of it in his journal.

At last the dispossessed aborigines would no longer impede settlement by the whites, and the way was paved for zealous land seekers and covetous speculators to get into this desirable section, to cut and sell the tracts of centuries-old pines. Lumbermen from the forests of Maine, from villages along the banks of the Penobscot, the Kennebec, the other St. Croix, the Saco, and Androscog-

gin rivers, were itching to get their hands on the vast stands of
virgin timber along this new St. Croix.

After the sanctioning of the Chippewa and Sioux treaties in
1838, there began the inexorable march of white men into the
Indians' hunting and fishing grounds along the St. Croix River.
The pioneers first staked their claims at the falls of the St. Croix,
then at Marine Mills and other valley villages. The ink was barely
dry on the treaties before the newcomers became squatters in the
valley. They built homes and sawmills on land that wasn't theirs,
then headed north along the river to search out and bring to
market the forests of white pine still belonging to the government.
Lack of title to the land in no way held back the growth of lumbering. Those who came into the valley to cut the trees felt that
the logs were rightfully theirs, both collectively and personally,
and that they could do about as they wished.

The United States government was slow to move in this new
and unfamiliar country, slow to survey these lands and sell them
—unless forced into action by the continuing demands of the settlers. For example, during 1844 President John Tyler and the Congress were urged to place the pinelands of the St. Croix and Chippewa River valleys on the market, or else the "outrageous waste
being committed on them" would inevitably ruin any value they
might have. Caleb Cushing, a wealthy Massachusetts politician
and speculator in property around St. Croix Falls, also complained to Washington in 1846 that a vast amount of timber was
being promiscuously stolen along that river. He, too, advised that
the region be offered for sale.

With so many lumbermen illegally claiming timber in the pineries, and squatters by the score pouring into the burgeoning
villages, the General Land Office of the United States in 1847
finally authorized a linear survey of the area, and employed geologist David Dale Owen to examine its mineral content. Writing to
his wife from Stillwater on July 21, 1847, Owen struck a note
which river travelers continue to sound when he complained of
the "Swarms of mosquitoes, buffalo gnats, gadflies and a host of
other small but excessively annoying insects which infest these regions during the last two weeks of June, all of July and the first

two weeks of August. . . . Only by dint of the greatest perseverance and resorting to every imaginable means of repelling their attacks we were enabled to get sufficient sleep."

By mid-1848 the first acreage along the St. Croix was ready to be placed on sale at the land office set up at St. Croix Falls. The opening of such an agency was of vital importance. It signaled the official start of legal colonization in the Indian country acquired ten years earlier; at that office the pioneer could file his claim, lay out his money, and obtain a patent to the property he wanted. On April 28, 1848, Samuel Leech, a veteran of eleven years' experience in the government's land office at Quincy, Illinois, was appointed receiver at St. Croix Falls, with Cornelius S. Whitney as his register. President James K. Polk on May 8 issued a proclamation announcing the public sales of government property to be held at the Falls, with the first auction to commence on Monday, August 14, and last not longer than two weeks. Not until July 4, however, did Leech write to his boss, Robert M. Young, that he was about to leave Quincy to open the first land office in the St. Croix Valley.

Leech's initial customer was James Purinton, a Maine lumberman whom we will meet later in the unfortunate story of a jinxed St. Croix village. On July 24, Purinton, then a resident of St. Croix Falls, purchased some 138 acres at Willow River on the east bank of the St. Croix and soon moved to that downriver settlement to construct a dam and build the first sawmill in what is now Hudson, Wisconsin. This initial acquisition of land in the valley was made under the provisions of the Pre-emption Act of 1841 which permitted a settler to buy up to 160 acres, provided it was for his own use and not for speculation and profit. Entry number two in the land office record book was made August 12, for the pre-emption of 108 acres in the village of Marine Mills acquired by Samuel Burkleo, Orange Walker, and Hiram Berkey—three partners in the Marine Lumber Company. This is the first record of the sale of land in what was soon to become Minnesota Territory.

Although the President's proclamation specifically stated that the first public sale was to start on August 14, it began two days earlier, according to a joint report made by Leech and Whitney

on August 31. To publicize this disposal of public lands the governmental agents distributed and posted throughout the area
many copies of the handbill. Accommodations at the Falls were
difficult to find. Furthermore, the first sale was hampered by the
availability of only one crier, or auctioneer, as was the second
which began on Monday, August 28, as scheduled, and continued
for twelve days, through September 9.

The initial purchase made during the two public sales was not
recorded until August 22, more than a week after the auction began. This entry in the land office records was for eighty-five acres
at Marine, which cost only slightly more than one hundred dollars. The same Marine lumbermen who made the earlier purchase
were again involved with two additional partners, Albert H. and
George B. Judd.

The over-all results of these two auctions were quite unsatisfactory. Only 746 acres were sold, Leech reported on October 8, and
he took in but $11,012. Furthermore, Leech stated, a great share
of the land disposed of during the first quarter of business was to
the south, along the Mississippi River and in the vicinity of St.
Paul and the Falls of St. Anthony.

Sam Leech was not only discouraged by the outcome of the
auctions, but he was also personally unhappy about the location
of the land office so far removed from the amenities of life. By late
August, Whitney had already asked for a leave of absence, plead-
ing sickness in his family back East. Leech used a different approach. He complained of the "remote situation of our office, and
the imperfect state of our mail facilities." Commissioner Young, in
his reply from Washington on September 8, acknowledged that
there would not be much land office business during the winter
months "at that distant & almost inaccessible point." The President, he said, would not grant an official leave, but Leech received permission, as Young put it, to "dispose of your time during the winter as you may see fit," provided suitable agents were
put in charge, "to be paid by yourselves," the commissioner was
quick to add.

Leech arranged to leave the office in the competent hands of
two trustworthy local residents, geologist George W. Brownell

and future Minnesota governor William R. Marshall, so he could spend a more pleasant winter down in Quincy. "I expect to leave [by] the first conveyance," he wrote to his superior at Washington on October 2, "whether it be by Steam Boat, Batteau or raft, the latter being the most common on the St. Croix River between this place and Stillwater." In the hope that he would not have to return to the upper St. Croix the following year, Leech strongly recommended that the land office be moved either to Stillwater or St. Paul. "I would greatly Prefer," he overtly hinted, "to reside in St. Paul than the town of Stillwater."

Receiver Leech, however, was evidently not too efficient a government officer. He got himself into hot water by overpaying his co-worker Whitney, and he was also responsible for a number of costly errors in making out land sale papers. "I will hereafter avoid similar omissions," he apologized in a letter written from Quincy. His superiors were not to give him that chance for very long. By February 1, 1849, Leech was back at St. Croix Falls, and the following month he received orders to move the land office to Stillwater. On the same day a notice was also written authorizing the establishment of a second office at Willow River (now Hudson), to handle all Wisconsin sales in the Chippewa land district. During June, Leech moved the books and office records to the new headquarters at Stillwater. He was then relieved of his position as receiver, but continued to serve in that capacity until late August when he permanently left the St. Croix Valley.

By the 1850s the lumber industry was growing steadily, and agriculture was slowly becoming the second most important occupation in the valley. An early, prophetic voice, the *Minnesota Republican* of St. Anthony, editorialized on June 21, 1855: "As Minnesotans, we must look to our soil for support, more than to pine logs. Not that the pine region is exhausted . . . but we never can be prosperous and independent until our luxuriant valleys, prairies, and meadow lands, are cultivated." By 1855 no one remembered Governor Dodge's 1837 statement at Fort Snelling telling the Chippewa that "This country is . . . not suited to the cultivation of corn, and other agricultural purposes." But perhaps a few recalled Ma-ghe-ga-bo's forthright reply during the Indian treaty ceremonies: "It is not true," he countered. "There is no better ground to cultivate than it until you get up to where the pine region commences." And Chief Kabamappa of the St. Croix knew it, too, for even in the heart of the pineries, up near the Eau Claire River, his gardens of corn, potatoes, and pumpkins flourished.

From the earliest days when the first lumber mills were established at the Falls of St. Croix and Marine Mills, settlers tilled the soil for sustenance, raising a few acres of corn, potatoes, and garden vegetables to feed the hungry mill hands. Just who should be named the earliest farmers in the valley is somewhat in doubt. But probably that honor goes to Joseph Haskell and James S. Norris who in 1840 commenced their agricultural pursuits as partners near the village of Afton. There they turned three acres of land in six days with four yoke of oxen pulling a cast-iron plow. Then they planted the pioneer's two staples—corn and potatoes. A year later Norris moved to a claim near Cottage Grove, Minnesota, and seeded forty acres of wheat, said to be the first grown in any quantity north of Prairie du Chien. The next spring he put in ninety.

It is known that in the early 1840s there was a "grist or flouring mill" at the St. Croix Falls lumbering establishment. Then about 1845 Lemuel Bolles built what his contemporaries called a "little corn cracker" close by Afton on the creek which today unofficially carries his name. This first privately owned mill in Minnesota had a set of small stones for grinding corn and flour of a coarse quality and served lower river residents until the mid-1850s when new flour and gristmills began springing up around other settlements like Hudson, Marine, and South Stillwater (now Bayport).

As early as 1847 a resident at St. Croix Falls complained in the *Prairie du Chien Patriot* that this fertile valley with its "beautiful farming country," lacked but one thing—"farmers to raise grain enough for home consumption and some to spare, instead of having to transport a large amount from the lower country every year." During 1849 excursionist-author Ephraim S. Seymour recorded in his book *Sketches of Minnesota* that in the neighborhood of the falls there were about a half-dozen farms under cultivation. When the 1850 census was taken, only three inhabitants of

Marine Mills listed themselves as "farmers," and there were but forty-eight farms in all of Minnesota's Washington County, which then included most of today's Chisago and Pine counties as well as a portion of Carlton County.

The region's first settlers migrated to find employment in the pineries, not to cultivate the soil and open the land. The lumbering business paid good wages, and in the beginning there was more ready cash to be had by working in the logging camps and at the mills. To clear the rich farmland of timber and to grub out the stumps and roots was a long, tedious job, and a costly one if you had to hire it done.

The difficulties and expenses farmers faced when settling on the land are pointed up by the experiences of David Wentworth, a Pennsylvanian who reached Minnesota with his family in May, 1846, and five years later settled in the Point Douglas region. Through the next eight months he completed and moved his family into a twenty-four-by-eighteen-foot log dwelling. Before the snows fell, Wentworth also broke, plowed, and planted twenty-five acres of farmland and constructed a sturdy rail fence around his property at the cost of more than $400. Until the 1870s, fields had to be fenced to protect the crops from livestock that was permitted to roam at large. In addition, Wentworth enclosed a garden plot of one acre, constructed several outbuildings, and made numerous other improvements at a total expenditure of over $700. So heavy were his expenses, that not until several years later was he able to make any payments on the property.

Small farms like Wentworth's, however, could not furnish the sustenance needed by the people of the area. Until the end of the 1850s, a great part of the food consumed within Minnesota had to be imported from out of the territory, brought in by steamboats from other regions to the east and south. The lumberjacks in the steadily growing camps along the Kettle, the Snake, and other logging tributaries of the upper St. Croix were fed with Iowa, Wisconsin, and Illinois produce. Frank Delano, warden of Minnesota's Territorial Prison at Stillwater, complained in St. Paul's *Weekly Minnesotian* in January, 1854, that not more than one eighth of the flour, pork, corn, oats, beef, and other foodstuffs needed by the men in the pineries was furnished by Minnesota farmers. But the time was not too distant, predicted Stillwater's editor Milton H. Abbott two years later in his newspaper, the *St. Croix Union,* when large, productive farms would line the road between St. Paul and Stillwater.

Perhaps "Old Uncle Reuben Spaulding"—whose writing style recalls an aspiring Bill Nye or an embryo Artemus Ward—was prone to exaggeration, but he mirrored the optimism of the age when he sent in one of his contributions to the *Union.* "Hurrah for continental America and the St. Croix Valley," he exulted. "I have been out to the farms, and boys such farms you never see; oats so stout I couldent waller through 'em—a hundred acres in a patch. Wheat, corn and tatters that make the very Arth groan; fifty acres of corn hoed with a hoss and harer, an awful crop, and a dollar a bushel. Why, the ground works so easy they call a hundred acre field nothing, a hundred and fifty purty fair, and two hundred a right smart chance. . . . And oh, the country, tell Aunt Suzan, its full of flowers, and if she could see the lake roll and plash beneath the arnest gaze of the sun, and laugh and sparkle in her dear old face, or see it in the still night with the heaven and Arth sleeping in its bosom; she'd love the St. Croix Valley."

The land was there—good, fertile land, the "best in the territory," many thought. As Nancy Nichols, wife of Stillwater's Presbyterian minister, wrote to her sister back East in December, 1853, "If a man has enough to purchase him a team, cows and tools and live upon [the land] the first year, he will succeed." There was, however, one drawback. A large portion of the spreading upland prairies on both sides of the lower river was being held by land sharks, speculators, and promoters of paper towns waiting for the kill. "Vampyres," one newspaper called them. The high prices such men asked for farmland in the valley retarded cultivation for several years. It took a financial crash—the Panic of 1857—and the end of feverish land speculation in Minnesota and Wisconsin to bring property back into the market at more realistic prices. The St. Croix area, nevertheless, suffered to a lesser degree during the depression than did other sections of the country.

It was the steady stream of logs which kept rolling down the river and the large amount of lumber being exported to Southern markets that helped many valley residents weather the financial storm. Others were not so lucky, and numerous settlers could not last out the hard times. Stillwater lawyer Gold T. Curtis explained to B. Douglas & Co., a Chicago credit agency, one reason why some improvident valley businessmen and farmers were quitting the valley to escape all Eastern debts. Overextended credit had been their ruin. "There is one thing at which I am much surprised," wrote the experienced Curtis early in January, 1858, after several unsuccessful attempts to collect bad debts, "it is the facility with which tradesmen, whether of any capital or not, obtain goods on credit, in Chicago, St. Louis, Galena, N.Y., & other cities. Experience will finally teach these cities that they should exercise at least as much prudence in sales to a Minnesotan as to men in their own cities."

By 1859 local newspapers could report that business was looking up and that at last Minnesota was becoming a grain-growing state capable of exporting its products. The land was being opened, the fields grubbed of stumps and roots, and the earth planted. "The past season," boasted the *Stillwater Messenger* on May 24, 1859, "is the first season that Minnesota has been a produce exporting state, and the change from an importing to an exporting community has been attended with visible and happy effects. With the large, increased breadth of territory sown the present season, and the encouraging prospects of fine crops and an active market, we think we can see that 'good time coming' very near at hand." But there had to be more men to till the good valley soil. In a land-advertising pamphlet of 1859, Oliver Gibbs at Prescott stated that the greatest need along the St. Croix continued to be for "farmers . . . who can develop the resources of the country."

One attempt to get men to settle the new country came on May 20, 1862, when President Abraham Lincoln signed the Homestead Act, a land measure of importance to home seekers and farmers; although speculators, through perjury and chicanery, reaped even more personal benefits. The act had but few restrictions. The hardy pioneer over twenty-one years of age or the head of the

family who could live on and improve the allotted 160 acres in
five years would be able to acquire the land for the payment of
fees. This law, enacted for those of poorer means, became opera-
tive in January, 1863. During the stress of the Civil War, there
was no great rush of land seekers into the unsettled portions of
the United States. But after the return of thousands of soldiers to
civilian life, it was not long before northwest Wisconsin and the
rest of the country were singing:

> The farm that Uncle Sam will give, will please you to a charm,
> Then come along with all your sons, and get the splendid farm,
> Your wives and blooming daughters, come bring along likewise,
> Uncle Sam will bid you welcome, come seize the glorious prize.
>
> Come along, —come along!
>   Don't be alarmed!
> Uncle Samuel's rich enough
>   To give you all a farm—in Polk County!

The farmers came, more plows turned the soil, more fields were
fenced. The farmer prospered. After the Panic of 1857 and the
opening of land to a growing rural population, spring wheat became the important cash crop and the agriculturalists' main source
of income. "At Hudson and Prescott and other points on the Wisconsin side," New York editor Horace Greeley wrote after a trip
up the St. Croix in October, 1865, "as well as at . . . all landings
in Minnesota the cry is Wheat! Wheat! Hudson is a pretty eastern
town . . . whose staple is Wheat. . . . Every steamboat goes
down the river with all the wheat on board she will take, and a
couple of wheat-laden barges made fast to her sides." Over in
Somerset, Sam Fifield of Osceola's *Polk County Press* said in July,
1869, that the wheat fields gave promise of one of the largest
yields ever recorded in the valley. "In fact," he added, "among the
bone and sinew of the land, the tillers of the soil, prosperity
dwelleth, and although hard times have come, they see in their
growing crops enough and to spare, and take courage and work
on with light hearts."

Lumber and wheat! Through two great panics and depressions,

these were the important nineteenth century income products of the land along the St. Croix until the great stands of pine were gone, and the earth could no longer tolerate the same crop year after year. In 1870, however, the *Stillwater Republican* reported that Washington County was generally acknowledged to be one of the best wheat-raising districts in Minnesota and western Wisconsin. Contributing to this reputation was Oliver Dalrymple's 2,600-acre "bonanza" farm at Cottage Grove, first started in 1864. In 1869 he had seven threshing machines operating on 2,000 acres of wheat.

But by the close of the nineteenth century, the end of logging and lumbering on the St. Croix was at hand. Farmers were planting their fields with less and less wheat and today's diversified agriculture was taking its place. When the wheat-growing centers shifted westward, dairying became popular. The Indians were pushed farther north into the region of poorer soil and the good land on both sides of the lower river was for the most part in private and white hands. The government had all but stepped out of the picture. In 1889 the second land office at St. Croix Falls, opened in 1860, was closed. And four years later federal authorities felt that it was no longer profitable to maintain the only other St. Croix Valley land sale office, the one at Taylors Falls.

The pioneer days were over. Lumbering gave way to agriculture and the economics of the valley became more stable. Horace Greeley's prediction of 1865 became a reality: "This region will breathe freer when its last pine log is cut, run, sawed, rafted, and sold."

Chapter Five

The Birthplace of Minnesota

THE ENTIRE valley of the St. Croix was a part of Wisconsin Territory when the first ax bearers from New England and the East streamed up the river to open the land and build sawmills at the Falls and at Marine. At that time the Mississippi River formed the western limit of the territory. Not until mid-1846, when Congress gave its approval for Wisconsin to work toward statehood, was there any hint of a change in that boundary. The enabling act designated most of the St. Croix River, instead of the Mississippi, as the territory's western border.

Wisconsin lawmakers had long taken it for granted that the new state's western line would continue to run up the Mississippi to Lake Itasca, especially since the boundary had been so delineated in the Ordinance of 1787. The area between the Mississippi and the St. Croix consisted of 26,000 square miles, including the growing settlements of Stillwater, St. Paul, and St. Anthony, as well as what one Prairie du Chien resident called "an immense pine region, the best probably in the world." Wisconsin did not welcome the loss of such riches, and a number of politicians, in spite of the action of Congress, continued to work toward the acquisition for Wisconsin of whatever land they could salvage west of the St. Croix. Nascent Minnesota was, in turn, eager to claim a sizable share of western Wisconsin.

Bitter were the complaints of river residents when they learned that part of the St. Croix Valley might be taken over by the projected state of Wisconsin. They argued that the interests of those living along both sides of the river were identical, and that it was wrong to divide the valley by a state line. Moreover, many St. Croixans apparently preferred to ally themselves with the fortunes of the future Minnesota because a vast wilderness separated their valley from the distant, settled parts of eastern Wisconsin.

There was talk, too, of establishing the Minnesota territorial capital somewhere in St. Croix Valley, and Massachusetts politician Caleb Cushing, who was the owner of large tracts of land along the river's east bank, hoped he might be named the new territory's governor. Valley residents made their first attempt to push back the Wisconsin line in 1846. The proposition that both sides of the St. Croix be excluded from Wisconsin (which was skillfully championed at Madison by St. Croix Falls resident William Holcombe, delegate to the first constitutional convention) was rejected.

At the second Madison convention in 1847, further futile efforts were made by partisans of both sides to alter the boundary line, one way or another, and this time George W. Brownell of St. Croix Falls fought vigorously on behalf of Minnesotans. After all the arguing and discussion, however, Wisconsin gained admittance to the Union on May 29, 1848, with the St. Croix River forming a part of its western border as originally recommended in the 1846 enabling act.

This decision left the delta between the St. Croix and Mississippi rivers a no man's land without government or law. Western valley residents, eagerly anticipating territorial status for the forgotten region, pointed up the need for organized effort with a gala July 4 celebration at Stillwater. A parade through the main street, music, the ritual reading of the Declaration of Independence, and an oration by Stillwater's Morton S. Wilkinson, the first practicing attorney north of Prairie du Chien, undoubtedly helped stimulate action. But a decisive move was slow in coming. Not until a month later did anyone in the valley openly question how the abandoned portion of Wisconsin Territory should be governed. On August 4, a public meeting called at Stillwater to discuss the matter was so poorly attended that the few men who did show up decided to try again with a better organized "convention." Eighteen self-styled "Citizens of Minnesota Territory," most of them

from Stillwater, signed the notice which called for the appointment of delegates who were "to meet in convention at Stillwater
on the 26th day of August."

On that day Joseph R. Brown, lately a member of the Wisconsin legislature, called to order in the county courtroom the "Stillwater Convention of 1848." The morning meeting was occupied
with preliminary formalities. At one thirty in the afternoon the
delegates reassembled to hear Joe Brown read what is beyond a
doubt the most important document ever penned in the valley of
the St. Croix. Following are the preamble and resolution:

WHEREAS, by the admission of Wisconsin and Iowa into the Union
with the boundaries prescribed by Congress, we, the inhabitants of
the country formerly a portion of said Territories, are left without a
government or officers to administer the laws: and

WHEREAS, by the omission of Congress to organize a separate Territorial Government for the region of country which we inhabit, we
are placed in the unparalleled position of being disfranchised of the
rights and privileges which were guaranteed to us under the Ordinance of 1787; and without any fault of our own, and with every
desire to be governed by laws, are in fact without adequate legal
protection for our lives or property: and

WHEREAS, having patiently awaited the action of Congress during its
late session, under the full hope and confidence that before the ad-
journment of that honorable body, a bill would have been passed for
the organization of a Territorial Government to embrace our section
of the country, we have been disappointed in our hopes, and cannot
believe that the omission of Congress to act in the premises can proceed from any other cause than the want of an adequate acquaint-
ance with the position in which we are placed, the character of the
country, its population and resources:

Therefore, be it *resolved*, That a memorial be addressed to the Senate
and House of Representatives in Congress assembled, and also to his
Excellency, the President of the United States, respectfully request-
ing that he will invite the attention of that Honorable body, in his
annual message, to action in the premises.

Resolved, That a delegate be appointed by this Convention, with full
power to act, whose duty it shall be to visit Washington during the
ensuing session of Congress, and there to represent the interests of

the proposed Territory, and to urge an immediate organization of the same.

Resolved, That a committee of three persons be appointed by the President of this Convention, residing upon the waters of the St. Croix, and three residing upon the waters of the Mississippi, who shall collect information relative to the amount of business transacted and capital employed within the limits of Minnesota Territory, and forward such information, as soon as may be, to our delegate.

Resolved, That there shall be a committee of seven appointed by the President of this Convention to act as a central committee, whose duty it shall be to correspond with our delegate at Washington, and to adopt all other proper means to forward the object of this Convention.

After the unanimous approval of these resolutions, Henry H. Sibley, then a fur trader living at Mendota, was elected delegate. He was to go to Washington, lobby on behalf of Minnesota, and, incidentally, pay his own expenses. Memorials addressed to President James K. Polk and to Congress were signed by all sixty-one delegates from the "several settlements in the proposed Territory" of Minnesota. The name for the new region was taken from a Sioux word meaning "water with clouds in it." After Attorney Wilkinson moved a vote of thanks to the officers, the Stillwater Convention of 1848 adjourned *sine die.* The *Prairie du Chien Patriot* noted at the time that "The citizens . . . are aroused to the necessity of having an organized Territorial Government and they have taken prompt and we trust effective measure to secure that object."

There were others, however, who undoubtedly realized that Sibley's informal appointment would carry little legal weight in the eyes of Congress. They argued that Minnesota East, as the delta country was called, remained nominally Wisconsin Territory —though considerably truncated—and John Catlin of Madison, former territorial secretary, felt that the laws in force before the division were still applicable. Through a series of complicated maneuvers, the audacious Judge Catlin assumed the perhaps questionable role of acting governor of the rump of Wisconsin Territory. He established his residence in Stillwater, and from there, as though it were the capital city, he issued a proclamation calling for the election of a delegate to represent what was left of the old territory. Late in October, Sibley was again chosen by vote to serve the people. He went to Washington where he conducted an eminently successful campaign that led to the creation in 1849 of Minnesota Territory. John Catlin, his work ended, disappeared from the St. Croix Valley scene. Today a bronze plaque affixed to a bank building at the corner of Main and Myrtle streets in Stillwater is the only reminder that in this rough-and-tumble frontier settlement the future thirty-second state was born.

Shortly before the acceptance of Wisconsin's state constitution by the people, another effort was made by St. Croix Valley residents to change the western boundary line. During the autumn that Sibley was being chosen for the second time to represent Minnesotans in the halls of Congress, a public meeting was held at the Falls trading house of Maurice M. Samuels. Indignant river residents strenuously objected to the division of the valley and again urged that it be placed under one government, preferably that of Minnesota, since the river was "the natural centre to which all the Business of the Valley tends." Denizens of the St. Croix firmly pledged themselves to stand united and "Unceasingly to use all honorable means in our power to procure the establishment of a boundary line East of the St. Croix Valley."

Brownell, who had unsuccessfully championed the Minnesota cause at the 1847 Madison convention, also stubbornly continued the fight, but with little success. In a letter dated January 28, 1849, which he wrote to Delegate Sibley at Washington, Brownell argued that there was still much feeling on the subject. With the letter he enclosed a lengthy account of several meetings held at the Falls earlier that month, and of the formation there of a "St. Croix Vigilance Committee." He urged that the grievances of east bank residents be placed before the Washington lawmakers. "We *know* we have friends in the present Legislature," Brownell concluded, "who entertain a sense of our wrongs & who have the moral independence to declare it with effect." Again, however, the efforts of St. Croix residents on the Wisconsin side were fruitless.

No friends in Washington stepped forward to help them, and little attention was paid to their requests.

The arguments went on into 1850 after Minnesota had become a territory and the St. Croix boundary line was an established fact. Wisconsin citizens of the valley were "all anxious to be annexed to Minnesota," reported the *Minnesota Pioneer* on February 13. "It properly belongs to Minnesota; and why it was not included in this territory, is a mystery to all well-wishers of the great west." The same newspaper felt that some of the Northwest's public figures were "negotiable," and slyly hinted that gold would buy off most of them. Just how these bribes should be effected, however, or in what way Minnesota Territory would go about annexing a sizable portion of Wisconsin land was never made clear. In the end, a number of Wisconsin families came up with the simplest solution of all. Those who preferred to unite their fortunes with the new Territory of Minnesota packed their chattels, loaded them on a flatboat, and moved bag and baggage across the St. Croix to the preferred west bank.

Even today, some residents occasionally voice the belief that an undivided St. Croix Valley should be either wholly in Wisconsin or in Minnesota. Forgotten, however, are those plans which at one time might have taken fire—to include St. Paul in the state of Wisconsin and to locate Minnesota's territorial capital somewhere in the valley of the St. Croix River.

Chapter Six

Lumber for the West

THE SAGA of lumbering along the St. Croix River is an important part of the pioneer's relentless advance westward across the continent. Along a vast belt of northern timberland the tree cutters moved in search of marketable coniferous forests to fell. From Maine to New York, from Pennsylvania to Michigan to Wisconsin and Minnesota the lumberjacks stripped the land; they cut the noble white pines to logs and milled the lumber. They helped fill the insatiable need of an expanding America.

In the St. Croix Valley, at what today is the sylvan, peaceful village of Marine, the prodigious lumbering industry of western Wisconsin and Minnesota had its start. Here was located the first sawmill in Minnesota and along the St. Croix to cut and market lumber commercially.

The beginnings, however, were small.

The first known white men to obtain permission from the Indians to cut timber and build sawmills on Chippewa land were three fur merchants trading in the wilderness country of the Mississippi and St. Croix rivers.

An agreement, dated at Pokegama on March 13, 1837, and signed by traders Warren, Aitken, Sibley, and by forty-nine Chippewa chiefs and headmen, permitted the whites to cut trees in an area one mile inland from the east bank and three miles from the west bank of the St. Croix. This limitation extended from Wisconsin's Namekagon River near present-day Riverside, where Highway 35 crosses the St. Croix, southwest to the Snake River, close by today's Pine City. Unspecified annual payments of goods were to be made to the St. Croix and Snake River bands of Chippewa over a ten-year period. In exchange for goods, clothing, gunpowder, and scalping knives—no less—the traders received the right to erect mills at the falls above the Dalles. In addition to the specified area along the upper river, they could also cut a particularly desirable "Cluster of Pines on and near the Sun-Rise River."

The grant was a good one, Warren wrote Sibley, "as large as we could desire" because, quite simply, it comprised all the valuable pines within easy access of the St. Croix. When this agreement was signed, what now is Minnesota (except for the military reservation at Fort Snelling) and a large portion of Wisconsin still belonged to the Indians. It was only by such special dispensations that anyone else could touch ax to tree.

The project of these three merchants, however, died aborning, for on July 29, the Chippewa ceded this land and much more to the whites, thus opening to lumbering the vast expanse of white pine forests along the St. Croix and Mississippi rivers. Warren, Aitken, and Sibley vanished from the St. Croix lumbering scene.

These men were not the only ones to eye the rich pines of the valley. Nor were they the only lumbermen who did not bother to wait until a slow Congress ratified a treaty and an even slower government legally opened the land to purchase and settlement. The Chippewa treaty had just been signed when in mid-1837 Joseph R. Brown, one of Minnesota's most ubiquitous pioneers, was reported felling timber and trading with the Indians on the west bank of the St. Croix at what is now Taylors Falls. Another early bird, Virginian John Boyce, traveled from St. Louis in a Mackinaw boat in the early fall of the same year, set up his outfit of eleven men and six oxen at the juncture of the Snake and St. Croix rivers, and thereby became the first man on record to take a logging crew into this region. Missionary Ely encountered Boyce camping near the mouth of the Kettle River. "He is in search of lumber," Ely recorded in his diary, "has about 1,400 pine logs ready to raft." Joe Brown soon departed for other, and nobler, efforts. No later trace has been found of Boyce.

The plans of another early speculator were to bear more permanent fruit. Almost immediately after the 1837 conclave at Fort

Snelling, Franklin Steele and a companion hurriedly left the fort
to stake a claim at the falls of the St. Croix. Traveling by canoe
and accompanied by a scow loaded with tools, supplies, and laborers, these men constructed a warehouse and two log cabins
among the rocky palisades at the foot of the rapids. Then on July
5, 1838, soon after both treaties with the Sioux and Chippewa
were ratified at Washington, the side-wheel steamer *Palmyra* left
St. Louis for this new St. Croix Valley settlement. The boat was
loaded with about fifty men—millwrights, carpenters, masons,
lumbermen, teamsters, thirty-six laborers, provisions for four
months, and tools and machinery for building sawmill and shops.
This squatter outfit could have produced the first sawmill in the
valley, but Steele was appointed sutler at Fort Snelling and after
1839 had little to do with the development of the St. Croix. Work
on the mill, a dam, and millrace was not completed until 1842.
The complicated story of this hexed village, however, must await
telling in a later chapter.

The 101-ton *Palmyra* was probably the first such boat to ply the
waters of the St. Croix. Its arrival at the Dalles astounded the
Chippewa, and the shrill whistle and puffing engine of this *ishkoté-
nabikwan*, "fire-vessel," aroused great curiosity. In their excitement, and perhaps to see what would happen to the apparition,
the red men rolled rocks from the high crags and fissured bluffs
down on the steamer as it lay at anchor in the eddy opposite
Angle Rock. The captain was equal to their enthusiasm. The
boat's bell clanged, its whistle shrieked, and its stack belched bil-
lowing smoke. The Indians, terrified, vanished.

By the end of September, 1837, excursionists and military travelers to the upper reaches of the Mississippi had carried the welcome news back to Illinois, Missouri, and other states that the far
northern timber regions along the St. Croix were at last about to
open for settlement. One particular village in Madison County,
Illinois, heard of the ratification of the treaties with special interest—an interest that was to be of great importance to the future of
the valley. This town of Marine Settlement, located on a gently
rolling, fertile prairie some forty miles northeast of St. Louis, was
founded in 1818 by a colony of captains from the Atlantic sea-

board. Only twenty-odd miles from Lower Alton, which in 1837 had the finest landing for steamboats on the east bank of the Mississippi, the prosperous community of Marine was also close to the great mid-continent highway, the National Road.

To this Southern Illinois area, in 1822, came Elizur Judd, his wife, three sons, and a daughter to open a tavern and post office on a well-traveled state road. When tourists from the northern region late in 1837 brought news of the treaties, talk over the bar at Judd's Tavern must have been enthusiastic about money-making possibilities in the unknown country. And perhaps, during the early months of 1838, it was at Judd's place that plans were formed for the organization of a new lumber company to exploit the St. Croix pine forests. Wherever it was that the discussions took place, we know that at least twelve men were in on them. The three Judd brothers, Albert H., George B., and Lewis S., were senior members of the group. Then there was David Hone from Cherry Valley, New York, who had only recently arrived at Marine Settlement from Cairo, Illinois; and Orange Walker of Vermont, a tanner who had settled at Jacksonville north of Marine. Hiram Berkey, a farmer from nearby Collinsville, the two Parker brothers, Asa S. and James M., former Vermont brickmakers, William B. Dibble, a twenty-three-year-old York Stater, Samuel Burkleo of Delaware, a Dr. Lucius Green, and one Joseph Cottrell were also among those who probably gathered at the Judd tavern. Two of the twelve men, Hone and Lewis Judd, the youngest of the brothers, were chosen to make an exploratory trip up the St. Croix to choose the best site for a sawmill.

In September, 1838, the two delegates left Illinois on board the steamer *Ariel*, which was bound for Fort Snelling. At the head of Lake St. Croix, a mile or so above the future location of Stillwater, the two left the *Ariel*, and poled a flatboat upriver to the falls of the St. Croix. There they found millwright Calvin Tuttle and other members of the Steele party busily constructing a sawmill. In their continued search for a site, Hone and Judd pushed north to the mouth of the Kettle River. But it was on their return trip that the two men selected the spot they thought best for their projected sawmill—about halfway between the falls and the head of Lake St. Croix, where a full stream (called Fall River by the Chippewa) cascades into the St. Croix. There they staked a claim at what was later to be the Minnesota village of Marine and returned to Marine, Illinois, for the winter.

In the meantime, three of Steele's employees at the Falls, Jeremiah Russell, blacksmith, millwright Levi W. Stratton, and Robert McMasters, a laborer, had learned of the Illinois men's plans and took advantage of this opportunity for some extra money. On December 12, the three opportunists headed south from St. Croix Falls over the frozen river, and at the spot where a few months earlier Hone and Judd had staked the land for their future lumber mill, Russell, Stratton, and McMasters jumped the claim and took over the potentially valuable site. McMasters was given the job of clearing four acres of land, building a log cabin, and keeping possession until the next April. His two companions then returned to the Falls to continue their winter work. When spring rolled around, Russell and Stratton paid the carpenter-caretaker one hundred dollars and moved into the cabin on the jumped claim. Then they settled back to wait for the return of the men from Illinois.

During the winter months of 1838 in Illinois, plans were in the making. A verbal agreement was reached among twelve of the interested partners to organize a logging and sawmill firm and to call it the Marine Lumber Company. A two-year schedule of contributions was set up to finance the venture, but the arrangement was at best a loose and informal one. There were no articles of incorporation, and if any record book was kept, it unfortunately is now lost. Apparently, though, there were four "silent partners" in the group who did not make the trip to Minnesota—Albert H. Judd, James M. Parker, Dr. Lucius Green, and Joseph Cottrell. The other eight chartered the side-wheel steamer *Fayette*, which they loaded with complete machinery for the mill, farming tools, household goods, cows, three yoke of oxen, and other supplies purchased at St. Louis. Late in April, 1839, they headed north from that city. Also on board, bound for the St. Croix, were a millwright, a blacksmith, and Mrs. Hone, who took the responsibility of cooking for "The Company."

On May 11, after a voyage of fourteen days, the *Fayette* reached Fort Snelling and on the following night the little steamer headed down the Mississippi for the St. Croix. Lawrence Taliaferro was greatly impressed by the intelligence and seriousness of the party. "I was pleased," the Indian agent recorded in his journal, "with the St. Croix Lumber Companie, all Eastern men of character and capacity for business. May all success attend their efforts."

A heavy rain on May 12 considerably raised the level of the St. Croix, covering dangerous sand bars, and the *Fayette,* the second steamer to ascend the hill-shadowed waters above Lake St. Croix, had no trouble reaching the Marine millsite the following day. There the colonists found Russell and Stratton expectantly awaiting them. Since the company's agents as well as the claim jumpers were squatters on public land, the Illinois men had no choice but to agree to the terms laid down by Russell and Stratton. For $300 these two worthies relinquished the land to its original claimants and returned to the Falls. Discounting the payment given earlier to their third partner, each was a hundred dollars richer for the winter's work of laborer McMasters.

The Marine Lumber Company men immediately began the construction of a mill. From the beginning, Orange Walker was the head boss, and under his direction it took but ninety days to complete this first commercial sawmill along the St. Croix. On August 24, 1839, the slow and cumbersome muley saw cut its first lumber and one of Minnesota's greatest industries was born. Because of the settlers' immediate need for shelter, a log boardinghouse was erected even faster than the mill. In that small, forty-by-twenty-eight-foot building, Mrs. Hone, reportedly the earliest white woman to reach the Marine area, continued her work in the culinary department. During the summer months, small gardens were cultivated which furnished the kitchen with corn, potatoes, and other vegetables.

The duties of the men were divided among the more active partners. Asa Parker and Dibble, for example, worked getting logs out of the pineries and floating them downriver to Marine; Berkey supervised the sawmill, and Walker attended to the company's supplies and finances. During the winter of 1839-40, however, only a small beginning was made. The inadequate up-and-down saw, driven by an overshot wheel with buckets, was able to produce only 5,000 feet of lumber a day. Out of 2,000 pines logged by the Illinois group at the mouth of the Kettle and floated down the St. Croix in the spring of 1840, the Marine sawmill cut 800,000 feet of lumber.

The first three or four years were extremely difficult, and to make matters worse, some of the absent partners were slow in paying their pledges. Walker, after a special trip to Marine Settlement, was unable to collect a single penny on Dr. Green's six hundred dollar indebtedness. "Money, what times for money," he complained on July 2, 1841, in a letter from Illinois to his partner Burkleo back in Minnesota. "I find it hard work to get some of our folks here to a settlement, but there will be no lumber turned out until I do get it. . . . Tell Asa and Dibble to hold up good courage as I am Satisfied we can make money out of the consern yet."

Tireless work and unflagging interest in their venture soon brought results, and about the mid-1840s the company began to prosper when it branched out by building a small store at Marine and establishing, under the direction of George B. Judd, a yard at St. Louis to handle the sale of Marine-cut lumber.

The 1840s also witnessed the beginnings of other lumbering mills along the river. In 1842 the St. Croix Falls concern finally cut its first log, and on March 30, 1844, John McKusick's sawmill company at Stillwater became operational. During that decade other St. Croix mills were established—by the Kent brothers at Osceola in 1845, the Mowers at Arcola in 1847, and James Purinton at Hudson in 1848.

When the English landscape painter Henry Lewis traveled the river with geologist David Dale Owen and accompanying surveying party in 1847, he noted in his book *Das illustrirte Mississippithal* that "the pine forests along the St. Croix are no longer equalled on the entire continent except along the Penobscot and Kennebec in Maine." By 1855 there were seventeen mills from St. Croix Falls to Prescott which five years later cut 28,000,000 feet of lumber. And by 1875 that figure had more than tripled to 88,500,-

ooo feet. Lumber was needed to build the West, and the treeless states of Illinois, Iowa, and Missouri looked toward the Mississippi and its tributaries—above all to the St. Croix—for the supplies.

At Marine Mills, Orange Walker's optimism and encouragement paid off for his company. This man, the firm's strong right arm from the start, soon became one of the village's leading citizens and lived on at Marine to a hale and hearty old age. During 1848 the organization was reconstituted on a firmer basis; the name was changed to Judd, Walker and Company; and eleven shares of capital stock were divided among the six remaining partners, Walker, Burkleo, Berkey, Asa Parker, and Albert H. and George B. Judd. When, beginning that year, land in the valley was finally put up for sale, the names of the partners appeared often on the records as extensive purchasers of pineland. During the early 1850s a new mill was built at Marine. Its machinery was refashioned and improved, and by 1855 the firm was rafting 2,000,000 feet of lumber a year down the river. The company also had an interest in a busy flouring mill at Marine, which first began operations in 1855.

There were, however, difficult years. The Panic of 1857 brought hard times to business generally. But lumbermen were able to weather the financial depression because of the great amount of cut boards exported from the valley.

In September, 1863, a serious setback occurred when fire destroyed the mill and many men in the village were without employment. All but one of the original partners, perhaps discouraged by the holocaust and the lack of ready cash, withdrew from the firm—all, that is, except Walker who still had faith in the concern. He then joined in partnership with Sam Judd, son of Lewis, rebuilt the mill, and about 1868 took in a former company clerk, William H. Veazie, to form the new firm of Walker, Judd and Veazie, a name that looms large in the annals of the valley.

The decade of the 1870s was perhaps the most profitable in the company's history, even though the mills at Stillwater had far outstripped it in production. During the first year the Marine company built a large, handsome store, which carried on an expanded

business in general merchandise and lumbermen's supplies. This building stands today as originally constructed, one of Minnesota's historic landmarks which is still being operated (by Ralph Malmberg, his father and brother) for the sale of general merchandise. By July 25, 1873, the *Messenger* reported that the proprietors were each month averaging $10,000 in sales, continuing to handle, according to their boast, "as many or more Goods annually than any other firm in the county." In 1873, too, the mill was almost completely rebuilt and much new machinery added, which considerably increased the company's output.

Bad times, nevertheless, were soon to come. In addition to the depression years following the Panic of 1873, log jams in the river at Taylors Falls in 1877, 1878, and again in 1882, also undoubtedly hampered work at the Marine sawmill. But it was the jam of 1883, when for fifty-seven days no logs broke through a narrow bend at the Dalles, which prevented the firm of Walker, Judd and Veazie from filling its contracts. The next year was even worse. During the dry spring of 1884, the river did not have enough water to carry the logs over the falls and down to the mill. Lumbermen soon learned the truth of the old saying, "low water, rusty saws." Nor, because of widespread depression, could the company obtain the large loan it needed to carry on business until the next season. Men had to be taken off the drive, and the company was unable to pay its workers.

The final blow, both literally and figuratively, came when a tornado ripped through the Marine area on September 9, 1884. Hardest hit in the village was the sawmill, with a loss estimated at $15,000. Its towering smokestack was demolished, a million feet of lumber blown away, and when creditors began demanding settlement of their claims, the company was forced into bankruptcy. Early in 1885, goods in the store were sold at cost, the lumber company's steamer *G. B. Knapp* was disposed of through sealed bids, and livestock, wagons, and implements were auctioned off.

During the month of June, 1885, the mill reopened under the ownership of Orange Walker's creditors and once again took the name Marine Lumber Company. For the next few years of financial recession it had a desultory existence, even after being taken over in 1888 by the Stillwater lumber firm of Anderson & O'Brien. Logs were occasionally cut, but most of the time the mill stood idle, and the lumberjacks and sawyers of former days went elsewhere to find work. Some time before 1895, a St. Paul resident gained control of the property, and then came the final, ignominious end for Minnesota's first commercial sawmill. The machinery was sold to Minneapolis and Stillwater firms, and the extensive frame buildings were torn down.

Today, all that is left of what was for a short while one of the largest and busiest lumbering concerns along the St. Croix are the gray and jagged stone ruins of the inaccessible and slowly disintegrating engine house. The remnants of this first mill to cut lumber in the St. Croix Valley stand along the river's edge, overshadowed by the surrounding, wooded bluffs and deep in a tangle of underbrush and rotted tree limbs, a lonely and forgotten reminder of the hopes of men and of the lusty lumber industry which did much to build an expanding America.

Chapter Seven

Hercules in Handcuffs

W HEN, in August, 1838, Methodist missionary Alfred Brunson, paddling upriver, viewed the young settlement at the falls of the St. Croix, he was first impressed by the swift descent of water. Foaming rapids plummeted through a boulder-strewn gorge, the water surging wildly over rocks in a channel narrowed by precipitous black cliffs of traprock—a fifty-five-foot drop in a series of cascades less than six miles long. Brunson noted the awesome beauty of this region of noble pines and cedars, and remarked as well on the activities along the east bank. Several cabins were already constructed and thirty or forty men were "preparing to build a mamouth saw-mill" for the St. Croix Lumber Company. After preaching what is said to have been the first sermon heard there, the missionary portaged around the falls and continued his journey north. Near the mouth of the Snake River he came across Franklin Steele busily getting out timber for building the dam and mill.

Although the sawmill at Marine was the first to operate in the valley, the adventurous lumbermen at the falls were the first to begin constructing a mill, and the settlement of St. Croix Falls which grew up around it became the area's earliest town. The activity that Brunson witnessed should have augured well for the new business venture, but from the very start this embryo milling village was jinxed, its bright future clouded by internal feuds, lengthy lawsuits, and disinterested absentee ownership.

Only one year earlier, toward the end of July, 1837, the St. Croix Falls Lumber Company was organized at Fort Snelling.

That was just two days after Chippewa Chief Ma-ghe-ga-bo, dressed in his most fantastic costume, on July 27 consummated the Treaty of 1837 by lifting a piece of paper from a map. By the twenty-ninth, when the Indians touched the quill and agreed to give up their St. Croix Valley forests to the United States, another document of a different sort was also ready for signatures. "Whereas Samuel C. Stambaugh," began this second piece of paper, "George W. Fitch, Jeremiah Russell, and Franklin Steele, by a verbal understanding heretofore had, agreed to connect themselves in the business of making locations, and erecting saw mills on lands to be purchased of the Chippewa Indians on St. Croix River and its tributaries."

Of the eight eager men who then signed the new lumber company's articles of association, six were government employees. Colonel Stambaugh, sutler and postmaster at the fort, as the first to sign was the apparent promoter of the group. If so, the company was off to a bad start, since Stambaugh had a reputation for "dissolute habits" and was not generally considered "a man who accomplished anything of note." Another partner was Norman W. Kittson, the future fur trader, who during 1837 worked in Stambaugh's commissary department. Dr. John Emerson, U.S. Army surgeon at the military post, also joined the group, as did Steele, who the following year replaced Stambaugh as sutler. The Reverend Daniel P. Bushnell, Indian subagent at La Pointe, and Russell, who was then employed as a farmer at that distant *voyageurs'* outpost on Lake Superior, were at Fort Snelling for the Indian treaty. They, too, added their signatures below Colonel Stambaugh's, as did a Dr. Fitch of Muscatine, Iowa, and one John S. McGinnes. These, then, were the eight men who held twelve shares of stock in the original St. Croix Lumber Company.

Less than two months later, Steele, Russell, Fitch, McGinnes, and probably Stambaugh left Fort Snelling for St. Croix Falls in a "birch bark canoe propelled by eight stalwart men," as Russell later recollected. There they located the millsite and two good stands of timber in the pine groves near the Sunrise and Snake rivers. Franklin Steele was left in charge as company agent to hold the land until the ratification of the treaties, and he probably remained in that area throughout the winter months. During the following spring, undoubtedly accompanied by some of the other partners, he traveled to St. Louis, where he purchased machinery and supplies, and engaged workmen and transportation for the return trip. After hearing of the Senate's favorable action on the Indian treaties, the packet *Palmyra* steamed north to the new millsite, first stopping at Fort Snelling to give an anxious citizenry the month-old news of the ratifications.

No two authorities agree on exactly who made that pioneering trip up the St. Croix aboard the *Palmyra*. We do know that by this time both McGinnes and Dr. Fitch were out of the picture, having sold their interests in the lumber company the previous fall to William S. Hungerford, late of Connecticut, and Georgia-born Richard M. Livingston, who in 1837 were partners in a St. Louis mercantile business. Although these two young men undoubtedly knew their way among dry goods counters, they had no experience in lumbering. As early as November, 1838, from all appearances, Stambaugh, Emerson, Kittson, Bushnell, and Russell were also no longer connected with the lumber company. A third new partner—one-eyed Washington Libby of Alton, Illinois—proved to be incompetent as the firm's second agent. Instead of tending the lumber mill, he took a few barrels of whisky and beads, and set himself up in a short-lived side line as Indian trader. By mid-September, 1838, he had sold out to David B. Hill, a lumber merchant of St. Louis. Another participant prior to 1840 was William Holcombe, likewise inexperienced as a woodsman, who worked on the company's books until 1842. Of all the men initially connected with the St. Croix Falls Lumber Company, Franklin Steele was perhaps the only one who might have organized a successful operation. But all too soon he also stepped out of the picture to devote full time to his more important land holdings at the Falls of St. Anthony.

The St. Croix Falls Lumber Company was not only unfortunate in its organizers, it was jinxed as well by the location of its mill. Although the immense water power tantalized the pioneer speculators, they soon found that the site was otherwise not well suited for the milling of lumber. Here was nature at its most rugged, and the workmen experienced great difficulties in building a dam and log boom. In fact, not until 1842 was the mill ready to saw its first timber, and even then the men feared that floods and sudden freshets might wash everything away. In 1843 such a catastrophe set loose the winter's cut of pine trees. After most of them were reassembled on Lake St. Croix, thirty miles to the south, enough scattered logs were still hung up along the river's shore line to furnish several ambitious St. Croix Falls lumbermen the where-withal to start Stillwater's first sawmill.

Almost from the start there were money problems as well as quarrels and litigations over ownership of the land among the frequently changing partners. It was not long before the despairing proprietors of the company were quite ready to sell out the mill, several stores, shops, and workmen's homes they had constructed. Either that or bring in new financial backing. Title to their land, however, was still vested in the government, and none of it could be legally placed on the market and purchased until it was surveyed and proclaimed for sale by the President.

Before the opening of the land office at St. Croix Falls in 1848, property transactions usually took the form of trust deeds. A business was disposed of by selling the pre-emptor's, or original settler's rights which, among other benefits, included the opportunity for first purchase. It became a moot question as to exactly who at the Falls could claim these pre-emption privileges on the mill property. In 1842, for example, it appears that through a series of forfeitures, purchases, and assignments of stock Hungerford, Livingston, and one William Risley, grocer and commission merchant of St. Louis, were the owners of the mill.

During the same year, 1842, James Purinton, a fifty-five-year-old New Hampshire-born lumberman and former stonemason from Old Town, Maine, arrived at the new settlement. Not too much is known of Purinton, but perhaps an epithet thrown at this man of "powerful physical organization" a few years later is a key to his character—or just one person's biased opinion: "So heartless a Villian as old Purinton," a valley resident said when Afton farmer James S. Norris was served with what some considered an unjust writ of injunction. For two years Purinton leased the mill and performed the duties of company agent. Then in May, 1844, he bought out the three partners, but he failed to make the required payments and the property reverted to the owners. Hungerford accused Purinton of being an adventurer, of taking over the mill without any means, and having no intention of ever paying for it. By early 1845 Risley had sold out, leaving the company in the hands of Hungerford and Livingston.

Copper on the Lake Superior shores was a topic frequently mentioned in the newspapers of the 1840s, and rich deposits of the red ore were believed to exist as far south as the falls of the St. Croix. Through the efforts of Benjamin H. Cheever, a Boston broker, lawyer Caleb Cushing of Newburyport, Massachusetts, became attracted by the reputed richness of these mineral deposits. In August, 1845, he associated himself with attorney Rufus Choate and reformer Robert Rantoul, Jr.—among other wealthy Bostonians—to form the St. Croix and Lake Superior Mineral Company. Late in 1845 geologist George W. Brownell went to St. Croix Falls, where he located two mineral permits for Cushing and his partners—one on both sides of the river at the falls, and the other along the Kettle, some miles to the north. Although nothing came of the company's intentions to mine copper along the St. Croix River, Cheever, during his travels in the country as Cushing's agent, noted the potentialities of the water power at the falls and was the first to interest the Eastern capitalist in the mill property as an investment. Its proprietors, too, felt that this might be a solution to their many financial embarrassments and frequent ownership controversies.

Cheever also solicited several other Eastern investors to join the projected acquisition of the St. Croix property, and undoubtedly made arrangements for James Purinton to proceed from the Falls to Boston and accompany Cushing on his 1846 trip into the St. Croix country. As Alice E. Smith described this moment in the life of Caleb Cushing in the *Wisconsin Magazine of History:* "A year and a half earlier Cushing had returned to his home from a voyage to the other side of the world where, as a representative of President Tyler, he had negotiated the first commercial treaty between the United States and China on terms highly pleasing to the merchants of New England. Temporarily released from public service, and probably interested in business opportunities that would help replace the sums spent on this trip . . . he was in a mood to listen to the stories of Western mining adventures that were the topic of conversation among his Boston friends."

In the meantime Richard Livingston, considering his St. Croix Lumber Company stock worth "less than nothing," went so far as to pay Hungerford $3,000 to take his share of this unwanted property and all its headaches off his hands. Then during the spring of 1846, James Purinton was back, having acquired the lumber company partnership belonging to the estate of another investor. Because of legal entanglements, however, this one-sixth share should never have been sold, a fact which was made quite clear in a later lawsuit. Purinton did not stay long at the Falls. About July 1, he set out for Boston to guide Cushing by way of Lake Superior.

By early fall, on the eve of Caleb Cushing's departure for the West, this was the situation at St. Croix Falls: Hungerford and Purinton, obviously not on the best of personal terms, were both claiming possession of the lumber company. In addition, one Isaac T. Greene, lumber dealer of St. Louis, was in the picture with a claim on an undivided half of Hungerford's share by reason of a $10,000 loan. He and Hungerford were also at odds. "I understand," Greene wrote to Joseph P. Batchelder who was playing both sides of the fence by doubling as agent for each man, "that Hungerford is doing a Great Business with his tongue . . . what the fool will do nobody can tell. . . . Don't let Mr. Hungerford have anything to do with any of the Business in any way whatever." Hungerford himself called this "interference."

On September 14, 1846, Cushing left the Madeline Island village of La Pointe. Accompanied by the Reverend Mr. Ely, by Cushing's business advisor Captain Paul R. George of Brooklyn, and by thick-set, swarthy James Purinton, they headed toward the mouth of the Brule in a four-fathom bark canoe with two Indians as a crew. On the seventeenth, they made slow progress because of the size of their craft which they soon found drew too much water. On Sunday, September 20, Purinton made a special request, contrary to an original agreement, that they be allowed to travel on the Sabbath. To avoid any unpleasantness, Ely finally gave his reluctant assent because of what Purinton insisted was "the urgency of his business affairs." Two days later the expedition crossed the portage between the Brule and the headwaters of the St. Croix, a part of which, according to Ely, was "excessively rough from fallen bushes and brush." Down the St. Croix, Cushing and his party traveled and on the twenty-seventh reached the mouth of the Snake, where Ely left them for his return to his Pokegama mission a few miles up that river.

At St. Croix Falls, Cushing and Captain George were house guests of the William Hungerford family; the speculators "shared his hospitality, under his roof, and around his domestic board for a period of ten days." On Octobr 1, Cushing affixed his signature to a declaration of trust with Hungerford, Purinton, and Greene. All three signed, but who was actually in possession of title to the land was a question which kept Wisconsin law courts busy with suits and countersuits for many years to come. An important provision of this initial trust deed was that a new corporation be formed to replace the old St. Croix Lumber Company, and that its stated purpose be to conduct, manage, and improve the property "to the best advantage for the benefit of said company." The nature of the reorganization, however, mystified everyone except Cushing and his partners. From the start they insisted that the new company was constituted, yet at no time did they say whether it was formed at St. Croix Falls or in Boston; nor would they produce adequate articles of association, lists of partners or stockholders, number of shares, and other specific information to satisfy the courts.

Caleb Cushing, after his ten days at St. Croix Falls, continued on to St. Anthony; then he went by steamer to Galena, and across country back to Boston. Undoubtedly he felt that the expedition had been worth while. He was convinced that this Midwestern area had great possibilities for the investor. But whatever plans he may have made for the future were soon disrupted. During May, 1846, the United States declared that a state of war existed with neighboring Mexico. After returning from his tour into Wisconsin, Cushing received an appointment as colonel in the army. Shortly before his departure for the battle front, he wrote to the Public Land Office in Washington urging a survey to bring the St. Croix Valley lands into the market. After he was mustered out during the summer of 1848, a year and a half later, political and family affairs continued to keep him occupied, to the almost complete neglect of his Wisconsin project. William Hungerford was left to carry on as best he could.

Meanwhile, commencing in mid-1847, improvements began at the St. Croix Falls lumber mill under what author-traveler Mrs. Elizabeth Ellet in 1853 called the most promising circumstances. Following a ten-day visit at the Falls made in June by Robert Rantoul, Agent Cheever let out a number of contracts for carpentry on one-story "cottage houses," to be done in a "plain, neat, substantial, workmanlike manner." A large store was erected, the mill improved, and a spacious hotel partially completed, when company partner Rantoul reported that "because of the unparalleled scarcity of money in Boston," he could not raise additional funds to keep the mill operating. Many of the activities at St. Croix Falls had to be curtailed and during late fall Hungerford hastened to Boston to complain. There he met overt hostility and was accused by one of the Eastern partners of telling "the most outrageous lies . . . all over town." For his part, Rantoul was informed by Hungerford that once he returned to the West, "all negotiations will close. . . . I shall then begin to act;" he wrote, "and whatever that action may be, you must not blame me for it." To this threat the Bostonians answered that "The guns are long enough and the powder plenty at this end."

At about the same time that Cushing was obtaining his release from the army as a brigadier general in 1848, the so-called "Boston Company's" property along the St. Croix was being placed on sale at the newly opened St. Croix Falls land office. Hungerford, refusing to give up the results of ten years of work and investment, was smarting from the neglect of Cushing who was too busy being nominated Democratic governor of his state to pay much attention to any Western land holdings. Convinced that he had a valid pre-emption right to the property, Hungerford entered his personal claim for the millsite. On October 8, he also filed suit

against Cushing in Crawford County, Wisconsin, to gain possession of these holdings—a concentrated plan, the Easterner said, to
"vex and harass" the company.

For their part the Boston investors offered no help in running
the mill, although one stockholder said that only $2,000 would
work wonders. Geologist Brownell, who had stayed on at the Falls
to direct building operations, complained directly to Cushing
about the lack of money, stating that the "improvements have
been carried forward under circumstances of grate pecuniary em-
barrassment," and that no one there knew "when, where & on
whome to depend." Undoubtedly discouraged by the turn of
events, both Cushing and Paul George thought of unloading the
St. Croix property so they could invest in the area around the
Falls of St. Anthony.

Nothing came of this idea, however, and in June, 1849, Caleb
Cushing made a second trip to Wisconsin, where he found his
affairs in a worse muddle than ever. Buildings, left uncompleted
because of the hard times, were rapidly decaying, and the base-
ment of the great hotel was being used as a summer resort for
cattle. Although it was rumored that Cushing and Rantoul
planned to settle permanently at St. Croix Falls, the general returned to Boston in August convinced that Hungerford was using
the pre-emption claim and lawsuit as a threat to force an advantageous settlement.

In spite of the appearance of the village, from time to time an
optimist arrived on the scene. "When the title to the property
shall have been adjusted here," Eastern traveler Ephraim Seymour hopefully reported during his August, 1849, visit, assuming
that such an event might happen, "and a regular steamboat communication established . . . this place, I doubt not, will grow to
a town of considerable importance." Yet the fight continued. On
September 11, another Bostonian interested in the company wrote
on behalf of Cushing to the General Land Office that Hungerford,
who was "notoriously bankrupt in character and fortune has
leagued with some one or two others of a similar character to
defraud us of our rights. He sets up a claim to a pre-emption on a
portion of the land without any foundation in law or equity, and

the only hope of himself and his associates is to compel us to *buy them off*, this we are not disposed to countenance."

By mid-century few could be optimistic about what was in store for the village of St. Croix Falls and its potentially valuable water resources. There was wishful thinking, but harsh reality continued to confront the residents. With the fight over ownership barely begun, it had already become in Cushing's words, a war of mutual extermination. It was also in the year 1850 that area newspapers took up the fight. The *Minnesota Pioneer* of St. Paul, for example, on February 13 stated that St. Croix Falls had a population of 400, and contained *"houses enough for four hundred more* which had smokeless chimneys." According to the 1850 census, however, the village could count only 164 inhabitants living in thirty-eight dwellings. "The streets are regularly laid out," the newspaper continued, "the buildings are neat and handsomely painted, the citizens are frank and hospitable, but . . . the great mill is still under an injunction—Hercules in handcuffs—having succumbed to law, which in all probability will hold sway over the place for years to come." Three weeks later a resident at the Falls painted a rosier picture when he questioned this statement and boasted that the "unfortunate dispute" was "in a fair way of settlement. . . . Our Hercules is unpinioned." Soldier-engineer James H. Simpson, at Fort Snelling, suggested that both the gentlemen should come down to earth and speak of what *is*—not of what *will* be.

A hearing between the litigants was scheduled for November 4, 1850, at the land office in Stillwater. Cushing, either overlooking or not heeding the notice, neglected to send a representative in support of the Easterners' claim to the St. Croix mineral lands. The government officers decided in favor of Hungerford's pre-emption rights, feeling that the Cushing case was poorly documented since he produced no evidence to support his case. Perhaps, too, they were influenced by the apparently disinterested manner in which the absentee claimants prosecuted the affair. At any rate, litigation of Hungerford's original lawsuit of 1848 continued until late in July, 1851, when Judge Levi Hubbell of the Second Judicial Circuit finally handed down his decision which gave possession of the property to William Hungerford.

Cushing's lawyers, who had not appeared in Hubbell's court-room, claimed they were not informed that the case would be heard in July instead of during the fall, as they expected. Infuri-ated by the decision of the court, the general was more than ever convinced that Hungerford was a villain and that the judge was thoroughly corrupt. He then set out to do something about it. "When judges are successfully approached by corrupting influ-ence upon one side," Cushing was advised by one of his lawyers, "I know of no defense except to use the same weapons." Earlier that month Judge Hubbell had unwisely given Hungerford an opinion on the validity of an indictment for perjury by Cushing. The "Boston Company's" lawyers played this for what it was worth, with Cushing himself eagerly joining the fray, to accuse the judge of collusion, dishonesty, and corruption, and to gather evidence against that "vindictive and dangerous" public official. The case of Hungerford *versus* Cushing not only caused repercus-sions in Wisconsin politics, but it also led directly to impeachment proceedings against Hubbell by his political enemies, a number of whom were lawyers in Cushing's employ. Although Hubbell was later acquitted by a large majority, his legal career was ruined.

Cushing immediately appealed the 1851 decision to the Wis-consin Supreme Court, and Hungerford seems to have tried ap-proaching his opponent for a settlement. On September 27, Franklin Steele wrote Cushing from New York that Hungerford was there and wanted to see him. "I think you had best come on immediately," he advised. During this period, too, Hungerford's New York attorney sent a letter asking the general's views "on an early and definitive adjustment of the differences between you and himself growing out of the St. Croix Mills matter." The law-yer hoped that Cushing would be disposed to make a proposition, but nothing came of these attempts at a settlement.

Cushing's appeal appeared on the Supreme Court's calendar for November, 1851, but the case was continued to a later date after what Cushing called "a great deal of talking and foolish discus-sion." This proper Bostonian tried many different angles to get at his enemy, but none more surprising than when he paid out a hundred dollars that spring of 1852 in an unsuccessful attempt to obtain prosecution against Hungerford for the offense of fornication presumably committed in New Haven, Connecticut, on February 28, 1851. When Cushing's appeal finally came before the Supreme Court early in 1853, that body reversed Judge Hubbell's decision, and the St. Croix property was theoretically turned back to the general. But Hungerford would not yield possession, and the lower court refused to obey the Supreme Court's order to appoint a receiver. Hubbell, a Cushing attorney reported, felt that "the opinion was a humbug and an imposition on his court."

This tangled lawsuit meant nothing but confusion and frustration to the long-suffering residents at St. Croix Falls. During the summer seasons the sawmill there was operated by either the "Boston Company" or the "Injunction Party"—whichever happened by legal decree to have temporary possession. "But," Mrs. Ellet commented, "the liability to be dispossessed and the want of capital to manage independently so heavy a business, or secure payment to the workmen by the employers, have the usual consequences, disastrous to enterprise." Yet for a while things seemed to improve, so long as Hungerford was in charge. At least that is what John P. Owens, the St. Paul editor of the *Weekly Minnesotian*, thought when he spent a week on the St. Croix.

"The old milling site," he reported on June 18, 1853, "which it would take all the Courts of Christendom . . . to decide to whom it rightfully belongs, is now wearing greater signs of active prosperity than it has since the famous 'Boston Company' laid the withering curse of their hands upon it. . . . Certain it is that Mr. Hungerford, who now has possession, is making the Falls look vastly more like a business place than it has for years. The mill has been refitted with new machinery the past winter, and is now driving ahead rapidly, day and night. . . . Things about the village wear a prosperous appearance; and if the property were only out of the law, there would be no more thriving, driving, go-ahead village in the State of Wisconsin."

At about this time Milwaukee attorney Frederick K. Bartlett, another Cushing lawyer, approached the problem of ownership from a different angle, one which ultimately seems to have been the most successful. He started purchasing the claims of Hunger-

ford's creditors and thus slowly closed in on him, shutting off all
sources of money. As early as September, 1853, Bartlett reported
to Cushing with a tinge of admiration that Hungerford was "almost entirely deprived of resources and funds . . . and . . . he
is failing in energy and his usual adaptiveness to adverse circumstances."

During May, 1854, Bartlett obtained a court order to take possession of the St. Croix mill property, and by fall he felt he had
made sufficient progress to move in. "I shall stop their crowing
effectually this time," he boasted, "or something will happen." Accompanied by a force of some twenty men—including Edgar C.
Treadwell, sheriff of Polk County, and John Kearney of Racine,
the deputy United States marshal—Cushing's attorney arrested a
fleeing Hungerford in Prescott and then proceeded north to take
over the property at the Falls. This was accomplished on October
5, with what Bartlett called "some little resistance or show of it
and attempts at evasion." According to one story, Hungerford,
"his family and servants" were forcibly removed from what he
called his homestead and farm. Historian W. H. C. Folsom added
that the St. Croix lumberman was then taken handcuffed to Madison, a short-lived humiliation which his family bore "with a forti-
tude worthy of the name and reputation of the father and husband." On the other hand, the *St. Croix Union* of March 27, 1855,
felt, along with "hundreds of residents in this valley," that Hungerford's family had been treated with the greatest kindness and
courtesy by being "allowed to remain until they could conveni-
ently pack up such articles of furniture and apparel as were not
sold to Mr. Bartlett, which being done the family left destined for
St. Louis." They headed south on October 15.

Throughout this period Cushing continued to be occupied with
other duties, first as a member of the Massachusetts Supreme
Court and later as Attorney General in President Franklin Pierce's
cabinet. St. Croix Falls and its problems were a long way off and
remained of secondary importance to the politician. In spite of all
that had happened, there was no letup in legal hassling, and during April, 1855, the question of ownership and occupation was
further complicated by a two-year lease of the mill property

which Bartlett negotiated with longtime Wisconsin River lumber-man Daniel F. Smith. This turned out to be another unfortunate arrangement, for Cushing later found himself plagued by court proceedings instigated and won by Smith. Although Hungerford was apparently not residing in the valley, legal attempts to get back the property at the Falls continued, even though attorney Bartlett reported to Cushing late in 1856 that he had effectively stopped credit to their adversary in St. Louis, Washington, New York, and Wisconsin.

The year 1857 brought a virtual end to the Hungerford *versus* Cushing case. Although the year started with a legal victory for the former, Cushing finally won out. On February 10, 1857, Judge John M. Keep handed down the decree of his circuit court after a lengthy trial at the Janesville, Wisconsin, courthouse. He first castigated both the litigants by stating that if they wished to argue lawsuits in his court, "they must make up an issue by a distinct allegation of the fact on one side, and a denial on the other, and not leave the Court to spell out an issue from vague suggestions on one side and doubtful insinuations on the other." The judge then went on to say that of those who signed the original declaration of trust back in 1846, the late James Purinton's claim to ownership was denied. Isaac Greene's only part in the picture was his right to demand payment of the loan to Hungerford made in April, 1846. Judge Keep, stating that "the law will enforce honesty and fair dealing," then ruled that Hungerford's pre-emption claim extended back to his first settlement at the Falls, and therefore he was declared the rightful owner. The trust deed of 1846 between Hungerford, Purinton, Greene, and Cushing was ordered canceled, and Hungerford was to be put into immediate possession. "It is if anything more outrageous than Hubbell's decree," was the only comment made by Cushing's lawyer as he prepared to force his opponent to an out of court agreement. Frederick Bartlett had a stranglehold on his adversary. Hungerford, who by this time had returned to the Falls, was in desperate need of funds for operating the mill and found it impossible to borrow money. "I have 'set the pins' here," the former Milwaukee lawyer wrote to Cushing on February 24, 1857, "and they could not raise a dollar."

By April progress had been made toward a final settlement, but since it was not yet accomplished to the general's satisfaction, during the following month he journeyed for the third and last time into western Wisconsin to complete the arrangements himself. The nature of this agreement is not known, for Cushing's correspondence tells nothing, and he furnished the newspapers with no details. As a result of the visit, Hungerford abandoned his long fight to gain the mill property.

Hungerford then joined with Augustus Gaylord of Connecticut to open at St. Croix Falls in the fall of 1857 a dry goods store with a stock worth $20,000. In 1861, Gaylord left for Madison to become Wisconsin's Attorney General. It is not known when Hungerford quit the valley, but some of his later years were spent in Monticello, Illinois, where he died in 1874. A neighbor in the St. Croix Valley called him an indefatigable worker. "The labor of his life was invested in the improvements of the company . . . and . . . he became a foe worthy of his steel." Together, Folsom concluded, Hungerford and Cushing "unitedly accomplished the ruin of their town." The bright future once planned for St. Croix Falls and its magnificent water power was never to be.

Caleb Cushing was now in control of the property at the falls, and newspapers of the area hailed the settlement—they called it an "amicable compromise," perhaps with intentional irony—and everyone rejoiced that the trammels of litigation were apparently over. Early in February, 1857, attorney Bartlett introduced into the Wisconsin legislature a bill to incorporate a new firm, the St. Croix Manufacturing and Improvement Company. To secure its passage "in this corrupt legislature," Bartlett wrote his employer, Cushing had to buy votes.

A fresh start was attempted. "The St. Croix Manufacturing Company has been at work about two months," reported the *St. Paul Advertiser* during September, "and in that time has effected an entire transformation of the town. Under the long paralysis of the recent lawsuit the place had stood still, the tenements had fallen into decay, and had been appropriated by strolling Indians." Advertisements began appearing in another St. Paul newspaper that the proprietors were ready to sell or lease lots, and

Cushing's new superintendent, Major Charles N. Bodfish, called on manufacturers of wagons, furniture, agricultural implements, paper, and other commodities to locate at the Falls. These notices were published in the area papers for two weeks, and then they suddenly ceased.

Cushing continued to neglect his Wisconsin interests and for long stretches would not even take the time to answer letters. "Why cannot you let me know what the company is doing," Attorney Bartlett complained, "and whether it will ever come to a *point*." During 1858, promotional literature was printed in New York at Bartlett's suggestion, but not too much progress could have been made, since internal difficulties and personality clashes continued to plague the company's efforts. After a visit to the Falls, Bartlett reported that Major Bodfish was in serious trouble. "With mutiny staring him in the face every day, without money or supplies, overwhelmed with debt . . . he does not know what moment he may find the whole company property fired & destroyed & himself without a man with him." Toward the end of 1861, the *Taylors Falls Reporter* stated that "the saw mill at St. Croix Falls, which has been standing idle for a long time, and is in a very dilapidated condition, is to be repaired and put into operation soon."

But idleness at the mill seems to have continued throughout the years of the Civil War. Then during 1865 came another reorganization, perhaps because of a suggestion from the new agent, Circuit Judge Henry D. Barron. The Chisago Mining and Manufacturing Company was incorporated. The purpose of Cushing's new concern was to "manufacture iron and copper ore." Although this company lasted into the 1880s, it apparently made no improvements. In 1881 it was still waiting for the anticipated boom.

As early as 1869 other river towns were making snide remarks about their neighbor. St. Croix Falls, said Platt B. Walker of the *Reporter*, is "a small place not likely to be much longer." Although the *Hudson Democrat* disagreed, feeling that the sister Wisconsin village would "within a few years . . . be more populous, and of greater commercial importance than Taylors Falls," others agreed with Walker. Osceola's comment was perhaps the most damning:

"The ruthless hand of time," said the *Polk County Press*, "has made sad ravages, and though the industrious relic hunters might find there a dam by a mill site, they would not find a mill by a dam site."

Bad luck pursued Cushing with each new venture on the St. Croix River. The formation in 1868 of the Great European-American Emigration Land Company, in which he held the position of president, was no exception. Through this new organization he hoped to emulate his neighbors in Chisago County and populate his Wisconsin lands with Swedes. Cushing, however, again chose an incompetent, spendthrift representative. This time it was smooth talking "Count" Henning A. Taube who was in charge of bringing Swedish emigrants to the St. Croix Falls area in Burnett and Polk counties, and whose mismanagement ended in complete disaster, as will be seen in a later chapter.

A letter written from Minneapolis on December 20, 1870, to a New York trustee of the company, stated that in casual conversation with St. Croix Falls residents, the writer found "quite a bitter feeling against Mr. Cushing . . . they claiming that were it not for his nonimprovement of the water power, the falls would today rival any locality in the State, for they believe the power there to be superior to that at St. Anthony." Cushing's correspondent then described what facilities the village had left: The ruins of a grist-mill burned because of feelings against Cushing, a half-broken dam, and a sawmill stripped of its machinery.

The town continued to be jinxed, and to remain an unfortunate example of absentee ownership at its worst. Small wonder that speculators like Cushing were feared, even hated on the frontier. "When Caleb Cushing 'passes in his checks'," commented the *Stillwater Messenger* in July, 1871, "and the unlimited water power of Taylors Falls is improved in consequence thereof, the gurgling springs and laughing brooks which abound on his possessions, will shout for joy, and the echo will resound with gladness throughout the valley of the St. Croix."

During the fall of 1874, the year that William Hungerford died in Illinois and only five years before the death of Caleb Cushing, J. Stannard Baker came to St. Croix Falls to become Cushing's last agent for the sale of some 45,000 Polk County acres. The real estate business which was started then is still carried on by his son, nonagenarian Harry D. Baker. For the first time, Caleb Cushing chose well, and Baker's arrival brought a definite end to twenty-eight long years of injudicious management. If only a man of Baker's ability and stature had been sent to the Falls in 1846, how different might have been the story of this village at the head of navigation on the St. Croix.

St. Croix Falls never fully recovered from the withering curse of the absentee Eastern speculators and their ineffective employees. When the Bakers moved to the village, there was another man in this family of gifted children who later remembered in his book of delightful reminiscences, *Native American,* that St. Croix Falls was made up of a mere handful of primitive stores, a weather-beaten mill, a blacksmith shop or two, a hotel and livery barn, and a few houses straggling along the hillside. That boy, Ray Stannard Baker, later became a nationally known writer of popular essays under the name David Grayson. Scholars remember him as one of the early muckrakers and author of the eight-volume Pulitzer Prize-winning biography of President Woodrow Wilson.

During the 1880s Benjamin Franklin Butler, controversial Civil War army officer and former governor of Massachusetts, purchased a portion of the St. Croix Falls property. In September, 1886, his son-in-law General Adelbert Ames was at the Falls to appraise the situation and arrange for sale of the land to Isaac Staples, Stillwater lumber baron. Of the twin villages Ames wrote his wife: "Great Expectations have been their bane. Instead of being flourishing manufacturing places they seem dead and alive in spots, the dead spots being the most numerous. There is no water power here utilized. The only dam ever built here has long since passed away and only slight traces of the foundation remain."

For a time before the turn of the century, Ike Staples owned portions of the old Cushing holdings, and in his lumbering pursuits made use of the area around the site of the old mill. Then in 1895 several hundred acres on each side of the river, including a large share of former Cushing property, were acquired by Minne-

sota and Wisconsin to form a popular Midwest recreational area
—Interstate Park. Finally, during 1906, a dam constructed by the
Minneapolis General Electric Company completely confined the
surging rapids that once were the falls of the St. Croix, and in
December of that year this great water power was turned to fur-
nishing Minneapolis with its first output of electric current
brought from outside the city. These facilities, soon acquired by
the Northern States Power Company, now generate electricity for
the surrounding area.

Today, the twin villages of the St. Croix Valley are popular
tourist attractions, and during the summer season activity centers
mostly in the park and at the Taylors Falls boat landing where the
Mullers' four sight-seeing yachts make regular excursions through
the scenic and unspoiled beauties of the Dalles which Fredrika
Bremer back in 1850 had called "one of God's beauteous spots of
earth." Since shortly after the turn of the century, the Muller family has also used this landing as an embarcation point for leisurely
floating trips downriver to Marine or Stillwater. These are advertised as the "lazy man's canoe trip," since there are no rapids or
portages and a two-mile current does most of the work, except
when sand bars demand some activity.

On the Wisconsin side of the falls, a few blocks north of the
through east-west traffic route, the larger village of St. Croix Falls
follows the even tenor of its quiet existence, serving throughout
the year as a shopping center for this upriver area. The power
company's man-made falls draw large crowds of viewers during
periods of heavy rains and high water, when the five-foot flash-
boards which top the dam are lowered and the umber water cascades Niagara fashion over the fifty-foot drop in a roaring, boiling, foaming spectacle. When we consider the natural beauty of
this region which has been preserved for the enjoyment of future
generations, it was by modern values perhaps fortunate that the
continued litigation between William Hungerford and Caleb
Cushing kept the falls of the St. Croix from being developed as a
manufacturing center. Here the bygone era can now be called
freshly to mind; today everyone benefits from the ineptness and
faulty judgments of yesterday's would-be exploiters.

Chapter Eight

A Slab and Sawdust Dynasty

EARLY in the 1840s four young men—John McKusick, Elam Greeley, Elias McKean, and Calvin F. Leach—traveled their separate ways out of the New England states to seek employment among the pineries of the new West. Ascending the St. Croix River from its juncture with the Mississippi, each found the work he wanted at the St. Croix Falls lumber mill, established a few years earlier. For a season or two they blasted rock, built dams, and got out timber for the new sawmill. These men were in the valley during 1843 when a caprice of nature—extraordinary spring freshets and a cresting river—determined their future. The heavy rains broke a log-holding boom above the mill and carried 400,000 feet of timber crashing thirty miles down the swift river to the quieter waters of Lake St. Croix. Fortunately for the owners, an astute riverman, said by some historians to have been Abraham Lincoln's cousin Captain Stephen Hanks, averted what had all the appearances of a financial disaster. He collected some of the scattered timber, rafted and then ran it to the Southern market—the first such raft, they say, ever to go down the Mississippi River.

Later that year, when the lumber company at the Falls paid the four men, they received as part of their wages the scattered logs which were still hung up along the St. Croix a few miles above the settlement of Marine. Using them as their initial raw material, the four Easterners pooled resources, and on October 26, 1843, signed a contract to go into business and build a sawmill. The site, which was chosen with the help of Jacob Fisher, a carpenter from the Falls Lumber Company, lay on his claim along the west bank of

99

the river near the head of Lake St. Croix. The narrow plateau facing the lake and backed by steep bluffs seemed an ideal location for a mill. Jake Fisher pointed out that water power to run the machinery could be supplied from a lake, later named for McKusick, located in the uplands west of what soon became the village of Stillwater. One month later building commenced on the land for which Fisher was paid $300, and John McKusick called the place after his home village of Stillwater, near Bangor, Maine. The name was appropriate along the St. Croix, too, for the new Stillwater also prospered as a lumbering town. When Nathaniel Fish Moore, president of New York City's Columbia College, traveled West to the Falls of St. Anthony in 1845, he found at Stillwater "a saw mill, a tavern, a country merchant's store, and some half dozen wooden houses."

Early in 1847 the *Prairie du Chien Patriot* predicted that "Stillwater bids fair to become to Minnesota what Milwaukee is to Wisconsin," and a year later there were five stores along the main street of the village, one of which was operated by John McKusick to sell supplies to the men working for his lumber company. There were also two hotels, a "flourishing school" built on land donated by McKusick, about twenty-five "very neat and well finished buildings," and the sawmill. A new frame courthouse was about to be erected by Jake Fisher, also on land given by McKusick, and the settlement could boast from one to two hundred residents. Half of them, being lumberjacks from the pineries, were considered "transient and floating." One of the village's most striking features was the long wooden viaduct which stretched high above its rooftops to carry water power from McKusick's storage lake in the hills down to the sawmill on the river's shore.

Elias McKean was the first to sell out his interest in the company to McKusick in October, 1844. Greeley followed suit two months later, and Leach's share, which had been held by Greeley, was also transferred at the same time. Tall, gaunt, pipe-smoking John McKusick (said to have borne a striking resemblance to Abraham Lincoln) was soon in complete control of the mill; he was to remain one of Stillwater's leading citizens until his death in

1900. His growing importance in the life of the city over the years is reflected in the reply made by a Stillwater schoolgirl when she was asked to name the discoverer of America. Her immediate and inspired answer was, "John McKusick."

Until approximately 1852 the McKusick sawmill had a monopoly on Stillwater's river business. It was, however, a small operation and far from the busiest in the valley. Until the 1850s Judd, Walker and Company, the lumber concern at Marine, and the mill at the Falls each handled far more timber than all the other St. Croix lumber companies and numerous independent loggers combined. Lumbering along the St. Croix during this period was an informal and helter-skelter affair. No log-catching boom stretched between the banks of the river to confine and control the floating timber. Sloughs served as inadequate collecting points where logs were either made into rafts for downriver shipment or sorted out to be manufactured into lumber at local sawmills. A rather hit-and-miss arrangement called the St. Croix River Exchange was developed, and to it each logger reported how many trees he had cut during the season. Then when rafting time arrived, he picked from the river what he thought he should have, paying little attention to the ownership marks stamped on the logs. This system presumed that millmen and loggers were accurate and honest, and would take out only as much as they put in. Each fall an attempt was made to count and assign ownership of the leftover logs hung up along the shore from the Snake River to Lake St. Croix. An annual tally was then taken, which was neither accurate nor satisfactory to the loggers involved.

Mutual dissatisfaction with this arrangement brought together eight valley lumbermen, among whom were McKusick, William H. C. Folsom of Taylors Falls, Orange Walker and George B. Judd of Marine, and William Kent of Osceola. To facilitate logging operations on the St. Croix, these men in February, 1851, organized the St. Croix Boom Company to catch and hold safely all logs at an assembly point, or boom, until they were sorted according to log marks, measured by those familiar with the lumberman's scale, and then rigged into rafts. The firm's charters from the legislatures of both Minnesota and Wisconsin authorized it to charge specified sums for this service, and stipulated that the river must at all times be kept open to traffic.

Within a year after its organization, the company completed a boom approximately two miles upstream from Osceola and six miles below Taylors Falls. To control the river, the firm sank huge piers at intervals from the Wisconsin shore to the head of a long mid-channel island still known to river travelers as Boom Island. Floating timbers chained between the piers diverted and confined logs in the slough, from the lower end of which similar barricades were stretched to the Minnesota side.

This first attempt to bring organization into the logging business was only partially successful and the company was plagued by financial and other difficulties. The slough on the Minnesota side was too narrow to allow sufficient boom space. It was frequently impossible to keep the river channel free of logs and open to traffic. For example, when the steamer *Asia* was unable to get through the floating timber in 1853, the boom company had to pay for the transfer of freight to Taylors Falls, a compensation stipulated in the charter. In addition, during periods of low water, lumbermen found it impossible to raft logs that were stranded high on dry land. Moreover, the three Stillwater members of the corporation soon discovered that the Osceola boom was located too far upstream, leaving them with no facilities to catch the valuable Apple River logs after they reached the St. Croix.

Beginning in the early 1850s, Stillwater, rather than the other villages along the St. Croix, rapidly became the lumbering industry's headquarters and principal supply depot for the St. Croix pineries. Starting in 1852, new sawmills began to spring up in the Stillwater area near the head of Lake St. Croix. At the end of that year, the valley's lumbermen noted a rapid rise in the milling business—in spite of high water which forced all the sawmills on the river to close for a short time, and a near catastrophe that put one of them temporarily out of commission.

This event occurred in May, 1852, when the rains, it is said, were torrential along the St. Croix, and the river rose dangerously. After several days of constant downpour, everything underfoot was sodden and thoroughly saturated. High upon the bluff behind Stillwater, McKusick's storage lake was overflowing. Early on the morning of May 14, the villagers were startled by a roaring and rushing of water. Pressure had ripped away the dam controlling the flow into the mill's viaduct. St. Paul's *Minnesota Pioneer* reported that an immense river of melted earth, rolling slowly, ate its way through the viaduct-shadowed ravine. Tree-laden topsoil, sand, and gravel plummeted out of the gorge, spreading wide when it reached the bottom and crossed the main street in what has been called the greatest movement of real estate in the history of the valley. Several stables, a half-dozen houses, and McKusick's mill on the village's waterfront were almost completely buried by muck and gravel. But when the townspeople took a second look they discovered that the catastrophic landslide had deposited some eight or ten acres of new real estate along Lake St. Croix. This, they found, gave the village (and undoubtedly McKusick as well) quite a parcel of additional land, plus an excellent steamboat landing, both of which many felt would "permanently advance the interests of Stillwater." (No other valley settlement could boast such benefits from the rains. At Osceola, the cascading waters dumped into the river only "hen coops, pig pens and other domestic arrangements." No new real estate there!)

The rains put McKusick out of business for only a short time. He rebuilt his mill, and Stillwater continued to flourish. New sawdust-burning steam sawmills, two of them financed by Southern and Eastern capital, were also built in the village, and by 1856 the firm of Schulenburg and Boeckeler from Missouri, and Hersey, Staples and Company out of Maine, had established the best mills in Minnesota Territory. Faced by such moneyed competition, it was not long before John McKusick abandoned his small milling operation and turned to the real estate business. His sawmill was torn down in 1871.

Frederick Schulenburg, a German-born lumber dealer who had been successful in St. Louis, began early in 1855 to operate a large plant which was located at the north end of Stillwater. For many years, the firm of Schulenburg and Boeckeler was the biggest log cutter in Stillwater, and during the 1870s it surpassed in production any single mill in Minneapolis. Almost all the boards from this sawmill were rafted down the St. Croix-Mississippi waterway to the company's lumberyard at St. Louis. Although his firm was of great importance to the economy of the entire valley until the end of logging on the St. Croix, Schulenburg himself, even though he lived in Stillwater, was never a force in its civic life.

That role was left to rival lumberman Isaac Staples, who established a small empire in the village and ruled it with a firm but benevolent hand for almost half a century. It was in 1853 that Ike Staples set out from his native Maine in search of good pinelands. He found them along the upper St. Croix in the area of the Snake River and its tributary the Groundhouse. Returning East, he persuaded another lumberman from his home state, Samuel F. Hersey, to invest in the future of the Minnesota country. Staples became the resident Stillwater partner of Hersey, Staples and Company, and in 1854 established a general store dealing in dry goods, groceries, clothing, and miscellaneous articles. "We want a regular 'down east stock' such as you would buy to carry to Maine," was the request he sent to Hersey for the purchase of carefully selected items. "Minnesota is a poor market for poor goods." Early that fall the frame was raised on the mill located just south of the village, and construction continued throughout the winter months. By mid-June, 1855, the mill of Hersey, Staples and Company was sawing timber cut in the woods by the company's loggers during the previous winter. That fall carpenters also completed a large boardinghouse for the millworkers. The Staples empire was growing.

By 1855 the census made by Sheriff Asa B. Green recorded a population at Stillwater of 1,482 persons, 700 of whom were "unmarried men and bachelors." And out of the seventeen mills along the river, the six near the head of Lake St. Croix employed most of the village's male population. Sawmills were crowding the river and the burgeoning settlement was favorably compared with the greatest of all Maine lumbering towns when the *St. Croix Union* predicted that it would be a second Bangor in the lumber trade.

Staples had an idea which helped make that prediction a reality. He thought that an additional boom should be constructed at

Stillwater, a suggestion which gained momentum after he acquired control during the mid-1850s of the financially embarrassed boom company at Osceola. "The lumbermen on our river have concluded to build the Boom near Painted Rock this present winter," Staples wrote Schulenburg on New Year's Day, 1856, "& are counting on you to take over one or two thousand Dollars of Stock in same." In this forthright manner Staples also persuaded the other local mill operators to co-operate.

Construction of the lower boom began shortly after a new firm was incorporated early in 1856 under the aegis, among others, of Staples, Martin Mower from nearby Arcola, and Folsom of Taylors Falls, who was the only carry-over from the old company. The men selected an admirable site a little more than two miles above Stillwater, where the river runs between steep bluffs and where long, narrow islands divide the St. Croix into several channels. For more than fifty years this spot was to be the great gathering place for timber coming down the river, a corral for retaining logs. To it went the massive spring drives from the upper reaches of the St. Croix and its tributaries; at this boom millions of logs were sorted, scaled, and rafted. The *Stillwater Republican* called the boom an "institution absolutely essential to our great lumbering interests."

At the end of the 1850s a visitor described Stillwater as "quite a stirring place." Just how stirring the village was in 1860 is graphically indicated by the editorial joustings of the two local newspapers—the *Democrat* and the *Messenger*. Editors Catlin P. Lane, a son-in-law of Isaac Staples, and Lovel F. Spaulding of the *Democrat* began the exchange with an attack on the village's moral stability. In the issue of December 8, Spaulding and Lane charged that the growing town of 2,380 residents was "the heaven of saloon keepers," supporting twelve regular bars and four so-called "places" which purveyed five-cent slugs of bad liquor. "We do not invite enterprising manufacturers to come and improve our magnificent water power," quipped the two editors sarcastically, "no such scheme was ever the subject of a moment's gossip here, —but there is always room and welcome for a new saloon or strychnine whisky depot." Andrew J. Van Vorhes, editor of the

Republican *Messenger,* countered with a strong defense of Still-water. "We venture the assertion," he editorialized, "that there is no city or village in the west . . . that contributes more to en-courage, or enjoys greater religious and educational advantages." Van Vorhes went on to enumerate the number of churches, Bible societies, and literary associations in the village. He did not, how-ever, deny the accusations made by the *Democrat.* Spaulding and Lane were also concerned about the young men of Stillwater. "Where will you find one in a dozen who promises well for man-hood?" they questioned. "Plenty can be found who will grow up into rowdies, shoulderhitters and drunkards. And what better can we expect of any community that encourages gaming, drinking and rowdyism?" Juvenile delinquents, 1860 style.

Two houses of ill fame across the lake in what was then called St. Petersburgh, but which has since taken the name of Houlton, especially drew the newspaper's attention. These "sinkholes of sin," the *Democrat* said, were operated by "Red Nell," Harry Mandeville, Perry the Pimp, and Mack Fortune, all of whom ob-tained girls from St. Paul and derived their chief support from Stillwater. Prostitutes were undoubtedly in good supply, since the capital city itself could boast almost half a hundred establish-ments catering to lumbermen and local citizens. Authorities in the valley also looked the other way while the rugged, woman-hungry river boys reeled off to Wisconsin for some drunken, ribald oat-sowing in the bagnios of St. Petersburgh. ("Red Nell" continued to operate unmolested, figuratively speaking, until 1876.)

Perhaps this picture of early Stillwater was somewhat exagger-ated, perhaps not. Certainly, valley life was rugged in settlements like Hayward and Barron along tributary streams and in the river towns of St. Croix and Taylors Falls, Marine Mills, occasionally Osceola, and especially at Stillwater when the hard-muscled, hard-drinking loggers and lumbermen headed north for the pineries in the fall or when, restless and eager, they returned from the spring drive, "as the Gauls and Goths in the eruptions into old Rome." Author Stewart Holbrook has called Stillwater "Minnesota's ear-liest whoopee-town." With energy to spare and money in their jeans, the lumberjacks were out to celebrate after an all-too-sober

six-month winter of dawn-to-dark labor and the rigorous confinements of camp life. "The money flies, you bet!" said one reporter
when the bar-pounding, lusty jacks hit town, "the chests expand
and the hats rest jauntily on the back of the head. . . . As the
drinks multiply they become more fiercely jubilant, and they
firmly believe themselves endowed with the strength of thirteen
or fourteen double, back-action steam engines, and if they don't
collide with each other (which is often the case) they stumble
against the strong arm of the law."

Reckless as they were from the very nature of their work, some
of these lumberjacks, to rid themselves of superfluous vitality,
would go on one immense, prolonged drunk—a blowout that the
St. Croix Union, a family paper, gently called "a sort of jollification." And sometimes they ended up in free-for-alls at the bordel-
los of St. Petersburgh. When sixty or more of these men—described by the *Stillwater Gazette* in 1875 as "a tough, rough, bluff
set of fellows . . . with muscles like whip-cord, hair unkept and
bearded like the pard"—would descend on the village from Ike
Staples' camp near the Groundhouse, small wonder that many
local residents stayed at home, closed their shutters, and perhaps
even locked their doors. Politician Ignatius Donnelly, on his first
visit to Minnesota in 1857, called them a "fine looking set of men."

Both Schulenburg and Staples remained prominent members of
the valley's slab and sawdust dynasty. The latter divorced himself
from Hersey, Staples and Company during the 1860s and was established on his own. He continued to be the propelling force in
both the business and social life of Stillwater. He had the drive,
energy, and imagination to make himself a wealthy man. His empire was widespread, encompassing banks, vast pinelands, logging camps, racing horses, lumber and flour mills, large model
farms which furnished supplies for his camps, and stores of varying types. He was interested in railroads and improvement companies, and also took on the private project of bettering the appearance of his hometown. "If Isaac Staples should remain in our
city a few years longer," reported the *Stillwater Republican* in
August, 1870, "it would begin to look pretty respectable. He has a
perfect mania for buying up old tumble down places and vigor-

ously transforming them." The newspaper went on to predict that in only a few years Staples would have the whole town rebuilt. Twelve months later he constructed a handsome mansion high on a bluff overlooking his city, and for many years it was a showplace in the valley. The building is gone now, the unfortunate victim of wreckers' bars, but any visitor, by visiting Pioneer Park, can get the same beautiful and sweeping downriver view the Staples family had.

Stillwater lumbermen, sometimes dubbed the "Minnesota marauders," were heartily disliked by their Wisconsin neighbors, who complained that although the logs came mainly from their state, they were handled only by Minnesota men. The *Hudson Star and Times* in 1870 felt that the boom company had built up a most merciless monopoly, that its owners had obstructed navigation, discriminated against all opposing lumbermen, and "made their odious corruption a stench in the nostrils" of valley lumbermen and residents.

Ike Staples was the butt of many such complaints and accusations. One disgruntled worker, during the depression years following the Panic of 1873, displayed his feelings in two verses which appeared, unsigned of course, in the *Gazette* on March 14, 1877:

> These pines, these oaks, these beautiful maples,
> The source of much wealth, belong to Ike Staples.
> In the fall of the year when poverty rages,
> He hires us up here for damned small wages.
>
> His clerk in the store with a white paper collar
> Weighs out the brown sugar, six pounds for the dollar;
> The books will be posted by the ending of Lent,
> And I'll find to my sorrow he don't owe me a cent.

That some river men thought Staples held too great a monopoly over St. Croix affairs was shown in 1875 when valley residents formed a "People's Line" to keep local steamboats like the *G. B. Knapp* on the river. In the company's regulations, stockholders were prohibited from selling their shares either to Staples or to Mississippi River Steamboat impresario William F. Davidson for fear one or the other might gain control of what shortly proved to be an unsuccessful venture.

What little personal information is available about Isaac Staples characterizes him as a compassionate man who did not refuse work to anyone deserving it, who would usually find some job for a physically handicapped person, and paid in cash even in hard times. He was, it is said, a fair and honest employer, and no one had real cause for complaint against him. Although local stories tend to gloss over faults and glorify virtues, we know that Staples gave life and vigor to the village of Stillwater. Certainly Stillwater would never have become the first city in the valley without him. During the 1880s Staples began to curtail some of his activities, and contrary to expectations he put up no fight when rival lumberman Martin Mower gained control of the St. Croix Boom. But almost to the end of his life, Staples remained the boss logger of the river.

Lumbering and the West's appetite for its product created the St. Croix Valley settlements; and logs were for over half a century the foundation of their prosperity. "Instead of remarking about the weather," the *Chicago Tribune* reported in 1865, St. Croix residents "speculate upon the number of logs that are coming down, and the chances of their getting choked at the dam." Down they came every spring, millions of logs, after heavy rains along the upper tributaries brought high enough water to float them. The villagers along the St. Croix gathered expectantly on the levees to watch the sure-footed red-shirted river drivers with their innumerable batteaux, wanigans or cook barges, and multifarious camp equipage follow the tumbling, groaning logs to the final sorting place at the Stillwater Boom.

Sometimes, however, a rampant torrent of hurtling logs piled up in spectacular jams, like a giant's game of jackstraws, between the narrow cliffs of the Dalles, and it often took weeks of exhausting and dangerous around-the-clock work by the foolhardy and courageous jam crews and whatever steamboats were handy, to locate the key pieces that would finally free the jumbled mass. When the jam began to move, the Taylors Falls newspaper described one of these events in 1865, "Stores are hastily closed, busi-

ness suspended, and people come running from every direction to see the 'sight of sights!'" Lengthy and complete blockades frequently resulted from such jams as the released timber, which gutted the tributaries and choked the main channel, moved slowly downstream. "If the navigation of the river is to be continually interrupted," complained the Taylors Falls editor on May 20, "we all may as well give up trying to improve and settle up this portion of the country, as with this, our only avenue of commerce closed, we can do nothing." And if boats like the *G. B. Knapp* were unable to pass around the boom and bump their way through the floating logs, then the Boom Company had to pay damages.

To the captains of passenger and freight steamers and to the residents of villages above Lake St. Croix, the company was a veritable Hydra-headed monster. "The Boom Company next winter," facetiously reported the *Polk County Press* of Osceola on July 20, 1878, "will build a narrow gauge steamer 1,000 feet long, with joints, to be used in navigating Page's Slough. Her head will be at Marine and tail at Arcola. They propose to have her twist through the slough like a snake." But in spite of the steady opposition and complaints that impeded navigation was bringing what Sam Judd of Marine called ruin and stagnation upon the valley above Stillwater, logs and lumber dominated the St. Croix, and the sawdust dynasty remained in complete control. One by one the upriver mills faded from the scene, but the massive spring drives continued to block the river, fill the boom, and keep innumerable tugboats busy on Lake St. Croix towing huge rafts of logs to the mills along the lake and down the Mississippi from Point Douglas to St. Louis. The St. Croix was second only to the Mississippi as a carrier of logs.

As long as there was timber to cut, the St. Croix Valley remained a great factor in the lumber trade of the Western states. The industry not only furnished profitable labor for thousands of men, but it gave the people of the Midwest from Minnesota to Missouri a constant and cheap supply of splendid building material. From 1840 through 1903 the estimated yield in board feet of St. Croix logs came to the astronomical total of over 11,250,000,-

ooo feet. The biggest trees were cut in 1879 when they averaged 176 feet in height. In 1890, the peak year of the lumbering industry on the river, close to 3,500,000 logs totaling over 452,000,000 board feet of lumber were guided through the boom.

At Stillwater, Schulenburg, Staples, and other lumbermen prospered. But the end was approaching in spite of such optimistic predictions as the one made in 1887 that it would be many years before the industry would begin to fail, if it ever should. The golden age of lumbering came and went during the 1890 decade when loggers and cutters had their most successful years, and then the precipitous decline in mill production began.

Although most St. Croix lumbermen were convinced that the "seas of forests" were inexhaustible, there were a few doubters who came nearer the truth. As early as the mid-1840s a visitor in the St. Croix Valley wrote back to a lawyer friend at Bangor, Maine: "There is not half the timber in this country that is generally thought to be, but what there is is all timber & of good quality generally. They are erecting any quantity of mills through this part of the country & using up the timber very fast." How quickly it was disappearing from the land few realized until the river and its tributaries' pine-clad banks were almost denuded. What the loggers did not cut they set afire, leaving behind a desolate burned-over region of charred stumps and scorched earth. As astute an observer of the lumbering scene as the *Mississippi Valley Lumberman* said in July, 1896, that "Even today there is timber sufficient to keep the big saw mills at Stillwater and vicinity in operation for many years to come." But only two years later the same paper made an about-face and predicted that the best days of St. Croix logging had passed.

By 1902 the *Messenger* foresaw the "total annihilation of lumber business" in three years. It was not, however, until eleven years later that the last drive of logs came down the St. Croix. On June 12, 1914, W. F. (Frank) McGray, the boom master who is said to have sent the first log through in 1856, hitched his final log—the very last to go through the great St. Croix Boom at Stillwater.

It was back in 1850 that the *Minnesota Pioneer* of St. Paul predicted there was enough pine to last fifty years—which is about the time it took to strip the mighty timberland of the Midwest. The primeval white pine forests of Wisconsin and Minnesota which so awed the Swedish traveler Fredrika Bremer in the mid-1850s were gone from the St. Croix Valley. The lumber industry moved into the Pacific Northwest; towboats and unwieldy log rafts, which once were such a familiar sight on Lake St. Croix, soon vanished from the river, and one way of life at Stillwater and along the whole length of the St. Croix disappeared forever.

Today Stillwater is a city of some 8,300 inhabitants where farmers from Washington and nearby counties sell the produce of their fields and dairy herds and purchase their supplies. It is a commuters' town oriented toward St. Paul, and an attractive, picturesque place of precipitous streets, charming old homes, and a historic courthouse whose handsome cupola and graceful arcade dominate the valley scene.

Stillwater is also an industrial town. Here and in the nearby suburb of Bayport are manufactured more than eighteen products, some of which are sold nationally. The Andersen Corporation at Bayport is one of the world's best-known makers of window units; and the Maple Island Creamery produces many kinds of milk products. Its ice cream, they say, is the finest for miles around. Along the waterfronts of Stillwater, Bayport, Afton, Hudson, Prescott, and Point Douglas pleasure boat marinas have become big business. Lake St. Croix is now the unencumbered playground of the Midwest and the once busy log boom area has become a pleasant, sylvan wayside park. The lumbering era is all but forgotten along the St. Croix, and the region has now become a recreational paradise.

Chapter Nine

The Prison in Battle Hollow

IT IS true that no great university was built along the banks of the St. Croix and no impressive walled garrison ever shadowed its waters, yet this river can boast one institution which has from time to time brought it a fame of sorts—the Minnesota State Prison.

Among the points stressed by Minnesota's Governor Alexander Ramsey in his message to the first territorial legislature on September 3, 1849, was the lack of a suitable lockup controlled by civil authorities. He strongly advised that "there should be proper and safe places of confinement" for prisoners in the new territory, and urged that the legislature ask the federal government for money to construct a prison. Governor Ramsey's suggestion was approved by the legislators, and in June, Congress appropriated $20,000 for the erection of a penitentiary.

Selection of a site was the next problem. A proposal that the prison be built in the village of St. Anthony was met by a majority of its residents "with the most marked contempt," according to the *Minnesota Pioneer* of St. Paul. Another suggested location was farther up the Mississippi and more toward the middle of the state, perhaps somewhere in Benton County. But this idea was rejected by the larger downriver cities, because the proposed site was too "far removed from the present and probably future centre of population." In February, 1851, the legislature designated St. Paul as the territorial capital and selected Stillwater, the thriving metropolis in the St. Croix Valley, to be the site for the penitentiary. The new prison would be erected on four acres of land in

Battle Hollow, location of the bloody encounter between Sioux and Chippewa which took place there in 1839.

Among penitentiary buildings completed by early 1853 were a three-story prison house with six cells and two dungeons for solitary confinement, a workshop, and an office, designed by Jake Fisher, constructed of material taken from nearby quarries, and located within an enclosure about 280 feet square surrounded by a twelve-foot wall. Outside was the warden's house, halfway up the south hill overlooking the prison. This building stands today, the home and museum of the Washington County Historical Society.

To manage the prison's physical plant, the territorial legislature of 1853 designated Francis R. Delano, one of the contractors, as the first warden, and he assumed office on April 4 of that year.

A native of Massachusetts, Delano had settled in Stillwater by 1851 and had there engaged with little success in lumbering. During his early years as warden, he built up a profitable private business on the prison grounds. With his own funds, he purchased and took into the government-constructed penitentiary about eight thousand dollars' worth of steam-powered machinery for the manufacturing of shingles, sashes, doors, flooring, wagons, and plows.

Security arrangements within the newly built penitentiary, however, left much to be desired, and escapes were frequent. During a ten-month period in 1856, seven men and one woman fled confinement. Their methods of escape were ingenious and varried. The hall floor was pried up; an iron cell door was lifted from loosened hinges; a burglar's bar was smuggled in, according to the warden's record book, by "unknown hands"; locks and shackles were picked; iron window bars were sawed; holes were dug through the outside wall. A writer for the *St. Croix Union* of Stillwater complained that the penitentiary was either badly constructed or its officers were grossly derelict in duty. Delano, however, convinced newspaper editor Abbott that the fault lay not with the warden but with the prison, since the walls and buildings were not "of the most approved and substantial kind." The fact that there were no night guards was never mentioned.

The warden, as stipulated by law, was obliged to accept temporary prisoners from Minnesota counties that lacked adequate jail facilities. The counties sending prisoners to Stillwater frequently failed to pay the lodging fees, and the warden found it increasingly difficult to collect from them. By the beginning of 1857 they owed Delano $700, and he claimed that he had "stood all the loss he could." Following an inspection visit to Stillwater, the prison committee of the legislature recommended that the warden should not be held responsible for prisoners if the counties were lax in paying for their keep. An act to this effect was approved on May 23, 1857, and Warden Delano immediately freed prisoners from Winona, Nicollet, and Houston counties because payments were not forthcoming from the county commissioners.

"There is something wrong about the Territorial Prison," reads a November, 1857, editorial in the *Weekly Pioneer and Democrat* of St. Paul. That was after the escape of an accused murderer from Le Sueur who was placed in the Stillwater prison for safe-keeping pending trial; "any person who desires it can escape from it, and the Warden does not even think it worth while to offer a reward, or notify the public." About two weeks later, the *St. Paul Financial, Real Estate and Railroad Advertiser* joined the fray by claiming that, "a canary bird in a 10 acre field, with the bar doors down at that, would be more safely caged." During the following week, the same newspaper expressed the opinion that "the Warden should have a fixed salary and no officers in the institution should have an interest in the contracts, or in the labor of the convicts; nor be the owner of any part of the tools or machinery used in the institution."

Scarcely had the year 1858 begun, when a new convict, perhaps to help prove these criticisms, led three of his companions in a successful jail break. Unobserved, they picked a large hole through the cell block's stone wall and, with the aid of a handy ladder, quickly cleared the inadequate exterior wall while the guard was attending church services in the village.

The United States government immediately stepped into the picture. The territorial legislature ordered a grand jury investigation. The jury members, in reporting to Judge Charles E. Flandrau, found Warden Delano and Deputy Warden Michael McHale "negligent and careless." A total of eight scathing indictments were brought against the prison officials for alleged neglect of duties. Delano, on the other hand, challenged the moral character of several members of the grand jury, most of them fellow townsmen. Without using any names, he accused one of "having been tried in a sister State for the highest crime known to the laws," and another of dealing "a little game of Chuck-a-luck" between the sittings of the jury. Delano also complained that the jurors spent exactly twenty-seven minutes at the prison and visited only three cells. Most of their time while there was taken up by the high jinks of a Stillwater "eccentric wag" and saloon proprietor named Emanuel Dixon Farmer who was a member of the jury. For example, the jurors locked Dick Farmer in one of the cells and released him only when he promised that he would supply free drinks for everyone present.

Realizing, no doubt, that the territorial laws governing the penitentiary were faulty, and aware of the need for reorganization and reformation of the prison system with the approach of statehood for Minnesota, Governor Samuel Medary was apparently loath to press charges against Delano and his deputies. During the early months of 1858 nothing more was heard of the grand jury indictments and the lawsuits were dropped. The prison's first warden remained in charge until the expiration of his term on March 4.

Not until August 19, 1858, was a new warden, acceptable to all factions, appointed. He was thirty-two-year-old Henry N. Setzer, a Stillwater lumberman and a prominent representative in the first territorial legislature. Setzer immediately resolved the thorny county prisoner problem. "There is no authority now existing," ruled the new warden when he refused to accept one such prisoner, "by which the State prison can be converted to the use of a common jail, to keep in custody persons merely committed for trial." Setzer and the state board of prison inspectors also clamped down on many lax methods prevalent at the territorial penitentiary.

A Democrat who was not amenable to the politics of Abraham

Lincoln, Setzer put himself on record as being unwilling to hold office under any "Black Republican administration." Thus, in December, 1859, he tendered his resignation. Before doing so, however, he touched on a subject that was to draw comment from all succeeding wardens until the old territorial penitentiary was finally abandoned in 1914 and the new Minnesota State Prison occupied at the nearby suburb of Bayport. He strongly recommended that the prison be removed from the marshy and unfit location in Battle Hollow, which, he said, would never offer enough space "to enlarge and improve the State Prison to make it fit and secure enough to answer the purposes of its erection."

John S. Proctor gave up his Stillwater hardware store to receive the prison keys from Setzer on January 16, 1860. Proctor served well for eight years under four Minnesota governors. His long tenure of office, during a period of spoils and great political favoritism, proved the wisdom of Ramsey's choice. At a yearly salary of $750, Proctor, according to the *Messenger* of January 30, 1866, "bro't order out of chaos which formerly adorned and gave a stench" to the institution.

In 1859 John B. Stevens of Stillwater, a manufacturer of shingles and blinds, had leased the prison workshop from the state for five years at a rental of $100 a year. He took over all convict labor, paying the state a generous seventy-five cents a day for each full-time worker. Thus began the contract system in the Minnesota State Prison, which ended only when the old prison was abandoned fifty-five years later. When Stevens' shingle mill burned in January, 1861, forcing the contractor into bankruptcy, George M. Seymour and his partner, William Webster, Stillwater manufacturers of flour barrels, took over the contract for prison labor. They established a wage for prisoner work scaled to advance from thirty to forty-five cents a day over a five-year period. Toward the end of the 1860s, Seymour joined with Dwight M. Sabin, soon to be a Minnesota and later a United States Senator, to form the new firm of Seymour, Sabin and Company. This concern continued to rent the prison shops and to employ the inmates, who worked in silence under guard, manufacturing numerous wood products.

Between 1860 and 1867, the number of state prison inmates jumped from four to fifty-two—an increase due, said the board of inspectors, to the "general carnival of crime which seems to reign over the whole country." This post-Civil War development caused overcrowding and made necessary the construction of new buildings. A three-story cell block was erected and an additional shop built by Seymour and Webster, contractors, and paid for by the state so that Seymour and Webster, manufacturers, could employ a larger number of prisoners.

The contract system exploited by these firms was for the first time criticized by a warden in February, 1868, when Joshua L. Taylor, another St. Croix Valley lumberman, was placed at the head of the prison by Governor William R. Marshall. Both Taylor and the inspectors could read the handwriting on the wall when they urged that inmates be allowed to work for the benefit of the state rather than for private concerns. They felt that the existing system was detrimental to Minnesota's financial interests and that the evils resulting from it were "positively injurious to the discipline and hostile to the reformation of the convicts."

Such criticism of the system notwithstanding, Seymour, Sabin and Company continued to expand. For example, the firm began making threshing machines in 1876 and its business so prospered, especially with the introduction of the nationally known Minnesota Chief threshers, that the company could soon boast of being the world's largest manufacturer of such machines. Its net profits for 1881 came to over $300,000. In May, 1882, the North Western Manufacturing and Car Company was organized by Sabin and "certain wealthy persons" representing large railroad interests. Sabin's original company was absorbed into this burgeoning concern, which continued to make doors, sashes, blinds, flour barrels, and threshers, as well as to take on the construction of portable and traction farm engines, and to manufacture freight and passenger cars for several Northwestern railroad companies.

In addition to prison labor, which the company's officers openly bragged they had obtained through an advantageous contract with the state, approximately twelve hundred civilians were employed in the prison shops and around the extensive yards that had mushroomed outside the walls. "It was never expected when the contract for prison labor was made," apologized the inspectors in 1884, "that the Manufacturing Co. of Seymour, Sabin & Co. would develop into the mammoth N. W. Manufacturing and Car Co. . . . Had that result been foreseen, the shop room would most certainly have been restricted, and also the number of citizen employees allowed within the prison grounds"

But the company, through agreements and contracts signed with the state, had established too firm a foothold to allow any fundamental change in the existing arrangements. During their twenty-two years of authority at the Stillwater institution, the contractors managed to assume virtually complete control over prison affairs. Almost from the beginning they alone were given the lucrative building contracts for additions, improvements, and repairs in and about the prison grounds. As a result, the money received annually by the state from Sabin's company for prison labor and rental of workshops was considerably less than the amount the government had to pay out to the same firm for constructing buildings and repairing the prison wall. The contractors even assumed the right to choose the prison guards and officers it wanted employed by the state. The evils of the contract system, first recognized by Warden Taylor, had multiplied.

Eventually, in 1887, the state legislature, yielding to pressure from the St. Paul Trades and Labor Assembly, ruled against prison labor contracts that would come into competitition with free enterprise, and plans were formulated in 1890 for the state to go into business on its own. Since a combine of cordage manufacturers was then charging unreasonable prices for binding twine, to the disadvantage of Minnesota and Wisconsin farmers, a binder twine industry was initiated at Stillwater, and this proved successful almost from its beginning. Prison-made twine, sold at a reduced price, meant considerable saving to the farmers of the Midwest, and Minnesota thereby established what was for many years the foremost state-account system in the nation. It remains today one of the major industries at the prison. At the same time, the power wielded by the contracting company had been greatly lessened, indicating that the contract system of prison labor was on its way out.

At the end of his two-year term, in 1870, Taylor declined reappointment because the salary of $1,000 a year was "not commensurate with the position and duties required to be performed." To replace him, Governor Horace Austin appointed, in March, Captain Alfred B. Webber of Albert Lea, Minnesota. An occasional attorney-at-law and part-time politician, best known as an ex-hotelkeeper, he was a political appointee with few qualifications for the position.

Less than half a year after his appointment, Webber summarily dismissed long-time Deputy Warden Robert R. Davis on the strength of accusations of theft made by a prisoner. Davis countered with multiple charges against Webber, including "dereliction of duty, violation of prison discipline, and corruption in office." The testimony presented to Governor Austin contained imputations that the warden, by this time nicknamed "Bull Beef" Webber, speculated for his own benefit in prison flour and beef; that he allowed wives to enter the prison to sleep with their husbands; and that one life convict was frequently permitted temporary freedom so he could go hunting in Wisconsin. Prisoner Nellie Sullivan, popular nineteen-year-old Twin Cities prostitute and Madam, continued to ply her trade behind the guarded walls at Stillwater where, according to the *Pioneer*, she "was permitted to make assignations with the male convicts."

Governor Austin finally asked for Webber's resignation, and in September he named another St. Croix Valley lumberman, Henry A. Jackman, a self-styled "very Black Republican," who for many years had served as a member of the prison board of inspectors.

Under Warden Jackman, the first major building program interrupted the routine of prison life, as "the old dilapidated and tottering Territorial buildings" were removed. The only original structure left standing was the warden's house. New and substantial accommodations for a maximum of 158 prisoners were erected by the prison labor contractors. The warden called the new quarters "an honor to the State, a credit to the builders, and a blessing to the inmates." Only two years later, however, the new cell block proved to be less of a "credit to the builders" than Warden Jackman had anticipated, for faulty construction made it easy enough for a prisoner to escape simply by crawling under his cell door and between the window bars.

The year 1874 was a hapless one for Warden Jackman. In May, Deputy Warden Eri P. Evans, who had been relieved of his recently acquired position, retaliated by charging the warden with fraud, theft, neglect of duty, and infractions of discipline. Both the warden and prison inspectors demanded an immediate and thorough investigation, which resulted in the dismissal of all accusations. The governor was handed 400 pages of testimony, but so far as is known he did not request Jackman's resignation. At about the same time, Alonzo P. Connolly, a St. Paul newspaperman, visited the prison and reported in the *St. Paul Dispatch*, of June 24, 1874, that many of the newly built cells were damp and absolutely filthy, and that some of the bedding was wet. Faced with continued criticism, and "feeling keenly the effect of these charges," Jackman submitted his resignation in July, 1874. Governor Cushman K. Davis appointed John A. Reed of Sterling in Blue Earth County to be the new warden at what one newspaper called "that miserable basin."

Warden Reed's twelve years at Stillwater were unsettled ones. The number of inmates more than quadrupled and the state found it difficult to furnish adequate living and working space as well as yard room for the convicts and for the ever-increasing number of civilians employed by Seymour, Sabin and Company. Until this time, Minnesota had without much trouble managed to expand its prison facilities to meet the slowly growing criminal population. But the 1870s saw a continuing need for enlargements to the physical plant.

Two fires early in 1884 were major catastrophes and the reconstruction necessary was not completed until mid-1886, with 582 cells and ample shop room and machinery to employ over five hundred workmen. Since the prison population at the time was only 387, there was enough space for years to come. The contracting company faced financial difficulties after the fire and was placed in the hands of a receiver. In spite of setbacks, all available prison labor was employed making engines and threshing machines. "Careful observation," reported the state board of corrections and charities, "has confirmed our good opinion of the administration of Warden Reed."

Outside the walls, however, trouble was brewing for the warden. In their report for 1886, the three prison inspectors spoke out strongly against accusations which had been leveled at those connected with the the institution. "Ambitious men, disappointed, scheming demagogues." Governor Lucius F. Hubbard was informed a few months before he went out of office, "cannot understand why it is that businessmen will accept such positions as these unless it is to ally themselves to rings and assist in defrauding the State." It became quite obvious that a change of wardens would accompany the next political shift.

The change came when Andrew R. McGill became Governor of Minnesota early in 1887. He did not reappoint Reed, but named in his stead Halvur G. Stordock, a farmer from Rothsay in Wilkin County. Two of the three prison inspectors resigned because of the governor's move "to make place for some of his political friends." Stordock was the last warden in Minnesota appointed by a governor.

Within a few months the new warden and the inspectors demanded an investigation of what they called prison irregularities and immoralities under Reed. The reasons for the request are obscure. The governor appointed a committee to study the accusations, and before they reached a decision several months later, many scandalous charges and countercharges had been advanced by Reed, Stordock, and their respective lawyers. Giving testimony were several convicts who must have spent a good part of their time trying to gather evidence (based on "vague suspicions," said the report of the investigating committee) by listening through keyholes and peering over transoms. In December, the committee reported that none of the charges against Reed was sustained; Warden Stordock was reprimanded, and Reed was gently censured. After the dismissal of the indictments, Stordock was restored to his position.

In 1889, the legislature tried to take political favoritism out of prison affairs by vesting all direction and control of the Minnesota institution in a five-member board of managers, which was made responsible for the appointment of the warden. In August, 1889, John J. Randall, a sixty-year-old coal merchant from Winona, was selected to replace Stordock. "Randall has a good record," reported the *Messenger*, "and will doubtless make a good warden." His short term of eighteen months was marked by several innovations of importance to the prison's future. The first steps were taken toward establishing a school. In 1890 a Chautauqua reading circle was organized, and this group remained an active and influential part of prison life for almost fifty years, until 1938, long after the collapse of similar experiments in the few other penal institutions which tried them.

Once again, however, disgruntled accusations from discharged prison officials were heard. They followed a now familiar pattern. This time the victim was Randall, whom many critics considered too lenient toward the inmates. There were others who felt that Randall was being forced out because he was not amenable to the wishes of the prison contractors. "Until the position is removed from politics," advised the *Gazette* on December 4, 1890, "the life of a warden in Minnesota will continue to be an unhappy one."

The first professional penologist to head the Minnesota prison was Albert Garvin, who assumed the post of warden in February, 1891. He had received his training at the Illinois State Prison in Joliet. This warden, whom the prisoners themselves called fearlessly progressive, did most of the spadework in establishing a grading system and a prison school. Garvin, however, remained at Stillwater only a year and a half before he moved on to become St. Paul's chief of police. His work was ably continued by Henry Wolfer, who was picked to head the state institution on his record of twenty years' experience as another Joliet-trained penologist. He took over at Stillwater in June, 1892, becoming the old prison's most distinguished leader and introducing a new era in prison management for Minnesota. Except for one year, Wolfer served as warden until 1914, when the Battle Hollow location was exchanged for new quarters at nearby Bayport.

During Wolfer's administration, reformatory methods were successfully introduced at the Stillwater prison with the granting of conditional pardons, with restraint, to deserving men. Ordered on an experimental basis by Governor William R. Merriam in June, 1892, pardons were authorized by state laws the following year. Although not the first to attempt reformatory methods, Minnesota was the first to apply successfully the parole law. The power of granting pardons rested solely in the hands of the governor until 1897, when a board, consisting of the governor, the chief justice of the supreme court, and the attorney general, was given the responsibility. A grading system for prisoners, which was continued until 1953, was instituted in 1893. At about the same time the school was established under Carlton C. Aylard, principal of the Stillwater High School, and it remains today an important feature of prison life.

Wolfer had been at Stillwater only two years when the Minnesota Thresher Company failed, throwing 350 inmates out of work. To give them employment, several shoe manufacturing contracts were let during the few remaining years in the old prison. The state itself began making farm machinery at the prison in 1907. Manufacturing of farm machinery and of cordage remain the major industries of the prison today. As historian Blake McKelvey has pointed out, "It was no coincidence that Stillwater was the best state prison in the country throughout the era."

An administrator of such stature obviously deserved a better plant in which to implement his program. The damp, poorly ventilated, roach-infested buildings were a disgrace to the state. "Bed bugs are so numerous," complained one of the inmates, "they drive the average prisoner wild with pain and annoyance. The air is foul. The stench is almost intolerable." In 1902 and again in 1904 Wolfer pointed out in his reports the need for a new prison. In 1905 and 1909 the Minnesota legislature finally provided for new buildings to be constructed a few miles south of Stillwater. The end of the antiquated institution in Battle Hollow approached rapidly. Extensive new structures at Bayport replaced the crowded quarters that were "not fit to keep hogs in, let alone human beings." By 1914 the final contract with a shoe company expired, and only then were the last of the inmates removed to the model new prison built under Warden Wolfer's careful supervision—a prison that for many years was considered the best penal structure in the United States.

The walls of the new prison whose tall water tower is a landmark for miles up and down the valley, enclose twenty-two acres and all the main buildings. The total capacity of the institution, which includes a 1,000-acre farm, is 1,450 men. Over the years, however, the prison population has averaged 1,200, evidence enough that Warden Wolfer, more than half a century ago, built well for the future. Today's warden, Ralph H. Tahash, feels that the Minnesota State Prison is still unique in several instances: "We are able to keep the total population occupied at some constructive activity," he has stated. "We also are unique in that we pay our inmates more for their labor than any other institution in terms of the size of the industry." Authorities at the prison point with pride to the effectiveness of the classification procedures, to its recreation program, and its research.

Little now remains of the old penitentiary in Stillwater's Battle Hollow. What buildings still stand are occupied by a creamery. The warden's house serves as a museum, and an historic marker drive-in has replaced the austere east wall which once ominously overshadowed the highway leading north out of Stillwater toward Dutch Town and Marine.

And what of the many thousands of malefactors who since 1853 have been locked behind the cold stone walls and iron bars of both the old and new prisons?

No inmates brought more notoriety to Minnesota's Battle Hollow lockup than three of the desperadoes, supposed partners of Jesse James, who took part in the robbery of the Northfield, Minnesota, bank and the murder of cashier Joseph L. Heywood. The Younger brothers received life sentences in 1876; Bob Younger died at the prison, and James committed suicide in St. Paul after he and his brother Cole had been released in 1901. The last of the trio lived to receive a pardon, write his autobiography, and become the "hero" of a number of books.

What is in store for the new prison's most widely publicized inmate cannot yet be said, for the barred gates of the state institution closed behind him only recently, December 7, 1963. On that day thirty-six-year-old T. Eugene Thompson, well-to-do St. Paul attorney, chairman of the Minnesota Bar Association's criminal law committee, and one of the drafters of the 1963 revised Minnesota criminal code, began a life sentence at hard labor for the hired murder of his wife, Carol. For nine months this tale of a man's double life gripped the nation's attention and spread the horrible details of a bungled, brutal, and bloody crime wide over the land in newspaper headlines and magazine articles. Tilmer Eugene Thompson, once a prosperous summer resident of Forest Lake in Washington County, has now returned as a permanent inhabitant of the St. Croix Valley—where on the books of the Minnesota State Prison he is known as number 21893.

Chapter Ten

Fun on the Frontier

LIFE for the pioneer was not entirely one of unceasing toil. Felling the trees, breaking the land, and establishing a home in the wilderness were hard work. But along the St. Croix, as in most of the new West, exuberant youth predominated. It was "Young America," according to the *St. Croix Union,* that took the lead in all activities, and somehow they also found time for fun, play, and relaxation.

Socially, the early settlers were easy to please. They needed only a few events to believe themselves "blessed with an abundance." In December, 1855, for example, two dances were being planned by Stillwater hotelkeepers Casper Haas and Isaac Gray— one ball to take place at the Lake House and the other at the Minnesota House. Three months earlier the "New Englanders," a traveling company, had presented a pair of instrumental and vocal recitals; and late in November the far-famed singing Hutchinson family came upriver to give a "glorious concert" at the Presbyterian church. All these festivities, in the short space of only three months, prompted the *Union's* editor to rejoice: "Great country, this, for entertainment."

In July, 1856, only a little more than ten years after the first settlement of Stillwater, the people of the village packed the same Presbyterian church to hear with enthusiasm a concert given by the great Norwegian violin virtuoso Ole Bull. Unlike St. Paul and St. Anthony, however, the St. Croix town was less than kind to Adelina Patti, the thirteen-year-old singer in Bull's troupe, who later became the most famous coloratura soprano of her day.

While St. Paul critics enthusiastically praised her and a St. Anthony reviewer commented mildly, "she is not a singer yet," valley listeners felt that her untrained voice was little more than endurable. The *Prescott Transcript* reported that "as an attempt to copy Jenny Lind, it was a miserable failure, and . . . we have heard no one praise it yet." The *Stillwater Union* on July 25 concluded that perhaps "Miss Patti thought we were a plebian, unsophisticated and uncivilized audience; perhaps she did not like the red-shirts that condescended to hear her music, and this is the true reason she sang so shabbily."

During the week of the Bull concert, the ever-popular Hutchinson family returned to Stillwater and gave another of their well-received vocal recitals. To make those few days *completely* festive, there appeared on the village streets an organ grinder with a monkey, much to the delight of "sundry juveniles and some children of a larger growth."

The only known theater plays the St. Croix area could boast in the 1850s were a few given during the winter of 1858-59, when a small group of amateurs formed the Stillwater Thespian Society and presented a number of dramas to capacity audiences. Since lecturers were seldom brought into the valley, Stillwater also had to depend on local talent. In 1853-54 there was a lyceum, or "lecture course," and Margaret Miller, a local resident, recorded in her diary that the meeting on March 3 was a "grand burlesque on the message of our governor and quite a slur upon the proceedings of the present session at St. Paul. We have some pretty smart men here," Miss Miller concluded, "when they set out to be anybody." This lyceum continued for a few years. Debates were held and members took turns giving talks on a great variety of serious, popular subjects until quarrels among the participants caused the organization to disband. Papers were also read by "the Ladies" until they, too, got miffed and quit. Nor was Stillwater the only valley town to seek self-improvement. There was a lyceum in Lakeland during 1853, one at Prescott, and another organized late in 1859 at Taylors Falls, the veritable outpost of civilization. These were the principal sources of interesting and profitable amusement during the winter months, and the members of the

Hudson Literary Society found them "the best way that long winter evenings can be passed."

Occasionally a temperance lecturer appeared and, as elections approached, well-known Minnesota figures like James W. Taylor and Colonel Daniel A. Robertson of St. Paul stumped the valley, giving speeches at Stillwater, Marine Mills, and Taylors Falls for one political party or the other. Only rarely did speakers of national importance reach the area. One such occasion, though, was the evening of May 28, 1859, when Bayard Taylor, handsome and celebrated world traveler, poet, and lyceum lecturer, spoke at Stillwater under the auspices of The St. Paul Young Men's Christian Association. His topic was "Life in the North," and the small audience of some two hundred thoroughly enjoyed his exciting stories. Many more people had been expected to attend but, because of bad weather, the boats from downriver failed to arrive.

Just how bad the storm was and how exciting life in the North could really be is demonstrated by the story of the *Equator*. This stern-wheel steamboat, a "fast, commodious and elegant packet," was in 1859 beginning its second successful year carrying passengers three times a week between Prescott and Taylors Falls. On the day of Taylor's lecture, which followed appearances in St. Paul, St. Anthony, and Minneapolis, the weather was windy and threatening as the boat left the levee at Prescott and headed north for Stillwater. On board were more than three hundred excursionists who expected to attend the talk by one of America's most popular speakers. Just beyond Catfish Bar across from Afton, black clouds loomed up and a forty-mile gale and slashing rain suddenly struck the ship broadside. Waves poured across the main deck and through the open hatches; in the cabin, dishes crashed. The engines stopped dead. If it had not been for the calmness and bravery of Mrs. John Lay, the engineer's diminutive wife, panic might have ensued among the frightened women and children. Just south of Hudson, the *Equator* was driven with much violence onto the Wisconsin shore. The force of the impact crushed the hull's stern, and the boat foundered in several feet of water. No sooner had Captain Asa B. Green and his officers safely removed all the cold, wet, terrified passengers than the cabin of the battered steamboat was blown off and dashed to pieces by the violence of the wind and waves. Thus it was that some three hundred prospective listeners failed to hear Taylor's exciting, vivid lecture on "Life in the North."

Throughout the long winter months, after the river had frozen over following the last "full of the moon" in November, very few visitors made their way into the valley and business slumped. Henry M. Nichols, minister at the First Presbyterian church at Stillwater since 1853, echoed the sentiment of many Midwesterners when in November, 1857, he anticipated the dreary months ahead: "I dread these long winters." In the spring the shrill whistle of the season's first steamboat was the most welcome of all sounds—and always awaited with impatience. It heralded the opening of navigation, which once again placed the people in contact with the outside world. When the *Excelsior* nosed its iron-bound bow into the sand at the foot of Hudson's Buckeye Street on April 20, to become the first arrival of the 1856 season, nearly everyone in that village ran eagerly to the landing to swing their hats and shout huzza! "The weather is still beautiful," said the *Taylors Falls Reporter* at the opening of the 1860 season, "the river is in a good stage for navigation and all that is needed to send a thrill of pleasure through the hearts of our citizens, to increase our business, and invigorate us generally, is the arrival of a boat, which we are daily anticipating." Each spring as soon as paddle wheels could churn the waters of the St. Croix, individuals and organized groups, rejoicing, made plans for trips on the river. Then life became gay along the St. Croix.

Steamboat excursions were an important, even essential, part of river life for many years. Packet boats like the *Kate Cassel* provided an occasional outing for the pleasure-starved residents of the valley. An especially festive trip was made by this boat in August, 1859; at Marine and Taylors Falls the volunteer Stillwater Guards paraded the streets in full-dress uniform, led by the Afton brass band. Even the big 162-foot *Falls City* managed the sand bars and the unpredictable channel of the St. Croix on the last day of July, 1855, to bring a large group of tourists from St. Anthony and St. Paul to visit the Minnesota and Wisconsin towns along the

river. During the decade of the 1850s some twenty-five steamboats navigated the waters above Stillwater, some on regular passenger schedules and others only once or twice to unload freight
at Marine Mills, Osceola, or Taylors Falls. These packets, which
contributed so much to summertime pleasure, ranged in size from
the large 226-ton *Minnesota Belle* to the little twenty-ton *Queen
of the Yellow Banks,* one of the most diminutive steamboats ever
seen on the river.

But no single vessel of these early years surpassed in popularity
the forty-one-ton stern-wheeler *H. S. Allen,* "one of the neatest
water crafts we have seen afloat" said the *St. Paul Daily Pioneer.*
The *Allen's* captain, former hotelkeeper Isaac Grey, boasted, as
has every captain who ever navigated an American river, that if
the St. Croix should entirely dry up, he would still be able to get
through on a heavy dew. "The little Allen made a trip to the Falls
this week," the *Stillwater Democrat* affectionately reported four
years later; "she was the first boat that passed the ice jam at
Kitchen's Point, and proud of her achievement came up, sporting
the stars and stripes on her bow of a size large enough to almost
cover her from stem to stern." With pride, the residents of the
valley called the *Allen* a "smart and lively little craft." Less than
one third the size of more elegant rivals, the *H. S. Allen* was popular with many groups and organizations from 1857 through 1864.
For picnics, especially on the Fourth of July, the smokestacks, the
decks, and cabin were gaily decorated with brilliantly colored
streamers and bunting, and a brass or cotillion band played for
dancing.

Sometimes the St. Croix boats got through without incident, but
at other times almost everything went wrong. In 1858, spring
came early and Captain Green of the *Equator* planned a gala
"Grand Excursion" on March 29 to compete with the *H. S. Allen*
for the attention of valley residents. Some two hundred guests had
accepted the captain's invitation to make the trip. Music and refreshments were provided, and the crowd was in high spirits. Enthusiasm was somewhat dampened when a careless deck hand fell
overboard and "an hour's fruitless search for him caused some delay." Early in the afternoon, just above Marine Mills, the steamer's

engine refused to work. The boat was stranded in midstream, and it looked as though the excursionists would either have to spend the night on board or swim to shore and walk home. To enliven the passing hours, some passengers danced while others worried whether the food would hold out. Humiliating indeed was the climax of this festive occasion when the rival *H. S. Allen,* on her homeward trip from the Dalles, rescued most of the passengers from the stranded ship and returned them safely to Stillwater. The *Equator* limped ignominiously back the following day.

Steamboats also brought another kind of entertainment to the valley of the St. Croix—that unforgettable event of rural life, the circus. On a bright morning in the middle of June, 1858, a steam calliope appeared at the Stillwater levee and, with music as strong as "100 Brass Bands and the softness and harmony of a Piano Forte," announced the arrival from St. Louis of two showboats— the *James Raymond* and the *Banjo.* The circus was in town! The *Banjo* had tied up at Stillwater the year before with Ned Davis' Minstrels on board, so the public knew it could expect some pleasant entertainment. The twin boats of Spaulding and Rogers' "Great Monkey Circus and Burlesque Dramatic Troupe" presented afternoon and evening performances in its "audience chamber" seating 800 enthusiasts. Featured were monkeys and trained dogs, bearded, giant, and pigmy women, Swiss bird warblers, and other curiosities—a greater variety of amusements, said the *Messenger,* "than ever before exhibited in the upper Mississippi Valley." At Hudson, where the troupe performed after leaving Stillwater, the story is told of a banker who contracted admission for the entire village, and paid the bill with what was then local currency—pine shingles. It is said that when the two showboats left Hudson they had on board enough shingles to cover the Gulf of Mexico.

Today, after the passing of a hundred years, another showboat, this one operated by the drama department of the University of Minnesota, has come into the St. Croix Valley to tie up at the Stillwater waterfront and offer such gala entertainments as *Under the Gaslight* and *Zoey, or Life in Louisiana.*

Even the far-famed Cardiff Giant, one of the most widely pub-

licized hoaxes of the nineteenth century, once came upriver by steamboat to visit Minnesota. That was in 1871 when P. A. Older's Museum Circus and Menagerie set up its exhibits first in St. Paul and then at Stillwater. This giant stone statue carved in the form of a naked man, over ten feet tall and weighing 2,990 pounds, was "discovered" on a farm near Cardiff, New York, in 1869. Chiseled in Chicago from gypsum obtained in Iowa, the "American Goliath" was shipped to Upstate New York where it was buried in 1868 and dug up by prearrangement a year later. Many believed it to be a petrified human, a "new wonder," until the highly profit-

able practical joke was confessed by the perpetrator, a Bingham-
ton, New York, cigar maker. "Come and see it," ballyhooed the
Messenger, "and judge for yourself what it is!" The local newspaper, however, did not mention which exhibit was the most popular, the Cardiff Giant, the Living Horned Horse, or the Wild,
Uncouth Sea Cow.

Although women attended such festivities and took an especially active part in steamboat excursions, many leisure-time activities of the period, including hunting and fishing, were popular
only among men. For organized pastimes, curiosity about baseball
and cricket began developing in the St. Croix Valley during the
mid-century, but not until March, 1860, were the young men of
Stillwater reported ready to form a baseball club. Interest in the
game grew to fever pitch during the 1870s. Hudson had a team,
Afton boasted its "Lone Stars," and Stillwater produced the
"Shanghais" and the "St. Croix Club." By 1878, however, valley
residents seemed to lose their enthusiasm for the local teams and
amateur baseball never regained the same kind of popularity in
the region. "Since the baseball fever died out in Minnesota,"
smugly editorialized the *St. Paul Pioneer Press* in 1878, "there has
been a great decrease of crime committed by juveniles, and public
morality is on a higher plane." Today, the Friendly Valley Softball
League has taken over—and few will forget the classic 1963
championship team that was Scandia's.

Prize fighting, although not specifically declared illegal by city
ordinance either in St. Paul or Stillwater, was obviously frowned
upon by local sentiment. The sport may also have been tacitly
forbidden, since at no time was it listed among those entertainments and exhibitions requiring licenses. Occasionally permission
would be granted for a mock sparring performance, such as the
one held at Stillwater's Concert Hall late in August, 1871, but that
was looked upon as mimic play and uproarious comedy. The
reaction was different, however, when serious fighters faced each
other in the ring, bare knuckled and out for the hundred-dollar
stake. Then the show became a "disgusting and brutal gladiatorial
exhibition." Ring fans would go to great lengths to see such a
fight, as would the police to stop it.

Popular pugilists of the time were "Bridgeport Tom" Wheeler, Johnny McCarty, George Coon, and Tom Nesbit; but the best publicized of them all was a "nobby hairdresser" from Jackson Street in St. Paul where he was known as M. Capit McDonald. In 1869 McDonald gave up barbering, took on the nickname "Red-Handed Mike" and challenged all fellow pugs. It was not long before the *Minneapolis Tribune* was calling him a "famous prize fighter and notorious rough."

Because of police attitudes, careful, discreet preparations had to be made for all fights. Down at Mankato, along the banks of the Minnesota River, the invited spectators for one of Red-Handed Mike's encounters were instructed to leave the city singly and in different directions, so as not to alert the officers. Similar precautions, not so well observed, were taken for an 1871 bout at Stillwater. "Yesterday evening," reported the local *Gazette*, "although the time and place of the much-talked-of prize fight had been kept a profound mystery, eager crowds were hurrying to and fro on our streets, and silently embarking in squads, taking possession of every available skiff, batteau, dug-out, or anything that would float, and gliding noiselessly over to the other shore." In Wisconsin there were no regulations against the sport. Although Red-Handed Mike McDonald beat Johnny McCarty's head to a bloody pulp with his bare fists, the Minnesota authorities were powerless to interfere since the fight took place out of their jurisdiction. The public had found the excitement it craved.

Sculling on Lake St. Croix also had its enthusiastic devotees during the 1870s and for about three years there was considerable rowing competition between the boat clubs of Stillwater, St. Paul, and Red Wing. One enthusiastic sculler apostrophised the "Idols of the St. Croix Boat Club" in this fashion:

> Come down to the river, My Bonnie Lass!
>   And a sailor's sweetheart be—
> The water is smooth as a looking glass,
>   And is waiting to mirror thee.
>
> Come down to the river, my sand-hill Crane—

My Flamingo-tinted Gull—
And see me pull till my arms are lame,
And how beautifully I scull.

The popularity of horse racing started early in the valley.
Fishers Course on the outskirts of Stillwater was already well established when the first issue of the *Union* on October 23, 1854,
called that area "The Long Island of Minnesota" and egged on
"Those who indulge in the sport of the turf . . . to make investments." Over the next thirty years tracks were developed at Hudson, Lakeland, and Franconia, but the center of these sporting
activities remained at Stillwater, where a driving park near the
Washington County Fair Grounds adjoining Lily Lake later became the principal racing spot for area horses. Of all the animals
to run in the valley, none was more popular, nor received wider
publicity in and out of the state during the 1870s than Foxie V.,
owned by William C. Veazie, partner in the Marine lumbering
firm of Walker, Judd and Veazie. Sporting journals and turf regis-
ters spoke of her swiftness and "staying qualities so essential in
winning races." Foxie V. was also a good money winner for her
owner.

Diversion for women in towns and rural areas was more restricted. As a rule they were kept busy in the home. There were,
however, church functions, teas, sociables, sewing circles, and
temperance meetings. The Marine Sewing Society in February,
1858, met at the Upper St. Croix Boom House and made a bed-
quilt which Mrs. Orange Walker presented to the Congregational
minister's wife in the name of the society. The combined general
store and post office was always a meeting center for discussions
and gossip. And then, of course, the women joined in many social
activities with the menfolk.

In the smaller settlements along the river, social life was much
simpler than in towns the size of Stillwater. At Marine Mills, for
example, about the only group activity outside the church was a
spelling school for adults and young people which was held once
a week during the winter months. Residents would make great
efforts to attend distant parties and celebrations, or just to go "vis-

iting." Of other pastimes, dancing was perhaps the most
tant, since it permitted the mingling of the sexes. Marine had the
advantage over neighboring towns because its young men seemed
to be exceptionally active in getting up dances. These were held
more or less regularly in the popular hotels run by Adam Lightner
and Mathias Welshons.

Holidays were always a source of fun and celebration throughout the territory. Christmas was usually a family affair, with gatherings around a gift-laden tree and the "singing of a sweet little
hymn by the children." The *St. Paul Chronicle and Register*
looked forward to the 1849 holiday season: "Christmas is coming,"
the newspaper said, "and every one is preparing to enjoy it. . . .
The grave and devout will be at church. Those that love worldly
pleasure will be at the several balls, or out upon sleighing, and
eating and drinking parties. The great centre of attraction for this
class is the ball at the 'Minnesota House,' Stillwater, on Christmas
night."

Thanksgiving, New Year's Eve, St. Valentine's Day, and especially during the mid-century, Washington's Birthday, often found
neighboring settlements joining the fun in whatever town had the
most to offer in the way of parties, dinners, or dancing. A Thanksgiving Festival held at Stillwater in 1854, was such a success that
the assembled guests from St. Anthony, St. Paul, Hudson, and
Marine Mills moved en masse downriver to Hudson, where the
dance was continued the following night. And when no big celebration was planned at Stillwater for New Year's Eve, 1858, a
large group of young people traveled by sleighs to Marine, to
dance the intricate steps of the "mazy" at a "new and splendid
hotel," the five-story Lightner House. They returned the next day,
"delighted with the music, and dancing, and above all with Lightner's sumptuous supper."

"The Glorious Fourth" was the most popular of all holidays, one
of symbolic import and rededication. Almost every community
observed the day, and there was always on the program an orator
and a local celebrity to read the Declaration of Independence.
Firecrackers, much patriotic fervor, and frequent visits of the
male populace to the saloons were the order of the day. It was a

time for danger, earsplitting noises, and general excitement. "Harangued the people in a grove," the Reverend Mr. Nichols recorded of the 1854 Stillwater celebration, "and sat down to a grand dinner." But of all the villages in the valley, none has more frequently and more enthusiastically observed the national holiday than Marine. Almost from pioneer days the residents of that small village have seldom let the anniversary pass without a proper observance. Although orations are no longer in fashion, and nobody reads the Declaration of Independence, the parade, church picnics, greased pigs, fireworks, and a Firemen's Ball are programmed, now as then.

No Independence Day celebration, however, equaled the almost twenty-four-hour "jollification" of July 4, 1859, at Stillwater. Between five and eight thousand persons were in town for the festivities, which got off to a rousing start at sunrise with the firing of a cannon. Later in the morning the fifteen-piece Afton brass band led a colorful parade through the decorated streets to Nelson's grove in the south end of the village. The parade included two crack military companies in full-dress uniform and a cone-shaped float drawn by six white horses and bedecked with banners, evergreens, and pretty girls. The German Singing Society, the Association of Turners, and many citizens in carriages preceded the final float—a giant wagon pulled by ten yoke of St. Croix oxen and filled with no fewer than seventy-six men, women, and children.

Just as the parade reached the picnic grove, a cannon blast from the steamer *Itasca* announced the arrival of celebrating excursionists from St. Paul and other points along the Mississippi and St. Croix rivers. The Turners tumbled, the German Singing Society performed, and the military, resplendent in their uniforms, marched. There were well over twenty toasts and responses at the grove before the jubilant multitude adjourned to the armory for a cold supper, or "collation." In the evening a ball was held in Sawyer's new hotel, called the largest in Minnesota, and the nightlong celebration was interrupted only by the whistle and bell of the impatient *Itasca,* calling the guests from St. Paul.

It was a day long to be remembered. Never before, and
since, has the St. Croix Valley seen such a Fourth of July celebration. "Oration, dinner, toasts, parade, firecrackers, cannons, lager
beer, drunkenness, rockets, Roman candles, dancing, shouting,
obfuscation generally," summed up the Reverend Mr. Nichols.

During Minnesota's early years, only hardy individuals and
small groups of entertainers would brave the rigors of travel in the
new country. With the influx of settlers during the 1860s, however, came improved transportation facilities, and residents along
the navigable waterways began to receive more frequent visits
from theatrical troupes, operatic companies, variety shows, circuses, and lecturers.

At the end of the decade, social life was more varied in the
lower St. Croix River villages. But during Civil War years there
were still complaints: "Great dearth of shows, negro melodists,
&c. for some time past," reported the *Stillwater Messenger* in
April, 1864, "and people young and old rush eagerly in crowds to
see anything that promises amusement."

By 1869 the Stillwater correspondent of the *St. Paul Daily Press*
was happy about the numerous forms and variety of amusements
going on in that St. Croix village. There were hops—informal
dances—every other week at Concert Hall; a Professor Jones gave
terpsichorean lessons on Saturday afternoons; frequent sleigh
rides were enjoyed to Marine and Osceola, Hudson and Prescott,
where there was always dancing. Add to these, two or three private parties a week and "to all appearances," the reporter concluded, "we are a community of revelers."

The croquet fad, which swept the nation following the Civil
War, reached the valley during the mid-1870s and so popular did
this "exciting and healthful" game become that the Fayette Marsh
family of Stillwater even brought in kerosene locomotive headlights so they could continue playing after dark. Others smugly
labeled the sport "Presbyterian Billiards."

During the 1860s and into the next decade, panoramas, a new
form of entertainment, found their way to the region. Stillwater
and Osceola were among the river towns where these forerunners

of motion pictures were unrolled, and although spectators viewed only one large painting at a time, they perhaps could get the feeling of movement. For the most part the scenes of historical or religious interest were thoroughly enjoyed, but at times local reactions became severely critical: "A collection of daubs," said Stillwater residents in 1864 of a series of Civil War paintings, "humbug!"

It was principally the people of Stillwater, Hudson, and other larger settlements throughout the Midwest, however, who benefited from such a varied diet of fun. Only infrequently did the smaller villages have a chance to welcome traveling theatrical troupes, although Medicine Shows entertained the people from time to time, and their barkers made good money hawking patented nostrums and bottled cure-alls. Occasionally such boats as the popular stern-wheel packet *G. B. Knapp* did the unusual. In May, 1867, for example, it transported (undoubtedly during very high water) de Haven's Great Union Circus from Stillwater to Taylors Falls. When the *G. B.*—which newspapers liked to call the "Gay Boat"—passed Osceola, a delighted crowd followed in the steamer *Pioneer* to see the Taylors Falls performance. And in mid-July of the same year a large party from that village and Osceola came down, the *Messenger* reported, on the "elegant little steamer" the *G. B. Knapp* en route to St. Paul and the scandalous leg show, *The Black Crook*.

Residents of the valley liked the informality of river travel. In fact a Western steamer was considered far more democratic than those plying the waters of the effete East. In this country, the Taylors Falls newspaper felt that a man "only had to stick his feet up somewhere, light a cigar, and let his jaw wag of its own free will and straightway he becomes acquainted with all his fellow travellers."

Excursions, moonlight rides, and Sunday School picnics on steamboats did not lose their popularity until after the turn of the century. By the 1860s fishing parties "with the ladies" were, according to the *Messenger*, "*the* thing of all others." Ice skating clubs, too, were formed at Stillwater and Taylors Falls about the

same time. With the river at their front door, St. Croix
always enjoyed a ready-made summer, and often a win[t]
ground. Not many cities can today boast an annual ice cream
festival in the middle of a frozen lake as can Stillwater.

Activities during the months of snow also usually included one
or two major funmaking events. In February, 1869, there was the
festive ten-mile sleigh ride of twenty couples from Taylors Falls
west to Center City. After a supper at the Forrest House hotel,
dancing, storytelling, and cards kept the "gay and gallant crowd"
up all night. A few tried to catch a little sleep, but, as one of the
celebrants insisted, time was too short "to waste it indolently." In
spite of these infrequent flings, and an occasional husking party
when the young people would shuck corn all day and dance
through the night, organized social gatherings continued to center
mostly in the local church, as they still do today. Sliding downhill,
and attending singing schools and mite societies connected with
the churches were the principal pastimes for residents of Taylors
Falls. In 1862 visitors to Hudson were bored. With no lyceum,
debating club, lectures, or reading rooms, all the entertainment
they had was watching the teams come into the village loaded
down with wheat. As late as 1884 the young people complained
that small hops at Welshons' St. Croix House at Marine were
"about all the amusement we can scare up."

Fundamentally, village life has not changed greatly along the
St. Croix. The available entertainments are still few and far between. For a few days each summer the carnival spirit returns to
valley settlements when Lindstrom celebrates its Karl Oskar Days,
when Stillwater sponsors its Playdays activities, and the two-
state villages of Taylors Falls and St. Croix Falls join to raise their
respective hells during "Wannigan Days." Movie theaters and
television have taken over from traveling companies and individ-
ual artists. Square dancing has replaced the intricate steps of the
once popular "mazy." And gone from the valley are the nationally
known lecturers, the theatrical troupes, the burnt-cork minstrel
shows, the panoramas, the "Indian" medicine performers, and
many of the unsophisticated amenities of a simpler, fresher, and

vanished St. Croix Valley. The greatest single alteration to a way of life came at the turn of the century when railroads were well established in the valley, when the automobile replaced the paddle-wheel steamboats, and when Fourth of July celebrations lost their feeling of spontaneous merrymaking.

Chapter Eleven

The Battle of the Piles

TIME was when villages along the St. Croix enjoyed fierce, back-biting rivalries and reveled in frequent, wordy quarrels with neighboring settlements. Osceolans, for example, seemed more than eager to make invidious remarks about Franconia, St. Croix Falls, or Sunrise City. And these arguments were avidly recorded up and down the river. Taylors Falls was a constant and some-times bitter rival of its twin village in Wisconsin. Stillwater, too, seemed continually at odds with the capital city of St. Paul. During the 1850s valley editor Abbott complained that although St. Paul depended on Stillwater for lumber, its papers would not acknowledge the fact. "They would," he said, "infinitely prefer to have their eye teeth pulled." These feuds were the special delight of newspapermen who eagerly fostered, reported, and frequently embellished them.

One of the first such disputes in the valley was the Prescott-Hudson imbroglio begun by Sam S. Fifield, Jr., in an article he wrote for the *Prescott Paraclete* during May, 1855. He boasted that his village on the St. Croix River had the same advantageous commercial location for the entire upper Mississippi Valley as had the city of St. Louis in the lower Mississippi River region. Prescott, Fifield claimed, was the only true head of navigation on both the Mississippi and the St. Croix. In low water, St. Paul was quite inaccessible. Steamboats could not even land at Hudson, he added, because of the extensive sand bar opposite and below the mouth of the Willow River. Fifield completely ignored the exist-ence of the valley's fastest growing community—Stillwater.

The *Hudson North Star* was quick to blast the *Paraclete* article, calling it "abusive, insulting black guardism" and a "complete tissue of lies . . . closely woven and cunningly contrived." The *North Star's* editor, "to put immigrants on their guard against such deceptions," heaped scorn on Fifield's vivid imagination and unbounded self-conceit which could create a St. Louis out of Prescott and make it "the metropolis of the great North-West." Rival editor Charles E. Young at Prescott countered in kind with the accusation that the *North Star* was "reeking in . . . filthy slang."

Another favorite trick was for one village to belittle the capacities of the other, as happened early in July, 1856, when H. M. Smith's Great American Circus was preparing to tour the area. Prescott, to make sure it secured the sought-after entertainment, represented Hudson to the advance agent as a settlement made up of "a small people . . . few in number." The circus, however, bypassed both villages, and chose Stillwater. "We thank you, Prescott, for your timely favor," was the Hudson newspaper's sarcastic rejoinder.

In 1869 Platt B. Walker of Taylors Falls called Osceola a "pleasant place." But only five years later the *Hudson Star and Times* could not have disagreed more: "Osceola is a perfect specimen of a dilapidated, dried up and *dead* town."

By 1870 Hudson could afford to be more magnanimous, since Prescott apparently no longer threatened as a competitor. "In the St. Croix Valley," the editor pontificated, "all the smaller towns are jealous of Hudson. . . . Prescott, Ellsworth, Osceola, Richmond frequently speak of Hudson in disparaging terms. This jealousy and war among localities is useless and productive of evil. A hearty rivalry is necessary and commendable; but to build up one section, it is not necessary to tear down the other."

Stillwater, however, was an ever-present threat.

During the 1850s Hudson and Stillwater had been rivals for a bridge across the St. Croix, but their hopes went aglimmering when the expected railroad never reached the valley. Early in the 1870s a similar struggle suddenly flared into open revolt. Stillwater was convinced that it would get the newly formed West Wisconsin Railroad to cross the river at the head of Lake St.

Croix. But Hudson won out, and the residents of the upriver town were indignant. They felt that their lumber interests would be greatly injured if the bridge were constructed at Hudson.

Nor was the Hudson newspaper an ameliorating influence. "Stillwater is without hope in the world," taunted the *Star and Times* on March 3, 1871. "They could have had a branch railroad from here, but the natural perversity and unhallowed ambition of their wicked hearts has lost them all. 'Oh, Stillwater! How oft would we have gathered thee under our wings, as a hen gathereth her brood, but ye would not.'"

Work on the Hudson bridge was begun late in March, 1871, for ice left the lake early that year. All seemed to be progressing satisfactorily until the weekend before actual war was declared. It was in mid-July when Captain Wyman X. Folsom was unable to maneuver his little packet steamer, the *Wyman X* and its barge of freight between the bridge pilings already in place. At the same time the stern-wheel towboat *Mollie Whitmore*, with a raft of logs for the Stillwater mill of Schulenburg, Boeckeler and Company, and the steamer *Imperial* pushing wheat-filled barges were also unable to pass the piers without splitting up their tows. The lumbermen at Stillwater had requested a 200-foot clearance, but it was obvious that this distance was being cut by more than half. Businessmen of the upriver city felt such an action constituted a dangerous obstruction to river navigation. The contractor, however, paid no attention to an injunction obtained by the lumbermen to cease and desist. In spite of the appearance of the Washington County sheriff, the pile driver continued slamming posts into the river's bed, doing it under the cover of darkness. "If Hudson people," warned the Stillwater newspaper, "or their allies in St. Paul, think . . . to injure our city and valley by methods so shameful and disgraceful . . . they will find themselves sadly mistaken."

The *St. Paul Press* believed that war was inevitable: "Stillwater is armed to the teeth." Opportunist Sturgess Selleck, Stillwater dealer in men's and boy's clothing, took advantage of the excitement. "The Hudson bridge," he advertised in the *Messenger*, "affects in no way the price of clothes, for Selleck has no *pier* to obstruct the sale of his large stock." The *St. Paul Dispatch*, on the other hand, accused the Stillwater natives of "lashing themselves into a fury" ever since Joe Schlenck, another haberdasher, reduced the price of his pants a dollar a pair.

At 8 P.M. on Thursday, July 6, the *G. B. Knapp* made a quiet reconnaissance downriver to Hudson and found the pile driver still hard at work. Back in Stillwater, this news was sufficient to set attack plans in motion. At five o'clock the following morning a fleet of steamboats, loaded mostly with raftsmen, rounded to at the Hudson bridge pilings and with the shout, "Boys, man the piles!" they immediately set to work pulling out the offending underpinnings and sending them adrift down the lake.

Exactly how many paddle-wheelers and men took part in this Battle of the Piles is not known. Minneapolis, St. Paul, and Duluth newspapers guessed wildly at from five to ten steamers and up to a thousand men. Stillwater would only say that there was a sufficient number of both. Actually, four boats played active roles, although others stood by to watch the goings-on. First was the stern-wheel rafter *Minnesota*—the flagship—commanded by Augustus R. Young, who the newspaper reported was as cool and collected as though he had on board "a Sabbath School Pic-Nic." Prior to battle, the captain is said to have addressed his crew in this fashion: "My brave comrades, if I should fall in this desperate conflict, as most likely I shall, you will rush over my mangled corpse and fasten to the other pile!"

Staunchly beside the *Minnesota* was Martin Mower's *Swallow*, a small steamer of "remarkable speed and activity," captained by Josiah Staples, nephew of Stillwater's first citizen. Also in the fray were the rafter *Louisville* under the command of Captain Ralph J. Wheeler, lumber partner of Edward W. Durant, and the newly built *Brother Jonathan* piloted by Captain Austin T. Jenks.

All opposition faded before this formidable onslaught. The Stillwater men and their intrepid boats had no interference as they pulled from the St. Croix some one hundred piers. By dark that night the mission was accomplished and three of the steamers were ordered back to home base—to return along "the American side" of the river. The *Minnesota* remained behind to foil any attempts of the bridgebuilders to start putting back the piles. All night its paddle wheels churned the waters of Lake St. Croix so that the pile driver could not be held stationary. At six the next morning valiant Captain Young returned to Stillwater, taking the pile driver with him, but not as a captured prize of battle. To the contrary, said the *Stillwater Gazette,* the politeness and urbanity of the captain so won the esteem of the pile driver's crew that they were delighted to accompany him to Stillwater to spend the Sabbath. The editor of the *Star and Times* thought the campaign a brilliant one, saying that it "no doubt will take high rank in the achievement of naval history."

With the Battle of the Piles so quickly brought to a successful conclusion, there was left only a meeting of the "High Joint Commission" to iron out details of the treaty. Representatives from Hudson and Stillwater, the latter including Frederick Schulenburg, Isaac Staples, John McKusick, and Ed Durant, met on board the *Minnesota.* While Captain Young served up a "splendid meal," the commission decided that a slight change in the plans for the bridge was practicable. The Hudson newspaper reported Stillwater very fair in its demands, even "conciliatory in tone." After several more meetings and conferences, the railroad company conceded that the error was theirs. With the signing of the peace treaty at the Sawyer House about a week later, the Stillwater lumbermen got what they wanted—a span of 140 feet on either side of the draw pier for the safe passage of rafts.

There were, however, two aftermaths to the Battle of the Piles. Six months later Ed Durant petitioned the city council for a payment of $260 to the four boats involved—a justified expenditure, he claimed, and cheap, for who else could remove a pile for only $2.60? Apparently the sum was paid, although over objections. "During the present winter," complained "XXX" in the *Messenger,* "a party of young bloods went outside the city limits to a whore house and demolished the furniture. Would it not be a good idea, now that a precedent is established, for our City Council to make an appropriation to defray their livery and whisky bills?"

With the second aftermath, the Battle of the Piles became his-

tory. In August, 1872, Joseph R. Carli, sheriff of Washington
County, a man, they said, of cheerful yesterdays and confident
tomorrows, optimistically submitted a bill for $60.00 to cover his
expenses on official duty during the misunderstanding. Undoubtedly Joe Carli was disappointed when the council allowed him
only $25.00. But then again, perhaps he wasn't.

Early in 1964 further rumblings of war were being heard in
the St. Croix Valley, and once again it was Stillwater *versus* Hudson. Ninety-two years after the Battle of the Piles, the Northern
States Power Company announced plans for the construction of
two gigantic twenty-story coal-burning electric generating plants
along the banks of Lake St. Croix immediately south of Stillwater.
Although Wisconsin residents in Hudson and River Falls were
the first to raise loud and long their howls of protest, countless
others from in and out of the valley soon joined this new battle
to preserve inviolate the clear water of the St. Croix River and
the fresh air above it. As they did in 1872, Stillwater residents
again blasted St. Paul—this time for trying to snatch from them
an apparent tax bonanza.

"It is easy to put a dollar sign on commercial value," commented James R. Wiggins, editor of the *Washington* (D.C.) *Post*
on a visit to St. Paul late in August, 1964, "but you can't estimate
in dollars the use people in the area will get out of a recreational
area. The St. Croix is a good example. Nobody has enough psychological insight," concluded the former Minnesota newspaperman, "to evaluate the importance of one watershed that hasn't
been exploited."

By mid-January, 1965, this "Great St. Croix Debate" was a
topic of national interest when U.S. Senator Gaylord Nelson said
at Stillwater: "Call the roll of the great American rivers of the
past, and you will have a list of the pollution problems of today. . . . The story in each case is the same: they died for their
country."

As this is being written, war cries continue to echo along the St.
Croix, and the battle is not yet over.

Chapter Twelve

Mail for Pioneers

OF THE five post offices established in the valley of the St. Croix during the 1840s, those at St. Croix Falls, Marine Mills, and Stillwater are the ones which today continue to operate under essentially the same names. A fourth office still distributing mail to river residents was first formed as Willow River on November 21, 1849, but three years later that name was changed to Hudson. In 1827, some thirteen years before the inauguration of mail service into the St. Croix Valley, the first post office in the upper Mississippi area was established at Fort Snelling. Up to that time, mail had arrived only occasionally at this remote military post. On January 28, 1826, for example, two lieutenants returned from Prairie du Chien with letters which, according to Major Taliaferro at the fort, were "the *first* for *Five Months*." Even after the opening of a post office at the fort in 1834 under Samuel C. Stambaugh, soldiers and chance travelers arriving from Fort Crawford at Prairie du Chien continued to bring with them mail addressed to isolated military men and settlers on the upper river.

Through the next fourteen years Fort Snelling remained the only post office north of Prairie du Chien. Tidings from the outside world reached the fort about once a month, but mail deliveries depended on the vagaries of weather and the carriers' abilities to make their way through the vast, uninhabited wilderness. Postal matter from the South and the East reached the upper Mississippi Valley via Louisville in Kentucky, Vincennes in Indiana, St. Louis, and Prairie du Chien. All communications for this region, therefore, had to be addressed to Fort Snelling, and it was up to the people living along the Midwestern waterways to get their own letters and newspapers from the military post as best they could.

The amount of mail that reached the sparsely settled northern country was small. It was expensive to send a letter, and few could afford the twenty-five cents charged to transport a single sheet. Most early nineteenth-century letters consisted merely of one piece of paper which was folded, addressed on the reverse side, and sealed with hot wax. In 1845 postage rates dropped to five and ten cents a half ounce, depending on the distance a communication had to travel; and in 1851, when envelopes were becoming popular, postage was again reduced to three and six cents. Fees were usually collected by the receiving postmaster. Postage stamps, first introduced in 1847, did not come into general use throughout the Midwest until the late 1850s. As rates were reduced, the use of postal facilities increased, as did the demand for new post offices. At the same time, complaints about infrequent mail deliveries multiplied.

Although service for some decades was unreliable and irregular, post offices were quick to follow the founding of frontier settlements. At Point Douglas an office known as "Lake St. Croix" was established on July 18, 1840. A year and a half later, Philander Prescott, the settlement's first postmaster, informed postal authorities at St. Paul that the "Mail carrier furnished this office only once with the Mail last Quarter." But during the 1840s correspondence was usually received semimonthly along the Mississippi. The schedules of steamboats could not be depended on since they came and went in those early years only when they could obtain large enough cargoes.

Philip Aldrich of Willow River, Charles Rouleau of St. Paul, Edward Worth from St. Croix Falls, Henry W. Crosby and Jacob Fahlstrom of Lakeland are among the men who carried mail by canoe or on foot in the St. Croix Valley during the 1840s. Crosby, for example, made two trips a month on the route upriver, for each of which he received six dollars. The northern terminal was St. Croix Falls where, also on July 18, 1840, another valley post office was approved and put in operation under the name "Falls of St. Croix." This was changed to St. Croix Falls in 1868.

The federal government established another St. Croix Valley post office at Stillwater on January 18, 1846, and lumberman Elam Greeley, one of the village's founders, was named postmaster. A few months later St. Paul received its office and, over a road which connected the two villages at least as early as 1847, "semioccasional" deliveries reached Stillwater. The weekly mail from Prairie du Chien, however, continued to lag, sometimes delayed weeks on end at post offices down the line. "During five months," reported the *Minnesota Pioneer* of St. Paul on April 28, 1849, "the communication between this part of the country and our brethren in the United States has been difficult and unfrequent."

The need for additional postal service in the St. Croix Valley soon became evident and resulted in the establishment on April 25, 1848, of the Marine Mills office. One of the founding fathers of the village, Orange Walker, served as its first postmaster. But his new position hardly affected his work as clerk and manager of the lumber company, since mail arrived only twice a month at the company store, which also housed the post office. He had not been long in office when he began to complain about the lack of mail facilities. On January 15, 1849, for example, he wrote to Sibley, then Minnesota's territorial delegate in Washington, that since President James K. Polk had reported the post office department "in a sound condition . . . we would be verry thankful if they would expend some of the surplus in sending the mail to this section." Walker continued as postmaster until May, 1869, and his compensation for nineteen years of service totaled $917.57.

During the late 1840s one postal route from the south was by land from Prairie du Chien via Black River Falls, Wisconsin, into the St. Croix Valley and up the eastern shore of the river. Minnesota residents had to cross the stream to pick up their mail as Dr. Aldrich walked this weekly land route to St. Croix Falls. Among those who were inconvenienced were two Stillwater residents, lawyer Henry L. Moss and William Holcombe. They pointed out to Sibley that their village and Marine Mills needed direct connections with Prairie du Chien; then, complained Moss, "our mail would not lie a week or more in the office at the mouth of St. Croix Lake." Perhaps as a result, direct postal service between Point Douglas at the foot of Lake St. Croix and Marine Mills was inaugurated after a road via Stillwater was opened.

Although practically new, the road on the Minnesota bank of the stream was rough and almost impassable for wagons in 1849, when Ephraim S. Seymour traveled up the valley and reported that after heavy rains it was even "too miry to travel on horseback." Seymour also tells of seeing one of the semimonthly mails from Stillwater arrive at St. Croix Falls. He was amused by the great excitement it caused as well as by the "exhibition of the genuine democracy of the citizens. The mail matter was emptied out upon a bed, about which all the citizens who were present gathered, and aided in assorting the mail, and selecting their own papers or letters. There seemed to be no distinction between the postmaster and others," he concluded, "as all seemed to be equally engaged in distributing the contents."

Another St. Croix Valley post office was authorized on February 21, 1851—this time at Taylors Falls. The first mail did not reach there, however, until the following April, and all it brought was one letter posted at St. Paul. The second delivery likewise contained but a single missile, sent from Keokuk, Iowa. In 1851 a new road was built from the capital city of Minnesota via Little Canada and White Bear Lake to Stillwater. Thereafter, a weekly instead of a semimonthly mail delivery was instituted from Stillwater to Taylors Falls and its sister city across the river.

The future for better communication between St. Croix Valley residents and the outside world appeared bright. Only the pitiful inadequacy of the road along the river's west bank remained a hindrance. The Wisconsin area from Hudson north to Osceola was during the early years so sparsely settled that there was little call for added mail service. Nathan C. D. Taylor, postmaster at Taylors Falls, urged Sibley to have the Minnesota road improved, then resignedly concluded, "but Suppose we must remain Contented untill we get *big* enough to make a noise." The *St. Anthony Express* in May, 1852, reported that scarcely a wagon would venture to travel the road from Stillwater to Marine. North from Marine a narrow way had been cut, "but in the summer," added the newspaper, "it is utterly impassable on account of mire and hills." As late as March 6, 1855, the editor of the *St. Croix Union* of Stillwater complained that the road was full of water, grass, weeds, stumps, and tree roots. "Jupiter! what a road," he exclaimed. "The goats upon the mountains could not have engineered a worse road." Postal service in the St. Croix Valley continued poor mainly because of such conditions. Censure of the postal system became especially strong and bitter during the 1850s, for adequate mail service was of primary importance to the early settlers. Holcombe summed up the situation when he wrote to Sibley from Stillwater on March 27, 1852: "Our mails . . . are sadly out of joint."

The state of Wisconsin did little for its far western settlers and the young territory of Minnesota, with almost no money to spend on highways, had to depend largely on the federal government to tie its settlements together. By 1853 a military road up the west bank of the St. Croix, which eventually would connect Point Douglas with Lake Superior, was completed to twelve miles above Taylors Falls. Great must have been the day in that same year when the first four-horse coach, perhaps carrying postal matter, reached Marine Mills! In 1854 mail was arriving triweekly at Stillwater, coming overland from St. Paul. Occasionally, too, a steamboat would bring it in. Carlisle A. Bromley, a liveryman at Stillwater, was the carrier on the land route, and he also ran a two-horse mail carriage once a week to Taylors Falls via Marine Mills. About this time, St. Croix Falls began receiving some of its mail more or less regularly from Hudson. The postal service on that route, however, bypassed Osceola, which had to depend on "the kindness of some self-constituted mail carrier" for its letters and papers. "A greater humbug than Barnum," complained the *Hudson North Star* in 1854, "is the whole postal system in these United States."

Most of the complaints of the 1850s were aimed at those who contracted to carry mails. Many were sadly and shamefully neglecting their duty. "The irregularity of our . . . mail," editorialized the *Union* on November 3, 1854, "has become a matter of so frequent an occurrence that we can thank our stars that it is no worse." The postmaster at Dubuque, Iowa, perhaps had the correct explanation when he asserted that in the entire Northwest there was no effective postal supervision. The Galena boats did not make connections with the trains; on the land route, mail piled up in post offices because it was left behind when there were paying passengers to carry. Schedules, too, were changed to meet the carriers' convenience. Since communications from the East were still "as angel's visits—'few and far between,'" the *Union* in March, 1855, proposed that "we declare ourselves independent . . . make a China wall around the Territory, let the world wag, raise beans and corn, and live 'unspotted from the world.'"

After 1854, when George E. Nettleton contracted to carry mail through the pineries of the upper valley from Taylors Falls along the east bank of the river to Superior, Wisconsin, the complaints started coming in from the residents of that northerly region as well as from the carrier himself. On April 21, 1856, Nettleton wrote to Washington that "By embracing Sunrise City & Snake river Dam you increase distance of my route some 45 miles besides compelling me to pass the mail over a road some 60 miles of which is not worked at all and impossible to pass with a horse." The difficulties of such a journey undoubtedly discouraged the contractor, for in October of the following year Denis Dean, a resident of Superior, complained that his city was without any mail connection with the East. The contractor, he reported, "has *refused to take the mail.*" Yet Dean conceded that it was a difficult route and "at this season of the year the mail has to be carried on men's backs for 100 miles." It took men of great strength and nerve, encumbered as they were with packs and rifles, to trudge day and night through the deep snow. By the summer of 1860 the road north was reported to be in good condition and there was no excuse, some thought, for the contractor to hire Indians to carry the mail, in violation of postal regulations. Furthermore, the bags and contents were "allowed to get wet and some of it is left behind."

Poor service was not always attributed to laxness on the part of

Mississippi River postmasters. During December, 1856, a petition signed by 133 residents of Taylors Falls requested the federal government to oust postmaster Porter E. Walker, brother of Marine's Orange Walker, because he did not give "general satisfaction" to the public. Walker, it seems, was also the local schoolteacher, and "during school hours," as the petition put it, "the most busy part of the day, the office remains closed to the great annoyance and inconvenience of many citizens having business" there.

By 1858, the year Minnesota was admitted to the Union, the valley's mail situation had been little improved. On the route up the west bank of the St. Croix from Point Douglas to Taylors Falls, three more post offices had been established—at Lakeland and Milton Mills in 1854, and at the proposed village of Vasa in 1857. The name of Milton Mills was soon changed to Afton. Vasa was a speculator's village a few miles above Marine, and its name was removed from the list of authorized post offices in 1860. On the east bank of the St. Croix an office at Prescott had been established on February 20, 1852; at Osceola Mills early in 1854; and at Kinnick Kinnick (now River Falls) during December of the same year.

By 1858 mail was being delivered regularly at St. Paul, but only after the appointment of a special agent to travel up and down the route along the Mississippi River to see that the carriers fulfilled their contracts. A St. Paul newspaper pointed out that this supervision gave the contractors no chance "to impose on the people as they formerly did." When mail reached St. Paul punctually, the St. Croix Valley benefited. There was a daily mail and stage service between that city and Stillwater, and sometimes three deliveries a week reached the post offices north of the St. Croix River's chief lumbering town.

Statehood for Minnesota brought no immediate solution to the further improvement of St. Croix Valley postal problems. Complaints about the irregularity of mail continued to come from those who lived along the river. The *Messenger's* editor, late in 1858, accused the post office department of "progressing backward" in its routing of mail into Stillwater. "Instead of sending our mails direct from the junction of the Mississippi and St. Croix —a distance of thirty miles traversed by daily steamers," said the newspaper, "our mail matter is sent to St. Paul, making a circuit of some sixty miles. . . . Will not some friend send the Post Master General a Pocket atlas of this . . . country?"

An attempt to improve the service early in 1859, when the steamer *Equator* made a few trips with mail from Stillwater, failed as the result of a disastrous storm on Lake St. Croix which completely wrecked the boat. Captain Isaac Gray's little stern-wheeler, the *H. S. Allen*, described as the "Regular St. Croix River U.S. Mail Packet," established service between Prescott and Taylors Falls in 1860. But the residents of the latter village decried the less than satisfactory results, which brought them only two deliveries a week. "We doubt if any other portion of the State," complained the upriver village, "is so poorly supplied with mail facilities as the St. Croix Valley."

Another steamer, Captain Oscar Knapp's *Enterprise,* joined the *Allen* in 1862, and on alternate days the two packets busily hissed up and down river, delivering correspondence to villages along the route between the mouth of the St. Croix and Taylors Falls. Contractors, however, found it almost impossible to give regular or prompt service because of frequent delays caused by low water, log jams, and occasional accidents or the breakdown of equipment.

During summer months the river towns received mail daily by boat, as well as over the regular land routes north from Stillwater and Hudson. But deliveries reverted to a three-a-week schedule in winter. For a number of winters after 1862 the frozen river proved a good highway for both passenger and mail stages, far preferable to the rough and sometimes snowless land route, although thin ice caused an occasional accident.

North of St. Croix Falls the lack of mail during the seasons of cold weather and heavy snow was more noticeable. During 1868, for example, a huge backlog of letters and papers accumulated at the Sunrise post office awaiting transportation to Bayfield and La Pointe on Madeline Island. Residents were convinced that postal officials at Washington had deliberately wiped the Wisconsin side of the river off their map—for the duration of the winter months, at least.

The summers of 1863 and 1864, which were marked by extremely low water, were difficult for all steamboats on both the St. Croix and the Mississippi. Captain Knapp complained that a good-sized pickerel, lying crosswise in the channel, interrupted navigation, and that his boat could no longer jump over the sand bars. During October, 1864, the Taylors Falls editor spoke for the residents of all upriver villages when he commented on the effects of a major log jam: "We, denizens of this Upper Valley are now . . . most effectually blockaded, completely shut off from any passenger communication with the outer world, save by the daily means of egress and ingress from our hermitage, in the one horse conveyance which carries our U.S. Mail."

Letters continued slow in coming. To the question, "Why is Osceola a poor town for old Maids?" a local punster answered, "Because it has no *Mails*." Valley newspapers do not record another mail boat on the St. Croix until 1871, when the *Wyman X* functioned for a short time after a stage line discontinued service because the road bordering the river was in such poor condition. As the stage driver put it: "This road is not passable, not even jackass-able."

On occasion a postmaster's day might be brightened by letters like the one addressed in 1872 to William Thing, clerk on the paddle boat *G. B. Knapp:*

> Uncle Billie we call him—his surname is Thing;
> He dwells in old Somerset, if he's not on the wing,
> In the good state of Wis., and the Co. of St. Croix,
> E'en this's the address of that bully boy;
> And should the young man to known parts be gone,
> I want the postmaster to forward this on.

The year 1873 saw the end of the Taylors Falls mail run. Daily deliveries were established between Stillwater and Marine Mills, and henceforth Taylors Falls received its communications via the inland village of Wyoming, which was served by a railroad. In 1875 a lone steamboat was again in the mail-carrying business.

The popular paddle-wheeler, *G. B. Knapp,* looking "as gay as a girl in a calico dress with a white apron" with "U.S. Mail" painted in large letters on its bulkheads, ran upriver daily from Stillwater. It had been used briefly in a similar capacity during June, 1866. George C. McNeal, a Marine liveryman who held the mail contract, found it more profitable to carry both mailsacks and passengers by boat rather than team. This arrangement, however, ended when McNeal disposed of his contract late in 1875. The venerable *G. B. Knapp,* for many years familiar to St. Croix River residents, was the last of the stream's mail boats.

A major route change was made early in 1876, when the mail was taken over a new post road through Marine Mills, across the St. Croix by ferry, and via Farmington Center, Wisconsin, to Osceola and St. Croix Falls. Throughout this period, and until the mid-1880s, four stage lines were making the run. Abraham Johnson, a prominent Marine farmer, lumberman, and livery stable owner who is still remembered in the valley as "Abe," was a long-time contractor on the mail route north out of Stillwater.

The end in the St. Croix Valley of the difficult and unpredictable "star routes"—as those not served by railroads were known— was at hand. When the Stillwater branch of the Lake Superior and Mississippi Railroad began carrying mail in 1871, the St. Paul to Stillwater star route was discontinued and mail service by stage ended. But sixteen years were to pass before the iron horse came to Marine Mills. On December 5, 1887, after the Minneapolis to Turtle Lake, Wisconsin, section of the Minneapolis, St. Paul and Sault Ste Marie Railroad, popularly known as the Soo Line, was opened, the star route through Marine and into Wisconsin was discontinued. The railroad began transporting all mail. At last the St. Croix Valley could boast dependable postal service.

Chapter Thirteen

People of the Wooden Shoes

FREDRIKA Bremer, Swedish novelist and gracious, observant commentator on the American scene, was ecstatic about the new territory west of the St. Croix and Mississippi rivers which she visited in October, 1850; "This Minnesota is a glorious country," she rhapsodized, "and just the country for a new Scandinavia."

Even as she wrote these words, two groups of Swedes were on their way to the "glorious new Scandinavia," the delta between the St. Croix and Mississippi rivers which was then the only land in Minnesota legally open for sale and settlement. Traveling upriver from Illinois during the third week of October, Oscar Roos, Carl Fernstrom, and August Sandahl reached Hay Lake, a few miles south of present-day Scandia. There the three young men, all in their early twenties, built a small log cabin and spent the winter. The next year they sold their claims to other Swedes—the Daniel Nilson and Magnus Englund families—and moved on, Roos to Taylors Falls, Fernstrom to California and eventually Iowa, and Sandahl back to his native country. Today a thirty-foot monument spears skyward to mark the spot where these first Swedish settlers located in Minnesota—the vanguard of many thousands to come.

In the meantime, a second and larger group, having set out from Sweden on the sailing vessel *Odin* during August, 1850, arrived at the port of New York on the last day of October. Since they had no specific location for a colony in mind, some of these immigrants ventured west by rail and steamer to the Swedish

settlement at Chicago. They spent the winter of 1850-51 in that
Illinois area and were not satisfied. It was there that the group's
leader Per Anderson received from his friend Ulrik Nordberg a
letter mailed from the newly established post office at Taylors
Falls. During the previous year, Nordberg informed Anderson, he
had prospected around the area and found just the right spot for a
colony of Swedes. It bordered a beautiful lake of bays and inlets
called by the Chippewa *Ki-chi-saga,* or *Kitchi-sasega sagaigan*—
large and lovely inland lake—and the deep-forested country was
sure to remind the land-yearning settlers of their native provinces
of Helsingia and Småland.

Nordberg himself was apparently persuaded to go to the region
by another Swede, an Indian trader and whisky seller whose
name was either Nils or Jacob Tornell. Tornell, however, did not
live long enough to enjoy the fruits of his invitation, for in 1848 he
was murdered by a drunken Indian to whom he had sold too
much firewater. But the earliest of all the Swedes to settle in Minnesota, if not in the St. Croix Valley, was Jacob Fahlstrom who
came to lower Washington County about 1840 and was a very old
man when the Swedish immigration began. He died in 1859.

In 1851, as soon as ice was out of the Mississippi and steamboats
were once again running on schedule, four Swedish families and
several bachelors left their friends in Illinois and headed for Minnesota. Debarking at Stillwater, they made the rest of the trip to
Taylors Falls by flatboat. There Nordberg was on hand to greet
them and help cut a ten-mile trail west through unbroken forest to
the shores of Chisago, the large and lovely lake. When these newcomers reached their destination, they liked what they saw. It did
indeed remind them of their homeland, with but one important
difference. Here in the St. Croix Valley was "a rich and stoneless
Småland." They would stay.

Chisago Lake has a number of small, level islands, beautifully
wooded with maples and elm, which lie high above the clear waters. In 1851, the newly arrived immigrants found only one man
living in the area. He was John S. Van Rensselaer, a young bachelor from the East who was cultivating a few acres of ground upon
one of the islands near the present site of Center City. All else was

wilderness. Little is known of Van Rensselaer except that a short time before the arrival of the settlers he had come to the Chisago Lake island, built his neat cabin, and furnished it with a choice library. There this educated "Hermit of Chisago" lived "an independent and happy bachelor's life," said tourist-author Mrs. Ellet, never mingling with others, but always welcoming those who came to him. But when one overly curious St. Paul newspaperman called him a "strange freak of human fancy," the resentful Van Rensselaer packed his books and moved a few miles north to another island in Sunrise Lake, away from encroaching civilization. "He appears happy and contented," announced the *Weekly Minnesotian* on June 25, 1853, "neither a misanthrope . . . nor a bigoted anchorite, nor yet a romantic fool." But, smugly concluded the paper, "we have no desire to invade his privacy."

And so, at Chisago Lake, the Swedes ended their long journey. There the colony settled down to build homes and farm the land. "Families have been pouring in," said Stillwater's *St. Croix Union* on March 6, 1855, "until the population has become of no small account to the prosperity of Minnesota." These hardy sons of Sweden, with their families, their big, ironbound boxes, and their air of strangeness risked everything for the vague promises of the unknown. They did not, however, cross a vast ocean in the spirit of reckless adventure which was attracting so many less desirable characters to the gold fields of the Pacific territories; rather, they ventured into this new and strange country because of religious troubles, hard times, crop failures, and low wages at home. The optimistic blandishments in the letters of relatives and friends who had already made the trip to America were a powerful influence, perhaps the most important single factor which encouraged them to travel west to the new Eldorado. In the new, young country they hoped to find freedom of worship, the opportunity to own land, and a chance to gain a living by honest labor.

The state religion of Sweden was Lutheran, as it is today. During the mid-1800s several doctrinal beliefs existed that were untenable to many otherwise faithful churchgoers who developed a certain dissatisfaction with the state church and welcomed the opportunity to go to America. When the settlers reached the Minnesota country, lay services were held in area homes as early as 1851, and three years later Lutheran congregations were started at St. Paul and Center City. The handsome structure with its exquisitely carved interior, which today dominates that village much as churches do in the old country, was erected in 1888 and is the third building to stand on this site. The original frame church was built in 1858. In it was formed the first Minnesota Lutheran Conference, the predecessor of today's Augustana Synod. And it was from this focal point of Swedish Lutheranism that numerous churches were formed in other villages of the region, at Scandia, Marine Mills, Almelund, and elsewhere. Here, too, is a monument to Per Berg, in whose log cabin the first services were held.

Sometimes, Yankee neighbors labeled these immigrants "quaint" and smiled at their homespun clothing, wooden shoes, and strange Sunday headgear of a heavy silk kerchief tied in a bow under the chin. But everyone marveled at their untiring industry and frugality. "They attend to their own business," said the editor of the *Union*, "and let the balance of mankind attend to their own." This admiration was widespread throughout the valley. "We have never seen a more respectable class of immigrant" was the usual comment of newspaper editors when steamers like the *Enterprise*, the *Galena*, and the *G. H. Gray*, or the *Northern Belle* landed families of Swedes at the river's levees. They received a hearty welcome from those "who feel an interest in the development of the vast resources of the great North-West."

While the immigrants at Center City were building their first homes of logs hewn out of the surrounding forest, they had to sleep in the open air or crowd into close, narrow quarters with friends or relatives. One family which arrived late in 1853 found the area so filled with newcomers that they were forced to spend several winter months in a cave. "I thought we would freeze to death before our house was ready," the father reported. Their food consisted of fish, game, and wild fruit until the land could be cleared and staple crops planted and harvested. Friendly Chippewa Indians often helped them with gifts of venison, although their painted faces, decorated bodies, and strange language occasionally startled and alarmed the settlers. The early Swedes in the

St. Croix Valley were self-sufficient, making their own clothes, furniture, utensils, and farming equipment. They spun linen thread from the flax they grew, and converted raw sheep's wool into wearing apparel. They fashioned bowls, dippers, carts, and even the shoes they wore from the trees on their claims.

During the summer months they cut, grubbed, broke, and culti-vated the heavily wooded land. So difficult was this work, most of which had to be done by hand, that in 1854 it was still the excep-tional Swedish pioneer who had more than eight acres cleared

and under cultivation. Yet four years later *Minnesota Posten,* the Swedish-language newspaper at Red Wing, reported that settlers who had been in the valley three years had tilled and planted from twenty to twenty-five acres each in this heavily forested area. "They are an agricultural people," said the *Stillwater Mes-senger,* "industrious, frugal, and orderly."

When winter came the men found they had to supplement their meager incomes by obtaining work at the St. Croix Valley lumber camps and in the busy sawmills along the river. Scandinavians, accustomed to the cold climate of northern Europe, were good workers for the lumber business. In the pineries, during the 1850s, laborers were paid from twenty-five to thirty dollars a month, including board. "We are not in want of anything," wrote one immigrant in a letter from Chisago Lake, "and the wages are good." Orange Walker, at the Marine Lumber Company's store, began giving liberal credit to the Swedes as early as 1854. By July of the next year, his business with these newcomers was good enough to warrant advertisements in the six-month-old Swedish newspaper *Hemlandet,* published at Galesburg, Illinois. The wooden shoe people had established themselves in the valley of the St. Croix River.

"The tide is now pouring in," reported the *Daily Minnesotian* late in 1854 when the steamer *Galena* landed 200 more Swedish immigrants at Stillwater—destination Taylors Falls. For the next thirty-five years they kept coming, these "young, robust men and women . . . well provided with means to secure for themselves comfortable homes."

Immigration agents both in this country and abroad played an important role in promoting the settlement of Minnesota, although the St. Croix Valley benefited from their efforts to a somewhat lesser degree than other areas of the state. As early as March, 1855, hopes ran high among river residents when Eugene Burnand, Minnesota's first immigration commissioner, visited the St. Croix area. Swiss-born Burnand, the man named by Governor Willis Gorman to fill the post, was in Stillwater on March 20 to acquaint himself with that city's resources. The *Union* optimistically reported him "*much* pleased," and predicted that the prospects for a large immigration to Stillwater and the entire valley during the coming season were "very flattering."

Two days later Burnand visited Marine Mills where, after a tour of the village, he and his local guide drove a few miles southwest, to the east side of Terrapin Lake and the home of John Swainson, one of the region's influential citizens. There, over a few bottles of mild Swedish beer—*Svensk-dricka*—it was reported that Burnand collected for possible future use much valuable information concerning the country settled on by the Swedes. "Unfortunately for us in this vicinity, *Han kan icke prata Svenska,* he ·

cannot speak Swedish." Thus the astute Marine host pointed out the real reason why the state's immigration commissioner, during two years' work in New York City, did little to induce Swedes to settle in the state. On the other hand, Burnand was patently successful with Germans, Luxembourgers, Belgians, Swiss, and French, simply because he was fluent in their languages. Yet in spite of this neglect of the Swedes, it has been estimated that during the 1850s the number of Scandinavians in Minnesota increased from twelve to about twelve thousand.

After the Civil War, immigrants came in even greater numbers. Railroads were being built into the West, where land was cheap and readily available. Through societies organized in Sweden, members made regular payments so that trips to America could be won through lotteries. In Minnesota, too, the Swedes formed money-raising organizations to help bring fellow countrymen to the state. For example, in February, 1869, Reverend Erick Shogren of the Center City Swedish settlement gave what was considered a splendid talk in Swedish before the Ladies Emigration Society of St. Paul. And on December 14, the *Stillwater Republican* reported that the Swedes of Chisago County had during 1869 sent $5,000 to the old country so that friends and relatives could "reach America and Free Homesteads." This was, the paper hastened to point out, an individual enterprise. Stillwater residents Peter Booren and John Siderly went themselves to Sweden during 1866 and each brought back a small group of young and eager settlers. Most of these enterprises were eminently successful, and hundreds of Scandinavians joined their compatriots in the new Swedeland of the St. Croix Valley. The swelling body of migrants filled Chisago County and settled in parts of nearby Washington, Kanabec, Mille Lacs, and Pine counties. And they stayed. In all America, as recently as 1943, no two counties could show so compact a majority of Swedish stock as Chisago and neighboring Isanti.

Occasionally, overoptimistic or fraudulent agents both in this country and in Sweden took heartless advantage of the frequently gullible immigrant. The Great European-American Emigration Land Company is a case in point. This most ambitious of all at-

tempts to colonize the valley of the St. Croix was organized late in
1868 by a group of Eastern capitalists including Caleb Cushing,
the wealthy Massachusetts lawyer and diplomat who many years
before had acquired a large tract of Wisconsin lands around the
falls of the St. Croix. The men involved as directors and trustees
nobly hoped to unite the interests of America and Europe, to
"protect the Emigrants" as well as make money for themselves.
The plan was to have the emigrants pay for the land at any of the
branch offices in Europe, purchase their passages to the States,
and then select the desired property on arriving at a chosen destination.

Henning A. Taube of Stockholm, "Count" Taube he was always
called, became general manager of the company. As it turned out,
the choice was an unfortunate one, for the Count was extravagant
in his use of the company's money, made enormous and wild
promises, and grossly misrepresented the true and extremely complicated legal situation at the Falls. To persuade Swedes wishing
to emigrate, Taube had published, early in 1869 at Stockholm, a
detailed pamphlet about Cushing's Wisconsin lands. With the title
Upplysningar für Utwandrare till Amerika ("Explanation for
Emigrants to America"), it gave an all-too-rosy picture of what
his fellow countrymen should expect in the Midwest. Then on
July 3, 1869, aboard the steamer *Nellie Kent*, Taube brought to
the east-bank village of St. Croix Falls his wife and son, and some
one hundred Swedish immigrants. "They all like America so far as
they have seen it," reported the *Polk County Press*, "and express
themselves as favorably impressed with Polk County, for the
building up of a city at the Falls." By the end of the month the
same Osceola newspaper estimated that over 1,200 had settled in
the area during the first half of 1869. It was soon learned, however, that the land in Wisconsin's Burnett and Polk counties advertised for sale and paid for with gold back in Sweden could not
be claimed because the title to it was not guaranteed. "After waiting for six months to get the promised deeds," complained settler
Albert Larson and others to Cushing early in 1870, "we now have
been informed that we can get the deeds to said lands, if *we again
will pay* [for] *the land*." They were convinced, perhaps justly so,

that someone, somewhere along the line was cheating them.

At the time, the entire area around St. Croix Falls was in a depressed state. The sawmill at the Falls, unused for years because of entangled litigations between resident managers and absentee owner, was dilapidated and useless. "The ruthless hand of time has made sad ravages," complained the local press. Undoubtedly to put to use elsewhere what little was left of the mill, a group of unemployed Swedish settlers completely stripped the building of all its machinery. The dam crossing the St. Croix River at the millsite had washed out, and a fine gristmill located a half mile below the falls had in retaliation been burned by angry settlers. The immigrants were on the verge of starvation, almost penniless not only because of the unemployment situation, but also because in many cases they had to pay twice for supposed railroad tickets sold to them in Sweden by unauthorized agents who quietly pocketed the money. Count Taube made a hurried trip back to New York to consult with the Emigration Company officials. He returned to the valley on September 1, 1869, more hopeful than he should have been. "My work is success," the Count wrote to Cushing in his broken English. Even the local *Taylors Falls Reporter* on September 4, thought everything satisfactory, announcing that "The Count will proceed to build up the town as rapidly as circumstances will allow."

The new settlers were sufficiently encouraged by the persuasive Taube to crowd the Taylors Falls' levee and wish him godspeed when the Count, his Countess, and offspring left for Sweden a few days later. General Cushing would solve all their problems, they were promised. Although Taube said he would be back early the following spring with another large colony to settle on the fertile Wisconsin lands, he never returned to the St. Croix Valley. Agent Isaac Freeland, in charge of the company's office at St. Croix Falls, was left to cope as best he could with a potentially dangerous situation. The settlers had received no pay for work ordered by Count Taube. Their rations were low and they could not obtain employment. "Hungry men in a strange land soon grow desperate," Freeland warned Cushing. A female resident, on the other hand, told a meeting of the St. Croix Falls Lyceum on

March 18 that "Nobody ever starved in St. Croix Falls yet, and nobody ever will."

Somehow, the settlers managed to get through the winter of 1869-70. Many of them worked rebuilding the old sawmill, and all lived in what the *Reporter* called "untenantable shanties," subsisting mainly on a diet of flour. This supply gave out by mid-March, 1870, and about twenty of the desperate, starving Swedes marched on the local headquarters of the Great European-American Emigration Land Company. They demanded that Freeland pay up at least some of their back wages so they could get food to eat. Hoping the issue would be forced, the immigrants took possession of the office where, with threats of violence, they kept the frightened agent prisoner. By the end of that first day they had coerced Freeland into giving them company due bills, which were honored locally. The partial cash payments apparently satisfied the settlers and they released the agent.

Valley newspapers reported no additional confusion or excitement among the Swedish immigrants, thus it is to be presumed that things shortly quieted down. Cushing's New York City lawyer, also an officer in the company, declined all responsibility and thought the Swedes should be scalped. "Neither of us can be expected to pay money to redeem Count Taube's wild promises," he wrote Cushing on February 16, 1870. Caleb Cushing and other officials quickly resigned from the company, but not before turning over sufficient money to make good their debts to the impoverished immigrants. The Great European-American Emigration Land Company folded, but the Swedish immigrants remained along the St. Croix.

Pioneer days slowly passed and the Swedes, prospering on the land, were no longer newcomers. In the 1880s, when mass immigration to the region had about ended, they could claim as theirs a good share of the valley. And by 1950, these settlers from the old world still formed the largest group in Minnesota's foreign-born population.

As late as 1885, however, local newspapers were still writing patronizingly about the "quaint characteristics" of the settlement at Swede Lake, as Chisago Lake is still called by most area residents. As the years passed, the Swedish settlers may have become less self-sufficient, yet they held onto their old customs. Wooden shoes were frequent items of sale over the counter at Marine's company store, for in 1882 a Center City resident was supplying them to that outlet in quantities of 200 pairs. "And he has orders for lots more," concluded the *Stillwater Gazette*. "Slowly and with seeming reluctance," complained an obviously Yankee *Messenger* reporter, "have they adopted any of the American customs." Fortunately, some lingering survivals of Old World traditions can today occasionally be found around Almelund, Chisago City, Center City, Lindstrom, and as far south as Scandia and Marine on St. Croix. In parts of Chisago and Washington counties, for example, the language of the first settlers is still widely spoken; even third-generation Swedish-Americans talk with a melodious, lilting accent. And this region remains the valley capital of *lutefisk* and Swedish head cheese—*sylta*. Until 1945 church services at Scandia were regularly conducted in the Swedish language.

Lindstrom and Chisago City had their most recent day in the sun in 1943 when Swedish actress Ingrid Bergman came to Chisago County to make a movie called *Swedes in America* for the Office of War Information. The feature was filmed at Lindstrom, local legend relates, partly because the community had the same name as Ingrid's first husband. But Chisago Citians hasten to deny this, claiming that Lindstrom has a straighter main street, that's all, and the picture was therefore easier to shoot.

Today's traveler along the highways and winding, hilly country roads can see by the names on the mailboxes that this fertile farmland section of the valley, with its trim villages and many lakes, remains predominantly Swedish. These are the same Rosengrens and Magnusons and Hawkinsons and Nilsons whose names were once so familiar as farmers in the lower valley and as part-time lumbermen in the pineries of the upper St. Croix. Swedish roots go deep in this land. Here still live the descendants of the self-reliant, rugged, wooden shoe immigrants who left the worn-out soil of their native land to pioneer on the farms of a rich and stoneless Smaland, the true Land of Canaan. This is indeed Swedeland, U.S.A.

Chapter Fourteen

The Paddle-Wheelers' Heyday

IN THE mid-twentieth century, it is hard to imagine that steamboats of sizable tonnage could possibly have navigated the treacherous, shallow sand bars of the St. Croix. Nor does it today seem credible, for example, that during a seven-month period in 1869 a total of some 230 steamers reached the Taylors Falls' levee to unload passengers and freight. Nowadays it is frequently impossible for any water craft but canoes and the smallest of flat-bottomed outboards to travel with ease the almost thirty miles of crisscrossing channel between Stillwater and Taylors Falls—except during the first rush of spring waters or the flash flooding of late August rains.

Yet in 1851 the 182-foot side-wheeler *Excelsior*, with a carrying capacity of 272 tons, reached the Falls without recorded mishap; and six years later the even larger *Metropolitan* of St. Louis managed to get as far as Marine Mills. When the *Minnesota Belle*, a veritable floating palace, tied up at the levee of that village in April, 1859, it was carrying a heavy load of freight for the local firms of Judd, Walker and Company and Ballard, Draper and Company. The *Stillwater Messenger* noted this trip, and boasted that "The largest class boats do not encounter the least difficulty in reaching Marine."

But on the capricious St. Croix, such large vessels were the exception rather than the rule. Over the years from 1838, when the *Palmyra* became the first steamer to travel the river and open a new era for the valley, down to 1916, when the little gasoline-powered *Olive* S. and *St. Croix* were the last paddle-wheelers to

operate regularly between Stillwater and the Dalles, the more active boats averaged about one hundred tons in capacity and nineteen feet in width. To navigate during periods of low water, all
had to be of light draft; if they drew more than eighteen inches
unloaded they were headed for trouble. The opportunities for
steamboat enterprises on the unpredictable St. Croix were limited.

During the heyday of river travel, which lasted from approximately 1860 to 1890, the river bed had not yet filled up with silt
and sand from eroding hillsides, adjacent gravel pits, and the cut-
and burned-over lands along the upper valley. In those years
about the only natural obstructions on a trip north out of Stillwater, during any but extremely dry seasons, were the "eternal or
infernal sandbar at the head of Lake St. Croix," and the so-called
Marine bar, a mile upstream from that village.

In dry seasons, such sand bars became natural deterrents to
river travel and when the pilot was unable to skate his boat over
the river bottom, he would sometimes be hung up for days trying
to extricate his grounded vessel, or patiently waiting for rain and
a rising river to float it off. Low water navigation was a prolonged
and very tedious business. When Dick McLagen's boat stuck fast
on a particularly mean bar at Osceola for seven days he threatened to lay claim to the land—the only trouble being that it was
mighty poor soil. When the *Blackhawk* went up the St. Croix in
1852, it struck sand bars a dozen times, and each involved a delay
of several hours. "In such cases," Mrs. Elizabeth Ellet reported, "it
was necessary to send out a boat with men and ropes, tie the rope
round some stout tree and haul the boat over." Often removing
the freight was the only way to lighten a packet sufficiently. In
August, 1860, the *H. S. Allen* got stranded on an obstreperous bar
three miles above Stillwater. The crew succeeded in freeing the
boat only after hours of work by digging a channel through the
obstruction with six yoke of cattle and heavy plows. During the
low water season of 1863, Captain Oscar F. Knapp of the *G. H.
Gray* suggested that the Minnesota legislature pass an act prohib-
iting the river's catfish from using what channel was left.

Another barrier to river navigation—the lower St. Croix boom
just north of Stillwater—especially irritated the steamboat pilot

because it was created by his fellow man. An essential part of the lumber industry, this marshaling area was frequently so filled with timber that the river would be completely blocked, sometimes twelve miles up to Marine. Rivermen held frequent indignation meetings, and the boom company paid heavy damages when boats could not pass upstream. The problem, however, was never solved. It remained to plague St. Croix captains until the end of river steamboating, for, in the long run, lumbering was economically more essential to the valley than excursions and the packet trade.

A hundred years can bring about many changes. Time was when residents along the St. Croix depended almost entirely on the river for transportation. It was their lifeblood, their glistening highway, and they desperately needed the stern-wheelers and "double wingers" to help settle the country, to bring in supplies, and to keep in touch with the outside world. There were no gold fields at Taylors Falls and St. Croix Falls to attract wealth seekers. These twin villages, only fifty miles from the river's mouth, were simply the end of the line. Boats regularly plied the St. Croix for one reason alone—to give service to the people of the valley. And during the early years, that service was no better than haphazard, or at least so it seemed to settlers on the river. Valley residents complained that "only semi-occasionally" did the villages north of Stillwater have the opportunity to welcome steamers. There were, to be sure, frequently announced plans to place regular packets on the run to the Falls, such as the side-wheeler *St. Anthony* in 1849 and 1850. But, as a St. Paul newspaper sadly reported of that boat, "The captain went elsewhere."

By 1849 Stillwater had developed what travelers called a good steamboat landing. Lumberman Edward W. Durant, a recorder of St. Croix Valley history, lists a total of thirty-four steamers which presumably traversed Lake St. Croix from 1840 through 1848. Although information for this period is meager, we know that some Mississippi River craft on their way to or from St. Paul made the round trip from the river's mouth through Lake St. Croix to land passengers and freight at the Stillwater levee. This village was six years old in 1849 and already a lumbering point of growing importance when James M. Goodhue, Minnesota's first newspaper editor, described it in his *Minnesota Pioneer* as "fresh as a rose in a flower pot." At the time, he was enjoying a St. Croix excursion aboard the steamer *Highland Mary* from St. Louis. But the *Mary* only reached the halfway point above Stillwater before grinding to a halt on the Marine bar. It could go no farther that late August afternoon. Freight had to be unloaded so the boat could move off and head back downstream.

Other boats came and went at irregular intervals until 1852 when for three months a diminutive stern-wheeler with the euphonious name *Queen of the Yellow Banks* made triweekly trips under Captain Albert Eames from Stillwater to the head of navigation at one dollar for the round trip. This boat was the first to provide anything like regular service on the upper river. The forty-foot *Queen*—Mrs. Ellet called it a "seven by nine" boat—could carry twenty tons; it burned one cord of wood every twelve hours, and looked like two lumberjack wanigans fastened together, with a pilot's wheel stuck in between. A St. Paul wag who signed himself "Splash" in the *Minnesota Pioneer*, called it a "little pet of a steamboat" which could run like a scared owl over a dry sand bar. "Success to the Queen" concluded Splash, "grease her bottom, captain, and shove her through."

A second steam craft of Lilliputian proportions, the *Humboldt*, also appeared on the St. Croix later in 1852 as a triweekly packet operating between Stillwater and Taylors Falls. The little *Humboldt*, a burlesque on steamboats, with an engine of one teakettle power, and looking like a large dry goods box with legs standing on a floating plank, was soon well-known throughout the upper Mississippi Valley. It was "a great accommodation to the people of the St. Croix," said John Philips Owens, editor of the *Weekly Minnesotian*, when he reported a trip on the boat in June, 1853. And curious spectators crowded the levees to see it. "She stops anywhere along the river," continued Owens, "to do any and all kinds of business, and will give passengers a longer ride, so far as *time* is concerned, than any other craft we ever traveled on."

During the fall of 1852 and all the following year the accommodating *Humboldt* served the valley well, up to the Dalles one

day, and back down to Stillwater the next. Other boats like the
Asia, the *Montello,* or the thirty-stateroom *Blackhawk* were only
occasionally seen on the river above Stillwater. In 1857 Captain
Edward C. Strong advertised the *H. S. Allen,* a packet which he
said would make regular trips north from Stillwater to Taylors
Falls. Another boat, the *New St. Croix,* joined the *Allen* on the run
to the Dalles, providing service when sand bars did not persist in
sticking their heads above water.

Packets running just between Stillwater and Taylors Falls, however, did not meet the public need. There was a gap of many
miles without regular steamboat service from Stillwater downriver to the levees at Prescott and Point Douglas where freight
was often left by St. Paul-bound steamers. To point up this fact,
an editorial in a December, 1854, issue of Stillwater's *Union* called
for a boat large enough "to ply at the several ports between Point
Douglas and Taylor's Falls and do business on a larger scale than
has been done heretofore."

Any results from the suggestion were a long time materializing,
for it was not until the spring of 1857 that a real attempt was
made to place a boat on the lower run. Then the 106-ton stern-
wheeler *Eolian* was brought in to carry mail and serve the lake
trade between Prescott and Stillwater.

The merchants of that city were very soon disenchanted with
the *Eolian.* Charges for freight from Prescott to the Stillwater
levee equaled, they said, what it cost to ship the same goods all
the way from St. Louis to Prescott. Hudsonians called the *Eolian*
a nuisance, to which the *Prescott Transcript* replied that "with a
certain class of gas-blowers everything is a nuisance that hails
from Prescott." The businessmen of Stillwater, complained the
Union, "are determined no longer to submit to such barefaced
imposition." Apparently this threat to boycott the *Eolian* was successful and the freight rates were lowered, for the steamer continued its Prescott-Stillwater run throughout the summer. By September, the same paper was on the best of terms with the boat's
chief officers, calling them "admirable."

Only a few years later the merchants and businessmen of the St.
Croix Valley found themselves mixed up in a situation far more

complex and lasting than the temporary *Eolian* dispute of 1857. In
an effort to break the near monopoly of a rival packet company,
William F. Davidson during 1860 expanded his Minnesota River
service of two boats and began running steamers on the Mississippi from La Crosse to St. Paul. As one of Davidson's admirers,
with more poetic license than truth, described him in the *Messenger* for August 30, 1872:

> Bill kem in the track with the derndest old craft,
> She was broke down amidships and bagged all abaft,
> And her chimneys they leaned at right angles away;
> But he writ on his wheelhouse: "I've kem yer ter stay!"

This competition for control of the upper Mississippi Valley
packet trade instigated a lengthy steamboat rate war and "Commodore" Davidson's canny and sometimes ruthless methods were
soon felt on the St. Croix. Captain Oscar Knapp's Franconia-built
side-wheeler *Viola,* belonging to the recently formed St. Croix and
Mississippi Steamboat Company, tried to enter the La Crosse to
Stillwater trade in 1865. Davidson apparently forced the *Viola* off
the Mississippi, and two years later the company, made up of St.
Croix Valley capitalists, went out of business in what was called
"a great fizzle." The strongest monopoly in all western steamboating was felt throughout the upper Mississippi.

Concern was occasionally expressed that St. Croix boats might
be tempted off the river by advantageous offers from the Commodore. For example, shortly after the *G. B. Knapp* was launched at
Osceola in June, 1866, the *Taylors Falls Reporter* hoped that Captain Knapp would keep his new steamer in the home region for
which it was built, and "not be enticed into the channels of the
Mississippi passenger trade." Since early May, Davidson had had
a packet, the *Enterprise,* doing business on the St. Croix and there
was general surprise when he withdrew it and came to an amicable agreement with Knapp in regard to the transportation of
freight above Stillwater. The *Prescott Journal* felt that by so doing
Davidson had "made himself many friends on the St. Croix."

> He'd run any boat in the trade out of sight,
> And wuz never seen nappin in daytime or night,

> But would land for a hail jist ter take in a dime,
> And the shippers, they said: "Give us Bill every time."

This feeling of good will, however, did not last long. The *Nellie Kent,* a 112-foot stern-wheeler expressly built at Osceola for Davidson and the St. Croix trade in 1868, was the first to bring a rate war and the Commodore's familiar boat whistle of two longs and three shorts to that river. Along the St. Croix price cutting and a fight for supremacy broke out in full force. All of a sudden, in the spring of 1869, there were four paddle-wheel steamers on the river, each trying to beat out the other to secure valley patronage. Davidson's *Nellie Kent,* the opposition Northern Line's *James Means,* and two local boats caught in the squeeze, the *G. B. Knapp* and the *Wyman X* of Taylors Falls, became the first of a long line of packets to take part in this comic opera affair. "A little competition is what we want," said the *Taylors Falls Reporter,* and that is exactly what the river towns got.

"Sell tickets at any price" seemed to be the order, and all along the Mississippi from St. Louis to St. Paul freight rates and passenger fares plummeted until the traveler could almost name his own price. Taking pleasure trips became cheaper than staying at home. Steamer clerks considered twenty-five cents the top price from Prescott to the Dalles, and rivalry to secure business and customers was sharp, even bitter, at every steamboat landing. How drummers for competing steamboats went after potential customers at Stillwater's levee is told in the *Stillwater Gazette* for June 30, 1875:

Agent for the "Nellie": I will give you a passage on my boat to Taylors Falls and return for twenty-five cents—twelve and a half cents each way.

Agent for the "Knapp": I will make you a present of a ticket up and back; it shan't cost you a cent.

Agent for the "Nellie": I will give you your fare up and back and furnish your meals.

Agent for the "Knapp": I will see that offer and raise him one. I will give you your passage up and back, furnish your meals, and give you a berth.

And the young lady in question? Wanting nothing to do with a berth, she chose the *Nellie*.

The general feeling at the beginning of the "irrepressible conflict" was that such a situation couldn't last, and that a compromise must soon be made. But the *Nellie Kent* held on as "the girl of the valley" until it had to be taken to the La Crosse dry dock for rebuilding in 1878. Many other boats like the *Ada B.*, *Maggie Reaney*, the *Lulu* came and went to keep the fight at fever pitch for thirteen long years, until 1880. Although some seasons were "hotter" than others, perhaps the most mixed-up and exciting period was from 1875 through 1877, when times were especially lively for shippers, passengers, and residents generally. A People's Line was formed by valley residents to combat Davidson's influence, and its charter contained strict regulations that stock could be sold neither to the Commodore nor to Isaac Staples, Stillwater's lumber baron. Denizens of the valley were hard pressed to decide whether they should be loyal to the local boats or patronize Davidson's *Nellie* whose clockwork regularity gave it the nickname "Old Reliable."

Races, too, brought excitement to St. Croix river travel, and the captains prided themselves upon speed almost more than anything else. "Hot Steamboating," the newspapers called it, and in their excitement the passengers forgot the risk. Sometimes the crew of the *Nellie* tied the coveted broomstick signifying victory to its flaming red smokestack after "sweeping the river"—but at other times the *Knapp* would puff and snort its way to triumph.

In their anxiety for river supremacy, boat captains would leave Stillwater at unpredictable hours in the morning, hurry up the river together, make only token stops at village landings along the route, and then dash back in the afternoon, still neck and neck. Steamboating on the St. Croix was fast becoming a farce. Residents of the valley were no better served than if they had but one boat. Merchants and businessmen complained that they could no longer submit to a monopoly "having its head in St. Louis and its tail in St. Paul." Complaints, however, did little good.

The local boats fought the competition as best they could with limited resources. But in the end it wasn't Commodore Davidson's competition, the price cutting and chicanery of the steamboat war, or the logs and the low water that brought about the ultimate end of packet trade on the St. Croix. The chief reason for the decline of steamboating throughout Western waters was the railroad. River business began falling off when the first iron horse entered the valley in 1870. This is mirrored in the statistics of three steamboats. During 1870 the *Wyman X* alone carried 5,776 paying passengers from Stillwater to Taylors Falls and return. In 1879, on the other hand, both the *Mary Barnes* (née *Nellie Kent*) and the *G. B. Knapp* together could count but 2,000 passengers up and 1,894 downstream.

At first the tourist trade boomed when boats started meeting the trains, the "upper" train at Taylors Falls and the "lower" at Stillwater; but the attractions of a trip on the river and through the Dalles faded fast after White Bear, Forest Lake, and Lake Elmo were developed as popular Minnesota summer resorts. From 1872 to 1879 there was much discussion, led mostly by politician Ignatius Donnelly, of building a ship canal from the head of Lake St. Croix to Lake Superior. This, it was thought, would bolster river traffic. But nothing came of the proposal and by the mid-1880s freight business on the river was nil. The one reason for boats being on the St. Croix—to give service to the people of the valley—was a thing of the past. The valley found itself better served by the railroads.

Several hopeful attempts were made after the 1880s to continue regular trips on the St. Croix. Captain Ben Knapp, Oscar's son, tried it in 1884 with the *Cleon,* another of the many steamers built in the Osceola boatyards. But the *Cleon* later that same year went to towing steamboat wood from the Franconia area to St. Paul. In 1886 the St. Croix River commerce consisted of two regular packets carrying freight and passengers to Taylors Falls. Excursions of Sunday schools, library associations, singing societies, and similar groups remained popular to the very end of the steamboating era. Whether the excursionists went down the lake to the elegant Chapin Hall House at Hudson or up to Taylors Falls to view a spectacular log jam mattered little; just so they were out on the water. Steamers were the essential agents of social life, and they did a bang-up business.

There were sometimes unusual, spur-of-the-moment trips like those during the extremely mild winter of 1877-78. The river had been free of ice for over a week when three intrepid St. Croix boats took part in as many different excursions. The *Aunt Betsey* and *Maggie Reaney* went out from the Jackson Street levee in St. Paul for short trips to the mouth of the Minnesota River and Fort Snelling on December 25 and New Year's Day. The *Ida Fulton*'s excursion up the St. Croix from Stillwater to the Dalles, on the other hand, lasted two days. A festive crowd gathered at the Stillwater wharf on Friday, December 28, to watch and cheer the ten o'clock departure of sixty-five passengers and a crew of nineteen. Only five hours before, the engineers had started preparing the boat and getting up steam—a procedure which usually took two days. Many of the men who went aboard were outfitted in black pantaloons, linen coats, straw hats, and carried fans; some of the passengers insisted they were bothered by mosquitoes. The food, reported the Osceola *Polk County Press,* tasted as good as "in the palmy excursion days of mid-summer." There was a reception at the Dalles House in Taylors Falls and dancing continued throughout the night until the weary celebrants had to board ship in the morning for the return home.

The biggest of all St. Croix excursions, on the other hand, did not take place until after the turn of the century. In early June, 1901, the Soo Line brought into the village of St. Croix Falls twenty-eight cars loaded with an estimated 2,000 railroad conductors who were attending a convention in St. Paul. After spending a few hours sight-seeing around Interstate Park, the tour crowded on the *Columbia* and the commodious *Lora,* which then made their way downriver to Stillwater.

But 1,100 retail grocers did not get to see the Dalles when they took a July, 1905, trip upriver from Stillwater on board the steamer *Purchase* and its excursion barge the *Twin Cities.* They could only get as far as Log House Landing near present-day Otisville, where they went ashore, ate lunch, and had their program of athletic sports. The *Purchase* carried only one more excursion of about eight hundred sight-seers to Taylors Falls in July, 1914; then quietly, with no fanfare but certainly not unwept, steamboating died on the St. Croix. The witchery of river travel had passed.

An era closed which fewer and fewer can now remember. Most of those who have lived their lives beside this placid stream recall best the quiet times of canoes and tiny, flat-bottomed craft propelled by the inevitable two-horsepower outboard motors and with minnow buckets trailing behind. Today the peace and wonder of the St. Croix they remember can still be theirs—but only from Monday to Friday. Weekends in the valley are now filled with the earsplitting staccato of high-powered speedboats, reminiscent of the time the old side-wheeler *Uncle Toby* lumbered upriver in 1851: "From the first we heard the boat down the river," said the *Minnesota Pioneer*, "until it went by and was unheard of in the distance above, was a lapse of nearly half the night." The sand bars, low water, and a channel too often the depth of a soup plate that once plagued the steamboat captains and pleasure tourists above Stillwater, are now regarded by some valley residents as blessings in disguise, for they provide protection against the noisy and frequently dangerous onslaught of an ever increasing flotilla of modern speedboats and daredevil water skiers.

Chapter Fifteen

Paper Towns and Forgotten Villages

THE ST. CROIX Valley can boast no spectacular ghost towns, no bonanza settlements or burgeoning villages which were abruptly abandoned, like those in the mining country of the West, and remained almost intact for future resurrection as period curiosities and money-making tourist attractions. Instead, travelers through the valley of today will find former logging and sawmill towns which have survived either as crossroads hamlets or small, sleepy, river villages like Franconia and Sunrise. And they will see almost no evidences of former prosperity. The decline of these once busy settlements was gradual, but inevitable after the St. Croix Boom Company and the larger, wealthier Stillwater saw mills took over, when river traffic declined, and settlements in the valley were shunned by railroad builders. The flour and lumber mills so necessary to the economy of an earlier day were abandoned to decay or fire, the stores and shops closed, and the homes of pioneer settlers were deserted, torn down, or moved to other communities. Such settlements constitute the forgotten villages of the St. Croix, places where people once lived and anticipated a prosperous future.

Paper towns, on the other hand, are something else again, for many of them never actually existed. Theodore C. Blegen, a distinguished Minnesota historian, has written that between the years 1855 and 1857 no fewer than 700 settlements were platted in his state, providing enough building lots for 1,500,000 people. Many of these villages, created only on paper by overoptimistic speculators, were doomed almost from the beginning. Had it not

been for the disastrous financial panic in late 1857 and the precipitous end throughout the Midwest of a land speculation boom,
residents along the St. Croix Valley might today be living in such
villages as Amador, Alhambra, Nashua, Fortuna, Neshodana,
Drontheim, and Sebatana. During the mid-1850s each of these
townsites was the surveyed and platted brainchild of one or more
visionaries who hoped for suitable compensation from the sale of
building lots. But the projected 100-foot-wide streets, and the
square blocks so magnanimously set aside by the proprietors for
public parks, seminaries, and courthouses were seldom if ever
built. The coming of hard times which sent farm prices into a
tailspin of deflation cut short all such dreams of wealth and the
carefully mapped towns remained brush and swamp and farmers'
fields.

Among these paper settlements were the twin villages platted
about 1856 by Dr. Carmi P. Garlick and M. G. Blackstone along
the St. Croix ten miles above Taylors Falls. According to the elab-
orately lithographed plat map, Amador on the Minnesota side of
the river was to be connected by ferry with Sebatana in Polk
County, Wisconsin. Both sites, the owners confidently promised,
would develop around the flourishing sawmill constructed at
Amador by the Minnesota proprietor a few years earlier. Dr. Garlick's village, his sawmill, his medical practice did not flourish as
expected and soon he left Minnesota for the Wisconsin village of
Osceola. Amador lives on as the name of the present-day township, but Blackstone and Sebatana seem to have vanished completely.

Gordon City—or Neshodana—once located near Danbury in
Burnett County, Wisconsin, one mile up the Yellow River from
where it flows into the St. Croix, is today completely forgotten.
Founded in 1855 by W. P. Graves, Milwaukee speculator, who
expended some $20,000 in building a dam and sawmill, it had
already disappeared by 1868 when a group of valley sportsmen
made a fishing excursion to the Brule River country. "It was the
result of the railroad excitement of that day," said Sam S. Fifield,
Osceola editor, who was one of the group. "The site was laid out
into village lots, with streets beautifully lithographed and adorned

with high-sounding titles; in fact it was a beautiful city to behold
—on paper. But like many an 'air castle,' it burst, and the explo-
sion 'busted' the proprietors, who retired with the old maxim, 'A
fool and his money is soon parted,' for their consolation. The mill
has been pulled down, the dam cut away, and nothing remains
but the birch bark wigwams of a few strolling families of Chippewas to mark the spot of the once 'proposed metropolis of the
Great Northwest.'" Another Gordon exists today, but it is farther
north, on Highway 53, just below where the Eau Claire River
flows into the St. Croix. In that village, at one time called Amick,
half-breed Antoine Gordon once lived and operated a successful
store and boardinghouse. Today it carries his name.

Fortuna, its birth also heralded by the publication of an attractive undated map, seems to have met a similar fate. Apparently in
the spring of 1857 the village was located, according to the proprietor W. A. Porter, in the midst of the great pine forests of the
upper St. Croix where the Point Douglas to Lake Superior military road crossed the Kettle River. The rock-bound spot had been
the site of a camp which one 1857 traveler on his way to Superior
described in the *Minnesota Pioneer* as a "miserable den." But
Fortuna had only recently been laid out, he continued, and he
thought that, because of good water power, it would prove "a
great lumber depot for the surrounding country." In May Fortuna
was named the temporary seat of Buchanan County, a governmental unit which disappeared in 1862, and is now the northern
half of Minnesota's Pine County. Although the name Fortuna appeared on county and state maps as late as 1881, only an occasional traveler or two mentioned its existence. Even today the exact location is in dispute, for there are some who say that after
1885 the present Kettle River community of Sandstone developed
on the site of old Fortuna. Others, like Grover Singley of St. Paul,
have evidence that the government road crossed the Kettle not at
Sandstone but at a beautiful, cliff-lined bend in the river, which
today is almost inacessible, about six miles to the north of that
onetime stone quarry town.

A few miles downriver from Fortuna, and only two miles north
of Sandstone, another Kettle River quarry village, Banning, flour-

ished from 1892 to 1912, and then quickly vanished. Today all that remains of this once thriving community of 300 persons, two busy stone quarries, and an asphalt plant are a few weathered concrete ruins which rise strange and ghostly among the birches and aspen, the sumac and second-growth pine. The wild beauty and peaceful quiet of this region known as Hell's Gate will soon be turned into a 5,000-acre state park.

Vasa is another village which has disappeared almost unnoticed from the valley, although for a while it seemed, if we are to believe the contemporary press, that this Washington County settlement on the west bank of the St. Croix might develop into a boom town. When Francis Register, a clerk for the Marine Mills lumbering concern of Judd, Walker and Company, decided to become a land agent, he made an arrangement with Benjamin F. Otis to release a tract of some three hundred acres about two-and-a-half miles north of Marine. Encompassing an area a short distance above present-day William O'Brien State Park, the land extended down to the river and included about two miles of valuable shore line. Late in 1856 Register, who was then twenty-seven years old, had this section surveyed and the plateau 400 feet back from the water's edge laid out into streets. He named his village Vasa, in honor of the Swedish king, to attract Scandinavian settlers. Land was placed on the market shortly after Christmas, 1856, and by the time a post office was established in February, 1857, sixty-one lots were already taken. "That too in the middle of winter," boasted Frank Register, "is not a bad beginning."

Considerable publicity and advertising in the Stillwater and St. Paul newspapers loyally spoke of a good steamboat landing, a steam sawmill, several flourishing stores, a "large and commodious" three-story hotel, as well as a number of substantial houses already built or "in the course of erection." At Vasa, said the *St. Croix Union* on August 21, there was "indeed every inducement which a new place could possibly offer to settlers. . . . We predict for Vasa a growing prosperity and first class position among western towns." The *St. Paul Pioneer and Democrat* was equally enthusiastic and urged all immigrants to look first at this new settlement.

But again the 1857 depression found a victim, and one by one Register's plans collapsed. First the sawmill failed after a partner pocketed what money there was and took French leave. Then in June, 1859, the settlement's name was changed back to Otis because it was found that another Vasa had been organized in Goodhue County. Finally, the *coup de grâce* came in 1860 when the post office was discontinued and Marine stepped in to vote a reannexation of the area. Vasa reverted to wheat fields, and proprieter Register, still owing a sizable bill for newspaper advertising, also took French leave of the valley to return East and become a prominent Philadelphia lawyer. Today the family name of early storekeeper John Copas has replaced that of Vasa. At the popular restaurant Crabtree's Kitchen and the 1875 schoolhouse along Highway 95, which now houses a gift shop, the modern motorist is near the hoped-for busy corner of Market and Fourth streets.

Amador, Sebatana, Fortuna, and Vasa are typical of the valley settlements projected and platted by land speculators. They lasted a few years, and then quietly disappeared, the victims of a great panic and depression. Other forgotten villages along the St. Croix, like Chengwatana, Sunrise City, and Franconia, successfully survived the crash of 1857, even flourished for a while, only to become ghost towns or bypassed villages when they were shunned by capricious railroads.

For an unknown number of years before the advent of white settlers in the Pine County area, Chengwatana was an Indian village at the mouth of Cross Lake, where the sinuous Snake River begins its final short run east to the St. Croix. During the early years of the 1800s there were at least two wintering fur posts on what was then known as the Rivière au Serpent, and the general locality had long been a gathering point for Indians and traders. Lumbermen from the lower valley first became interested in the region of the Snake, it appears, during the late 1840s, and by 1849 Elam Greeley had constructed a dam there for sluicing logs down to the St. Croix. Three years later the settlement consisted of several log houses and a hotel. Judd, Walker and Company of Marine Mills, also believing in the timber-cutting potentialities of the area, early in 1856 joined Greeley to build a sawmill below his dam and lay out the village they called Alhambra. By then it was a stopping place on the government road being built to Lake Superior. Alhambra, however, could not have paid off, for the same Marine firm and a group of speculators from St. Paul and New York in the late 1850s resurveyed the settlement, this time reverting to the old name Chengwatana, which in the Chippewa tongue means "pine village." To stimulate the growth of their investment, the proprietors made several attempts during this period to settle groups of Belgian and German immigrants at Chengwatana. But apparently their efforts were in vain, for at no time did the population of the village exceed a hundred persons.

As small as it was, Chengwatana for about a decade had the distinction of being the largest valley settlement north of the Dalles. After February, 1857, this village was the county seat for the unsettled wilderness of pine forests and logging camps that was Pine County. From all appearances, Chengwatana might even have developed into a prosperous lumber town. The proprietors, however, committed the fatal error of trying to dictate to a railroad backed by the powerful Philadelphia banking house of Jay Cooke and Company. In August, 1869, journalist and free-lance writer John T. Trowbridge accompanied an excursion into the Minnesota country sponsored by the owners of the yet unfinished Lake Superior and Mississippi Railroad. He described in detail his trip by train from St. Paul, fifty miles north to Rushseba and from there by wagon to Duluth, the embryo port city on Lake Superior. By that time tracks were being laid along the west side of Cross Lake directly opposite Chengwatana, and the village of Pine City, platted during the same year, was beginning to develop. "Chengwatana should have had the railroad depot," Trowbridge wrote in the April, 1870, issue of the *Atlantic Monthly* magazine, "but it made the common mistake of setting too high a price on what it deemed indispensable to the [railroad] company, which, accordingly, stuck to its own land, and put the track on the other side of the lake. . . . It is the railroad that makes towns," concluded the author, "not towns that make the railroad."

By 1872 many plans were afoot for the expansion of the new

Pine City. It already had a steam saw and shingle mill employing fifty men, as well as a stave factory where thirty men held steady jobs. There were two hotels, two general stores, and a schoolhouse which doubled as a church. When the log drives came tumbling down the Snake River in the spring, reported the Taylors Falls newspaper, "they bring an accession of three or four hundred men and a wild time generally ensues during their stay." Chengwatana with its ninety-odd residents, its few wooden houses, huts of half-breed Indians, and a small water-power sawmill was definitely on the decline. The final blow came after the fall election of 1872 approved the removal of the county seat to the fast-growing village of Pine City. Chengwatana, on the wrong side of Cross Lake, decayed and died. Today there is not an original building left, only summer cabins stretching along the shore of the lake, and this settlement that might have been is now lost in oblivion and as dead as the shortest lived of the pre-1857 paper villages.

Sunrise City, like Fortuna and Chengwatana, was also on the government road—the first stop after Amador going north from Taylors Falls. By 1856 this settlement which borders the Sunrise River a short distance from its confluence with the St. Croix had a sawmill and a population of twelve to fifteen families. That was enough for the *Pioneer and Democrat* to call it a "place of respectable advantages," and for the village to be platted in July of the following year. In spite of snide remarks published in neighboring newspapers, Sunrise grew slowly until 1869. The Osceola *Polk County Press* on December 18, 1867, for example, advised its upriver rival to rename the settlement Sunset, for it was "not of rapid growth, nor fortunate in its settlers. When one neighbor gets mad with another, the custom has been to set his house on fire, kill his hogs and chickens, poison his dogs and cats or pull down his fence and let another neighbor's cattle destroy his crops." Almost as disagreeable was another comment made by a Stillwater editor who suggested that the name be changed to Sundown. "The sun don't rise there," said the *Messenger*, "until three or four weeks after it makes its appearance at other places."

By 1869, Sunrise reached the peak of its prosperity with 300 inhabitants, a sawmill, two gristmills, four hotels, two stores, a schoolhouse, but only one saloon. A good share of the village's well-being was due to the location there, from 1860 to 1868, of the regional land office for the public sale of acreage in the St. Croix Valley. The gradual decline into obscurity began during the final year of the 1860s, after Jay Cooke's railroad was built through North Branch about ten miles to the west and the land office had been moved downriver to Taylors Falls. When trains started running from St. Paul to Duluth in 1870, the once heavy traffic on the government road came to an almost abrupt end. Sunrise City struggled along. From time to time there were hopes that something might happen to restore the economy of the village, as when John S. Van Rensselaer, the onetime hermit of Chisago Lake, left his island hideaway in Sunrise Lake in 1874 to build an unsuccessful cheese factory at Sunrise City. But not until twenty-one years later, after all hopes had died that the "City" would ever live up to its name, did this forgotten village officially become just plain 'Sunrise." Shortly after the turn of the century Sunrise enjoyed a temporary boom as the Arrow Line, a projected railroad to link the Twin Cities with Superior, began grading and laying track in the vicinity. It proved, however, to be another abortive project.

Today little is left of old Sunrise City. But it is entitled to a place in history. Local residents boast of its being the birthplace of motion picture actor Richard Widmark and like to point out that Lorenzo O. Lowden, the former postmaster of Amador, had a son Frank, who was born in 1861 in a white clapboard farmhouse which still stands about a mile south and a little west of the village. That son, Frank O. Lowden, became a two-term governor of Illinois and a leading contender for the Republican presidential nomination in 1920. A deadlock, however, resulted in the choice of Warren G. Harding as a compromise candidate. Four years later Lowden refused to take second place on the ticket for the office of vice-president of the United States.

Another state governor to come out of the St. Croix Valley is Warren P. Knowles, son of a county judge in Pierce County, Wisconsin, who was born in River Falls and since 1935 has practiced law at New Richmond. Elected lieutenant governor of Wisconsin in 1954, he was one of the few Republicans to gain governorships

in the 1964 Democratic landslide. The small town of New Richmond—3,316 persons—now boasts of being the second capital
city of Wisconsin. Governor Knowles reciprocates this affection:
"I have a great devotion for the St. Croix," he said in a post-
election interview. "It's been home all my life." U. S. Senator Gaylord Nelson, former Wisconsin governor and the son of a country
doctor, was also born in the valley—at the village of Clear Lake,
on the road running north from New Richmond to Turtle Lake
and Almena.

Franconia, about three miles south of Taylors Falls, was another lively river town which the railroad from St. Paul to Duluth
bypassed in 1870. But unlike Sunrise City and other settlements
on the St. Croix above the falls, the railroad's snub was not the
only reason Franconia is now a sleepy settlement of a few homes
and summer cottages without even a sign on Highway 95 to show
visitors where to find it. This mill town depended on its lumbering
business, and on the continuance of river traffic for the transportation of wheat and steamboat wood for the downriver market.
While those facilities existed, Franconia mushroomed into life and
was a busy spot. But after the St. Croix Boom Company gained a
powerful stranglehold on the entire valley during the mid-1880s
and made no attempt to keep the steamboat channel open, one by
one the saw- and flour-milling towns of the valley above Stillwater
were left to a leisurely economic demise.

Although Franconia was never a large village, at one time the
flats by the river, which are now planted to corn and potatoes,
were squared off into platted streets. Dominating the numerous
homes, the stores, hotels, factories, and saloons which about filled
the area, was the handsome four-story stone flour mill built in
1864 by the Luxembourg immigrant, Paul Munch. Near the
water's edge stood the sawmill and shipbuilding yards—about
where today's fishermen launch their boats. During the 1860s a
number of lumber and wheat barges as well as two, perhaps
three, sizable paddle-wheel steamboats were constructed at Franconia, one of which, the 130-foot side-wheeler *Viola*, played a
small part in the transportation story of the St. Croix.

With the usual optimism and loyalty of early newspapers the

Taylors Falls Reporter in 1865 was certain this river village would become a place of note. On August 1, 1896, however, the *Polk County Press* announced that the village of Franconia was about to sell its jail and other property and go out of business. As the century ended, a requiem for the nearly abandoned village was held downriver at the Osceola Methodist church one August Sunday in 1899. Although the text can nowhere be found, we presume that out of Franconia's downfall the minister drew a pointed moral for his own village. The title of his sermon that Sabbath day was "A Visit to Franconia and Its Lessons."

Anyone who has driven down the steep gravel road which winds into the placid remnants of Franconia, who has walked along the boulder-lined shore north of the landing, or canoed up to the lower Dalles and Rocky Island (the Chippewa's *minissabik*), perhaps the most popular of all river camping spots, will realize that on weekdays, free from the din of outboard motors, the peace and calm of the St. Croix at Franconia have indeed made it a far different place from what the ambitious pioneers of 1865 might have wished it to be.

Unlike other St. Croix Valley towns, railroads and river traffic meant comparatively little to the settlement at Arcola, which grew up after 1846 around the spacious and beautiful home built by lumberman John E. Mower and the sawmill of his bachelor brother Martin. Situated only seven miles above Stillwater, near the north end of what was called Buck Horn Prairie, Arcola had no communication difficulties with the outside world. The mill, constructed there in 1847 and rebuilt in 1852, was kept busiest prior to the establishment in the late 1850s of the logging boom a few miles to the south. Martin Mower's real prosperity, however, came about because of his shrewdness, his business acumen, and the extensive river frontage he owned, for the use of which he was able to secure large blocks of stock in the St. Croix Boom Company. By such manipulations, during the 1880s, he gained ascendancy over Ike Staples, control of the corporation, and a stranglehold on St. Croix transportation.

Arcola itself consisted of little more than the Mower homestead, a well-stocked store, blacksmith and carpenter shops, a schoolhouse, and a half-dozen or so homes built by mill employees. At one time, according to valley historian William H. C. Folsom, a town was platted there, but no one seems to have bothered to record it. From the beginning, therefore, the Mowers obviously had no plans for its growth nor for any of the "great things to come" promised by the proprietors of so many other valley settlements. Throughout the years of Arcola's history the statement made in 1854 by territorial prison warden Frank Delano has held true: "It makes no pretentions to a village." As a bona fide ghost town, Arcola perhaps leaves much to be desired.

About twenty years before the panic of 1857 wiped out the plans of many land speculators in the valley, two settlements began to develop on opposite shores of the St. Croix where it flows into the Mississippi. Point Douglas on the west bank, and its counterpart Prescott in present-day Wisconsin, were rivals for about a decade, until the latter village with its better location won out in the competition for survival. At first, though, it appeared that Point Douglas would be the one to triumph. When Prescott's Landing, in the 1840s more widely known as "Mouth of St. Croix," was still an Indian trading post, Point Douglas could boast the best general store in the area where most supplies were purchased for inland settlements. In addition, it became the regular stopping place for steamboats to take on wood for fuel and to transfer passengers and freight bound up the St. Croix Valley. The Minnesota Packet Company was also offering semiweekly steamer service from Galena, Illinois, and one of its two stops along the St. Croix was at Point Douglas where the line kept a resident agent to handle the business. By 1850 the *Minnesota Chronicle and Register* of St. Paul predicted that the Minnesota village would soon be "among the most prominent settlements of the Territory." It was even considered a possible location for the territorial prison. But Point Douglas reached its peak only four years later when it had two stores, a sawmill, two hotels, a school, and fifteen to twenty "neat and well finished homes." That was the time, too, of the most intense intervillage rivalry, with each of the settlements, as Mitchell Y. Jackson of Lakeland recorded in his diary, "claiming to be great towns in the future." But both were too close to St. Paul to amount to much, he added.

Prescott soon took the lead after it was surveyed and platted in 1853. By the mid-1850s, following the development of an improved levee, an excellent steamboat landing, and adequate storage facilities, the Wisconsin village almost immediately became a port of call for Mississippi River boats. St. Croix packets, too, bypassed Point Douglas. They began making regular trips from Prescott north when the stern-wheeler *Eolian* was put into service during 1857 to link Lake St. Croix with boats already plying the upper river between Stillwater and the Dalles. Point Douglas, also soon overshadowed by neighboring Hastings on the Mississippi, slowly faded. Over the ensuing years, railroads and highways played havoc with the settlement's original plat, so that today it is difficult to imagine where the once-prosperous village of Point Douglas stood. Bordering close on the highway, there are left only three of the original homes and the old school building, which are today sandwiched between split-level ramblers and a well-filled junk yard and automobile gravesite. These remnants are hardly sufficient to remind motorists, as they wind down the long hill to cross the river into Prescott, that along this narrow point of land there was once a busy steamboat landing, a flourishing sawmill, and for a while, a short distance back up the hill, a thriving valley community.

The competition of frontier days was relentless. To survive, villages and projected settlements had to be endowed with the combination of a good location, the right leaders, and money. Stillwater was fortunate in its site which could be equaled nowhere in the valley. In addition, astute lumbermen like Isaac Staples settled there during its infancy, bringing with them the confidence and especially the financial backing of Eastern and Southern capital. Such a fusion, at the right time, helped make Stillwater the entrepôt for the entire St. Croix Valley. On the other hand, the dreams and work of people like Frank Register, Dr. Garlick, and Elam Greeley died aborning because the men lacked the business ability and almost unlimited funds of Ike Staples. They could not survive the difficult times following the 1857 panic, and their platted villages, which were poorly located for such grandiose plans, disappeared as completely as though they had never existed.

As the years rolled by, those towns which lived through the depression were soon economically blighted by the ascending powers of the St. Croix Boom Company and the Stillwater lumber barons. Railroads, too, contributed their share to changes in regional economy. They cut across and sucked away the river's life. Today, however, there is retribution. Trains are quitting many parts of the valley, the tracks are being torn up, and depots abandoned. Highway traffic and pleasure boating are now bringing a certain amount of prosperity back to some of the forgotten villages along the St. Croix. And Prescott, Afton, Arcola, Marine, even Osceola, are fast becoming commuter towns. More and more they are being built up with year-round homes for families who earn their living in Stillwater, Hudson, and St. Paul.

Chapter Sixteen

Health and Pleasure Seekers

"**O**N MONDAY, the fourth of June, I set out . . . by land, to the Falls of St. Croix," wrote Ephraim S. Seymour, a tourist from New York State, after he left St. Paul and began a walking journey to Stillwater and the Dalles. This was one of several trips he made through the new territory of Minnesota during the summer of 1849 with the express purpose of writing an account of his experiences. One year later, when his book entitled *Sketches of Minnesota, the New England of the West* was published in New York, he became the first to record in detail what he saw of the villages and countryside along the lower St. Croix.

Many tourists before Seymour enjoyed what came to be called the "Fashionable Tour"—the steamboat trip on the Mississippi from St. Louis and Galena to the Falls of St. Anthony and Fort Snelling which were great points of attraction from the mid-1830s through the 1850s. But no one, it seems, bothered to branch off from the main river, head north up the tributary St. Croix, and then write about it at more than newspaper length. No one, that is, until Seymour came into the valley.

This York Stater was an entertaining commentator on the local scene, doing the things and asking the questions one would expect of a tourist intent on getting out a book. He obtained information about Stillwater from lumberman John McKusick and concerning the upper valley from William H. C. Folsom, a resident of Taylors Falls. A visit to the Reverend William T. Boutwell on his farm near Stillwater provided Seymour with a mass of material about the onetime missionary's experiences among the Chippewa and

Sioux. Seymour described local scenery and valley settlements from Willow River, now Hudson, to St. Croix Falls, showing himself to be a factual reporter who had little desire to embellish or poetize his descriptions.

In 1850 twenty-four-year-old Edward Sullivan, on a pleasure jaunt from his native England, traveled by birchbark canoe the Brule and St. Croix waterway from La Pointe on Lake Superior to Stillwater. He made the trip in the fall of the year and, as he later wrote in his book *Rambles and Scrambles in North and South America,* "the foliage was just acquiring its autumnal tints (nowhere more beautiful than in America) and the change . . . to the varied foliage, was very pleasing." As he descended the St. Croix the wonders of the river seemed to him more and more remarkable. "One hour of such lovely weather and beautiful scenery," concluded Sullivan, "fully repaid us for all our hard doings." His crystal ball was clouded, however, and one of his predictions remains as remote today as it was over a hundred years ago: "Who can tell whether three hundred years hence the banks of the Ste Croix may not be studded with smooth lawns and villas like the Thames."

Some twenty miles above what Sullivan called the "Chute de Ste Croix," his party met four men canoeing upstream—"They seemed a rough set, and we imagined they were traders." Sullivan's error was immediately corrected. One of the men was the Honorable Aaron Goodrich, the able and erratic first chief justice of Minnesota Territory doing the circuit courts. The encounter was more than the young Britisher could understand. "Fancy our judges going the circuit in birchbark canoes," he commented, "sleeping in the open air, and living on salt-pork and potatoes!"

Elizabeth F. Ellet was another tourist who went back to New York and wrote a book about her experiences in the western country during 1852. In *Summer Rambles in the West,* she describes in detail her upriver trip from Stillwater. It was made on the sidewheeler *Blackhawk* which the *Minnesota Pioneer* once described as a boat "of considerable prow-ess, but rather short aft." Unlike Seymour, Mrs. Ellet was poetic, almost breathless, in her descriptions of the scenery. Yet, in spite of tortuously long sentences, her

rhapsody on the Dalles of the St. Croix remains one of the best descriptions of that major tourist attraction. Few writers have since equaled Mrs. Ellet's eloquence:

Within a short distance of the termination of our voyage, a scene presented itself which nothing on the upper Mississippi can parallel. The stream enters a wild, narrow gorge, so deep and dark, that the declining sun is quite shut out; perpendicular walls of traprock, scarlet and chocolate-colored, and gray with the moss of centuries, rising from the water, are piled in savage grandeur on either side, to a height of from one hundred to two hundred feet above our heads, their craggy summits thinly covered with tall cedars and pines, which stand upright, at intervals on their sides, adding to the wild and picturesque effect;

the river hemmed in and overhung by the rocky masses, rushes im-
petuously downward, and roars in the caverns and rifts worn by the
action of the chafed waters. These sheer and awful precipices, mirrored
in the waters, are here broken into massive fragments, there stand in
architectural regularity, like vast columns reared by art; or some gigan-
tice buttress uplifts itself in front of the cliffs, like a ruined tower of
primeval days. One slender shaft, a solitary pillar, is seen; the top
formed like a chair, in which an eagle might build its nest. A high and
hoary cliff in front, seeming to bar further progress, appears the end
of the river. But a sharp turn to the left discloses the rapids; just before
us stand two solid enormous masses of rock like the abutments of a
bridge, and a notch between them is the landing place.

With the published accounts of authors Seymour and Ellet,
tourism got its start along the St. Croix. These two volumes and
Edward Sullivan's record of his more rugged canoe trip down the
length of the St. Croix to Stillwater were, however, both a beginning and an end, for no other book-writing tourist traveled the
river. After Seymour, Sullivan, and Ellet, those who ventured the
St. Croix and wrote about it did little more than put together
short, inadequate articles which today lie buried deep in the forgotten files of local newspapers. Where they exist, these accounts
seem to have been penned mostly by publicists for the St. Croix
Valley. As in the rest of Wisconsin and Minnesota, promoters
were intent on making out a good case for the area's maligned
climate. The remainder of the country, they felt, was prejudiced
against its "Arctic temperature," and they went to the other extreme and publicized absurd statements in favor of the unequaled
climate and its miraculous benefits to the sick and ailing.

Seymour was one of the first to claim that the valley's salubrious
air was a cure-all for malaria and consumption. For example,
when he found a Galena friend fishing along the banks of Bolles
Creek (now officially known as Valley Branch) near present-day
Afton, he noted that the once-ailing fellow townsman had become
"quite robust and healthy." He regarded St. Croix air as "far superior to quack medicines and expensive nostrums."

For many years preposterous promises were made on behalf of
Minnesota's varying and frequently extreme climate. No weather

was more moderate, said the most avid promoters, none less subject to abrupt changes! T. Dwight Hall, lawyer and land agent at Hudson, published a pamphlet in 1857 on *Hudson, and its Tributary Region* in which he extolled the clear air and boasted that "Fever and ague, the terrible scourge of the regions further south, is speedily driven away before the pure and refreshing breezes which come down from the northwest, and thousands of individuals from the States below have already found here a safe retreat from their dreaded enemy." The Reverend C. H. Marshall, first Congregational minister at Hudson, claimed in his 1858 Thanksgiving sermon, entitled "The Healthfulness of our Climate," that "A healthier State there is not in America," and went on to specify that the St. Croix Valley, above all others, was "the healthiest of all parts of the land."

Such exaggerations appealed to those afflicted with lung ailments, and they came by the thousands in search of renewed vigor. Malaria victims—sufferers of the "ague," "chills and fever," "the shakes"—also sought relief in the Minnesota-Wisconsin border country, away from what one essayist called the "poisonous exhalations" of the lower Mississippi swamps. The pure, clean northern atmosphere, they said, was free of the contamination so often found in the river bottomlands to the south. Oliver Gibbs, a dedicated Wisconsin land salesman at Prescott, claimed in a publicity brochure dated January, 1859, that only on the swift-flowing St. Croix, and along *his* side of the river especially, there were no "swamps and stagnant pools to poison the air."

Cornelius Lyman was operating the Marine House when traveler Seymour questioned why he had left "the fertile soil and sunny prairies" of Sangamon County, Illinois, for this seemingly similar northern clime. "He stated, in reply," reported the author, "that he had been severely afflicted with the ague in southern Illinois; that his constitution had become nearly broken down by the disease. Many of the young men of his neighborhood came up to work at the Marine Mills, and he noticed that all returned with recruited health, although suffering with ague at the time of their departure." Lyman went on to say that when he reached the Marine levee in 1844 he was scarcely able to walk from the landing to the mill's boardinghouse. Yet almost immediately his health was restored. Only once, the hotelkeeper concluded, was there malaria in that area of the St. Croix Valley. That was, he said, "when a sudden fall in the river, after an extraordinary rise, left water to stagnate in low places, and caused a few cases among the aborigines." The Indians, on the other hand, attributed their chills and fever to the arrival among them of so many white settlers.

Yet the whites, like the red men, also occasionally suffered malaria—even in Minnesota. Richard Hall, Congregational clergyman at Point Douglas, described a general outbreak of the malady along the St. Croix when he wrote to his brother George on September 22, 1852. He was, with many other residents of his village and of Prescott across the river, "quite reduced at present by fever and ague. I have had three attacks of it within six weeks past," he said, "but have succeeded in breaking it each time by the use of quinine. Minnesota has had the reputation of being entirely exempt from this disturbing disease but there is certainly enough of it at this present time about this point to characterize it as Fever & Ague country. It prevails principally on the river. People back up upon the prairie seem to be quite exempt from it."

Perhaps the greatest advertiser for this Midwest region was Editor Goodhue, who through his newspaper the *Minnesota Pioneer,* according to historian Blegen, intoxicated himself with his own superlatives when writing about the territory. Influenced by tourist-bureau-type palaver, the curious came, some in search of health and others to view the beautiful scenery. Many visited and, cured, remained as permanent residents. Others did not survive their illnesses, but there was little publicity about them. The rest returned East or South, and a few recorded their experiences.

Handbooks like *Tourists' and Invalids' Complete Guide and Epitome of Travel* found a ready market in the East and beguiled many a health seeker to the banks of the Mississippi and St. Croix. New York editor Horace Greeley, on his 1865 visit to Stillwater, recommended the entire upper Mississippi area to the ague-ridden and the cough-weary. During his widely quoted speech at Hudson he said: "I note the general robust health of her inhabitants as her best recommendation." The pineries of the upper St.

Croix as far north as Lake Superior became a Mecca for consumptives. "Pine emits an odor," said the *Stillwater Messenger* during the winter of 1866, "peculiarly healing and highly beneficial for invalids, hence it is no uncommon thing for small parties to take up their quarters in the wilderness, and spend the winter there with numerous gangs of lumbermen."

> For health comes sparkling in the streams
>   From Namekagon stealing;
>   There's iron in our northern winds,
>   Our pines are trees of healing.

Toward the end of the 1870s it was generally recognized that the invigorating climate of this area was, in the long run, conducive to good health. By then it was no longer necessary to belabor the point and make exaggerated and unsubstantiated claims about the weather and its miraculous healing powers.

There was, however, one additional effort to advertise the St. Croix Valley as a health resort. That came in 1873 when Ebenezer Moore opened his St. Croix Mineral Springs two miles below the village of Osceola and a short distance north of beautiful Buttermilk Falls. It was his hope that the medicinal waters on his property would bring in both tourists and money, and the *Messenger* hopefully predicted in August that Osceola would soon become one of the most prominent watering places in the Northwest, a popular resort for both invalids and pleasure seekers.

Two years later Moore sold the springs and forty-nine acres to a Wisconsin partnership from Eau Claire. "Thus dawns . . . a bright future for the village of Osceola," said the *Polk County Press*. The large, elaborate Riverside Hotel was soon constructed on a rocky promontory 200 feet above the river, and opened to the public in May, 1876. It was a two-story, green-trimmed and gray-painted building surrounded by two wide piazzas and topped by a large cupola from which could be seen a magnificent panorama of the valley. The dining room seated 200 guests and the grounds were landscaped to include a driving park for horse races, a large trout pond, a deer park, decorative peacocks, and a black bear. The public, however, did not patronize the hotel, even though Dr.

Otis Hoyt of Hudson and others testified to the outstanding hygi-
enic and remedial effects of the waters, and the steamboats *Nellie
Kent* and *Maggie Reaney* made regular passenger stops at the
hotel's landing.

The plan to develop Osceola into a "Saratoga of the West" did
not succeed. Financial difficulties developed, and there was talk of
moving the building into Osceola. During December, 1885, the
Riverside Hotel burned to the ground. A later use of the mineral
springs came in 1903 when a concoction made of mineral water,
fruit juices, celery, and kola was placed on the market. For some
reason—perhaps because of its name or ingredients—Osce-Kola
never gained widespread acceptance or popularity.

In the meantime, after the death in 1852 of publicist Goodhue,
another method was combined with the health angle to persuade
tourists, especially those from the South, that Minnesota was an
ideal, cool summer retreat. "Miserable sun-burned denizens of the
torrid zone," apostrophized Earle S. Goodrich, editor of the *St.
Paul Pioneer,* in 1854, "come to Minnesota all ye that are roasting
and heavy laden and we will give you rest." And almost from the
earliest days efforts were made to house comfortably in the valley
these fugitives from the sweltering South. In his book Seymour
mentioned that a new hostelry at Marine Mills would soon be
ready "for the accommodation of tourists." During the 1860s the
Marine House received its main support from downriver
boarders, and twenty-three years after it was built this "pleasant-
est stopping place in the valley" underwent a complete renova-
tion, the better to attract Southern tourists. By June, 1857, the *St.
Paul Advertiser* was boasting on Marine's behalf that "to the invalid, the pleasure seeker, as well as the sportsman, no place affords
more ample inducements for sojourn and recreation."

Hotels were also being constructed at Taylors Falls, Osceola,
and Hudson, and the large four-story Sawyer House in Stillwater,
located where today's attractive and popular Lowell Inn stands,
was built during 1857. That was the same year Napoleon B.
Thayer, merchant clothier of St. Louis, and his family started their
annual summertime pilgrimage into the St. Croix Valley, the vanguard of thousands to come. Every year until 1882, with few

exceptions, the Thayers visited Stillwater and stayed at the Saw-yer House. Summer cabins were also being built along Lake St. Croix. "The day is not far distant," predicted the *Messenger* late in 1858, "when nice cottages . . . will reflect their white and danc-ing shadows from the bosom of Lake St. Croix."

During 1860 the *Stillwater Democrat* was worried that what it called the "intermeddling propensities of Abolition fanatics" would keep nearly a hundred wealthy Southerners and their Ne-gro servants from spending the summer along the shores of Lake St. Croix. Such an influx of money was not to be scorned. "Ours is generally a law-abiding, order-loving people," the newspaper con-fidently assured those Southern tourists wanting to come north to Stillwater. "The good sense of our people would frown down any attempts to render our visitors, their families and servants un-happy and uncomfortable while they should be pleased to honor us with their presence." This invitation, with its promise of safe conduct to slaves, was issued only eleven months before the out-break of the Civil War.

After Appomattox, Southerners returned to the St. Croix Valley. For example, a Dr. Dewey, said to be of St. Louis, became a regu-lar summer visitor at Marine and in 1877 claimed, as had the Hudson minister almost twenty years earlier, that the St. Croix Valley was "the healthiest country in all the American continent." These were only two of the many families who sought out the area for summertime pleasure. It was following the Civil War that Taylors Falls also began developing as a resort town. By 1869 every boat traveling to the Dalles, usually stopping first at Osceola to view the impressive cascade, brought a load of excursionists and tourists to fill the village's hotels and private homes. "Right glad we are to welcome them," said the *Taylors Falls Reporter* on July 24, "and hear their expressions of delight at the glorious scen-ery, the bracing atmosphere, the beautiful views and fine fish-ing. . . . The beautiful scenery along this river has been the boast and pride of our State and the source of more pleasure to tourists than any other part of the whole Northwest." When the railroad reached Stillwater and the St. Croix Valley in 1870, soon to be followed by a line through Hudson connecting Chicago with

St. Paul, crowded steamboats ran more or less on schedule to the falls in connection with the trains. Four years later over five thousand persons visited the Dalles from all parts of the United States.

The iron horse brought many changes to the valley, and residents of Taylors Falls late in 1879 rejoiced that during 1880 railroad tracks would finally reach that village:

> And when we want to travel
>   No more we'll have to crawl
> All the way to Minneapolis,
>   Stillwater or Saint Paul.
>
> Then three cheers for Washburn's railroad,
>   Join voices one and all,
> Goodbye old lumbering steamboat
>   And Donnelly's ship canal.
>
> Rumbling through the ledges,
>   Skimming o'er the vale,
> Won't it then be jolly—
>   Riding on the rail.

As railroads followed the valley and linked together more and more villages, thus easing the difficulties of travel, not only did the smaller river towns like Marine, Osceola, and St. Croix Falls benefit, but inland lake resorts were quick to develop. Center City, Lindstrom, Forest Lake, Lake Elmo (which in 1879 was rechristened from its original name of Bass Lake) are only a few that became more accessible and burgeoned into full-fledged attractions for vacationists during the latter half of the nineteenth century. Extensive accommodations were built to house travelers, especially at Forest Lake and Lake Elmo, and gaily decorated boats plied the waters of several lakes in the area. At Forest Lake, for instance, the *Germania,* last of the twelve paddle-wheel steamers built at the Osceola shipyards, was used during the 1880s for the entertainment of guests at Michael Marsh's hotel.

Art, too, drew tourists into the St. Croix Valley before the end of the century. A summer colony for painters, run by Douglas Volk, the first director of the Minneapolis School of Art, brought numerous visitors to Osceola beginning about 1891. In addition, there was the added attraction of perhaps occasional visits from the painter's well-known father, the distinguished Leonard W. Volk, founder and president of the Chicago Academy of Design, who was said to be the only sculptor to make a life mask of President Lincoln. The elder Volk for a number of years owned a summer place on Poplar Lake a few miles northeast of the village. He died at the Hotel Cascade, Osceola, in August, 1895. More than five decades later this Wisconsin art colony had a parallel in a similar school at Stillwater operated for a number of years by Mrs. Josephine Lutz Rollins who later joined the faculty of the Department of Art at the University of Minnesota and now lives in Minneapolis.

During the last five years of the nineteenth century two events took place which mark the beginning of the St. Croix Valley as we know it today. In 1895, through the persuasive powers and hard work of St. Paulite George H. Hazzard, the Interstate Park was formed and he became its first superintendent. This joint enterprise of Wisconsin and Minnesota, the first interstate park to be established in the United States, set aside for public use almost 850 acres of that choice scenery in the Dalles which had so impressed Mrs. Elizabeth Ellet back in 1852 and still attracts thousands of tourists each year. A recent Wisconsin governor, now U. S. Senator Gaylord Nelson, has called the outlook from Summit Rock "Wisconsin's most spectacular view." The Minnesota side was that state's second park and the entire region remains today the St. Croix Valley's chief adornment.

There are also two other sections of natural beauty along the river which have been earmarked for the perpetual use of our citizens. St. Croix State Park, formed in 1943, is located twenty miles directly east of Hinckley in Pine County, Minnesota, where the fast-flowing, rock-bound Kettle River joins the main channel of the St. Croix. It extends north of the Chengwatana State Forest for twenty-one miles along the river and covers more than 30,000 acres of what was once productive lumber land. Although for many years a wasteland followed the ax, this is now a beautiful second-growth forest of pine, spruce, and hardwoods interspersed with open meadows which form ideal conditions for many deer, an occasional bear, and numerous other types of wild life. The William O'Brien State Park was established during the 1940s on 256 acres of wooded, rolling countryside along State Highway No. 95 just north of Marine on St. Croix. This closest park to the metropolitan area of St. Paul and Minneapolis with its mile of river frontage on the St. Croix, honors a St. Croix and Kettle River lumberman. Future plans call for the opening of yet another state park along a six-mile stretch of the Kettle at the Hell's Gate location of the ghost town of Banning.

Since 1945 the Wisconsin Conservation Department has been developing the Crex Meadows Wildlife Area (in Burnett County a mile northeast of Grantsburg) into the valley's greatest outdoor showplace. Once called the Big Meadows and extensively used by the Chippewa as a hunting ground and for the harvesting of cranberries and blueberries, the white man's exploitation of the region began in the 1890s. First the land was drained and turned into farms; then in 1912 a St. Paul rug manufacturing company purchased the area and for some twenty years harvested the Crex meadow grass for carpets. The twenty-five thousand acres now owned by the State of Wisconsin are slowly being restored to attract waterfowl during the spring and fall migrations and to increase the production of fur-bearing animals. This has been accomplished by the erection of nearly nine miles of dikes and fourteen water-control structures which have created 8,570 acres of flooded marsh.

Here also is prairie land as the early pioneers saw it, a wildlife haven created by the controlled burning of some fifteen thousand acres. "Our objective," the area's manager Norman Stone has recently said, "is to return Crex to its prairie condition and our best tools are fire and dikes." With this reversal of the land to its natural state, the birds, too, have come back—the sandhill cranes, snow and Canada geese, pheasants, ducks of all kinds, teals, a great variety of shore and upland birds, and high in the treetops the great blue herons have built their rookery of some 135 nests.

Today Crex Meadows each year draws many thousands of hunters, local trappers, naturalists, bird-club members, and sight-seers. Next to the Dalles at Interstate Park, it is the most popular of all tourists sights in the St. Croix Valley. A similar state-owned development in Minnesota is the Carlos Avery Wildlife Management Area close by the mouth of the Sunrise River, which will eventually be developed along the lines of Wisconsin's Crex Meadows.

Following the establishment of Interstate Park, the second end-of-the-century innovation was the opening in 1899 of the Electric Interurban Railway between St. Paul and Stillwater, financed by, among others, the St. Paul "Street Car King," Thomas Lowry. From then until 1932 this easy trip of one hour from the Twin Cities, via Wildwood on White Bear Lake to Stillwater, spurred the development of summer cottages along the banks of Lake St. Croix and brought many tourists and sportsmen into the valley. To publicize this event, about thirty young people made up a trolley party early in September—the first one organized in Stillwater —and thoroughly enjoyed a trip to Wildwood and return. For some reason, however, resort hotels never succeeded along the lower river.

Street cars and the coming of horseless carriages to the valley eventually brought great changes, but the beginnings were small. During the summer of 1900 a Mr. Lewis of Minneapolis created considerable stir on the streets of Taylors Falls when he appeared there with the first "automobile carriage" seen in the St. Croix Valley. "They may be plenty in a few years," predicted the *Polk County Press*—but how many, would have astounded the newspaper's editor. Then one day in July, 1901, Robert C. Wight, secretary of the Chicago and Great Western Railroad, donned his linen duster and cap, piled his family in their new White Steamer, fired it up, and bumped his way over unpaved, rutted roads from St. Paul to Stillwater. At last, said the local newspaper, Stillwater had come to realize "that autos are a good thing." By 1907 there were only 500 of these wonder buggies in all Minnesota, yet nine years later Stillwater alone could count 201 registered vehicles.

Trolley parties and auto trips became the order of the day, replacing the once popular steamboat excursion. With this great extent of valley playground becoming yearly more accessible, it appears to have been about 1912 that out-of-state tourists and visitors from the Twin Cities began in earnest to pick out their favorite campsites and purchase river shore property from the pioneer farmers. This was invariably on the more accessible Minnesota side because of better transportation facilities and the region's proximity to the Twin Cities. Not until after World War II was there any extensive development of the Wisconsin shore line. By 1914 many new homes were reported being built along the banks of the St. Croix and names like Sanborn, Ingersoll, Peabody, Strickland, Dunn, and Heath, most of them from St. Paul, became familiar in the valley. This migration from city to country has continued unabated. Today, as St. Paul and its businesses spread east, reaching toward Hudson, so property up the river is fast becoming more sought after for the construction of year-round split-levels and the restoration of century-old farmhouses and village dwellings. The St. Croix Valley, it appears, will soon become suburbia.

Chapter Seventeen

"A Fine Country for Sportsmen"

O VER the years, the St. Croix has meant many things to many people. For the fur trader the stream was a highway to the pelt market, and the lumberman thought of it in terms of trees and boards. For the ailing it was sometimes a surcease from pain. But perhaps the river has meant most to the sportsman. Now the furs have disappeared, and the great pineries produce no more lumber. Hunting and fishing in the valley, however, continue as they have since explorer Jonathan Carver caught "exceeding fine" sturgeon in Upper St. Croix Lake and tourist Seymour on his 1849 trip said that the lower valley was "a fine country for sportsmen."

During the earliest days of settlement, hunting and fishing were more necessities than sports, for it was essential that the pioneer table be supplied with venison, bear meat, prairie chickens, geese, ducks, and fish. From time to time, though, there were pleasure expeditions by local nimrods to what in the 1850s was called the "bear hunting ground" ten miles south of Taylors Falls. And when a prize was brought back, Adam Lightner delighted in serving it at his Marine Mills hotel for the pleasure of valley travelers and local gourmets. Down at Prescott a General Bear Hunt was advertised in the local newspaper, a two-day excursion for "all who desire to share in the sport." And about the same time Peter F. Bouchea of Hudson (then called Buena Vista) tempted hunters from home and business cares in more poetic form:

Come on then, ye sportsmen with high boots, rifle and blanket, and I will shortly conduct you to the forests where my forefathers, as they

chased the swift elk and the huge black bear, would proudly exclaim,
> No pent-up willow huts contain our powers,
> But the unbounded wilderness is ours.

Over a hundred years later, the huge black bear can occasionally
be seen along the banks of the St. Croix's upper and wilder
reaches, as well as in the large restored forest of St. Croix Park.

Timber wolves and wildcats, which often howled much of the
night, were a constant menace to the pioneer farmers' livestock,
and from time to time bounties were paid for their pelts. They are
still hunted around Almelund, close by Taylors Falls, and railroad
men up at Solon Springs get glimpses of, but have not yet caught,
an aged, shaggy, three-legged wolf roaming the pine barrens.
White-tailed deer were and are still plentiful. One early hunt into
Wisconsin's Apple River region netted four Hudson men 133 deer
which they brought back piled crosswise on sleighs, "like sticks of
wood," reported the *North Star*, "supported by high stakes." In
spite of the wholesale slaughter of deer by Indians during the mid-
1850s, and the forebodings of settlers that the animal would soon
disappear from the land, they became so numerous in the bordering hills that during 1871 three to four tons of venison were being
shipped weekly by steamer out of Taylors Falls, destined for the
Washington Market in New York City. Locally this meat sold for
six cents a pound.

Another favorite sport during the heyday of steamboating was
shooting geese from the vantage point of boiler decks, and frequently both passengers and crew members of the *G. B. Knapp*
and *Nellie Kent* returned home with a brace or more of succulent
birds. Paddle-wheel packets would also be chartered by groups of
hunters, but sometimes such trips were more expensive than had
been anticipated. When, in the fall of 1870, ten Stillwater men
secured the Osceola steamer *Knapp* for a hunting spree on Lake
St. Croix, each goose, counting boat rental and "extras," cost two
dollars and fifty cents.

Since those days of unlimited bags of game and strings of fish,
laws have been enacted to regulate how much the sportsman can
kill or catch, thereby safeguarding the propagation of wildlife.
Perhaps the valley is not today the hunters' paradise it once was,

but much game is still there for the hordes of hunters who now crowd the uplands during the season. Bow-and-arrow hunting at St. Croix Park in October is popular, and Spooner, Trego, Gordon, and Solon Springs are favorite jumping-off places for eager gunmen.

Game laws, however, did not come soon enough to protect one species of bird which we find often mentioned in the earliest annals of the St. Croix. The highly edible passenger pigeon which in vast numbers frequently darkened valley skies has long been extinct. During September, 1855, the *St. Croix Union* reported that in Stillwater, "Early in the morning they visit the Oak Openings around the town and feast upon acorns. Many of them are killed by Sportsmen," concluded the newspaper. In September, 1869, Charlie Staples killed twenty of these birds with but one shot. Over on the Osceola Prairie, Ebenezer Ayers fired his double-barreled gun into a flock and brought down fifty-two pigeons, which was a local record of sorts. After the 1860s the passenger pigeon seems to have fled the hunters' guns and the valley's encroaching civilization, only to find its final and unhappy end elsewhere—the great unsolved riddle of ornithology.

As with hunting, so there has always been fishing along the St. Croix. For centuries fish had been a staple in the Indian's diet and centered his life on the river. English explorer Jonathan Carver in 1767 singled out Upper St. Croix Lake for its excellent sturgeon. Indian agent Henry Rowe Schoolcraft, when he traveled the river on government business in 1832, was the first to mention the trout in the same lake; during April, 1839, the Reverend Edmund F. Ely also remarked in his diary that "The River abounds in fine Fish." Artist Henry Lewis in his book *Das illustrirte Mississippithal* noted during the 1847 trip he and geologist Owen made up the St. Croix on the side-wheeler *Cora* that the fishing for pike and trout was excellent. "While we were busy sketching," the English traveler noted, "our guide caught 185 such fish with a hook in two hours. . . . He picked out the best ones and threw the rest away. When we criticized his cruel and wasteful behavior, he answered simply, 'Where they come from there will be more for a long time.'"

Down at Prescott in the 1850s the river's bank at the mouth of
the lake (after school hours) frequently resembled "a cane-brake
with an army of bull frogs in it—boys with long poles—bamboo—
after fish." It was not, however, until the 1860s that fishing in the
valley began receiving any special attention as an important pastime. That was when the *Messenger* noted it as a favorite sport
with many of Stillwater's residents. The ladies, too, began joining
these outings, and the Dalles of the St. Croix were popular for
what the *St. Paul Pioneer* called "piscatorial amusement." Although trout were mentioned in the early records and can still be
found in smaller tributary streams like Crooked Creek in St. Croix
Park, smallmouthed bass and walleyed pike were and still are the
chief game fish along the entire stretch of the St. Croix, but especially in the river's upper reaches.

Today, the smallmouth can be caught in almost all portions of
the St. Croix. The quantity of this species, however, as well as of
other large game fish, is determined by the cover that is available,
by the depth of the pools, and by the presence of a boulder-and
rubble-strewn river bottom. Walleyes prefer a fast current and
generally the largest concentrations can be found in the rapids of
the upper river or near the mouths of tributary streams. The channel catfish also seek fast water and are usually hooked in those
locations favored by bass. A good fishing place for rock sturgeon
is in the deeper pools from the mouth of the Namekagon to the
Yellow River. One of the finest spots for bass and pike is at the Kettle River rapids adjoining St. Croix Park where rock outcrops,
varied topography, and a long divided section of river are outstanding features. A good rule of thumb for the angler to follow in
fishing the St. Croix is to avoid sandy bottoms which produce no
invertebrates to attract hungry fish. There are numerous stretches
of this type. Look, rather, for a section with boulders and rubble
and a minimum of sand. And remember that nearly all the larger
game fish are caught in holes where there is cover. Such conditions will give the fly-rod enthusiast a good location and many
hours of fishing satisfaction.

Cane-pole fishing, on the other hand, is best in the slow running
waters of the lower river and lake. Along the St. Croix below the

hydroelectric dam, especially in the tourist area of the Dalles and through the hidden, shaded sloughs where crystal springs tumble or drip from sandstone cliffs, will be found the mud and channel catfish. "You will be a little surprised," writes Kit Bergh in his *Minnesota Fish and Fishing*, "when you start traveling the catfish circuits to find you have no competition to speak of. While the lakes are crowded with water skiers and fishermen . . . the land of the catfish is often a lonely place. You can actually have miles of river to yourself!"

Wisconsin's northwestern lake district, all within the valley of the St. Croix, brings rich rewards to the fisherman. Within Burnett County alone, a region dubbed "The Fish Bowl" by local publicists, there are 318 lakes and five rivers which provide as great a variety of fishing as one could wish, from trout to muskies. Yellow Lake, too, on the Yellow River at Webster, Wisconsin, is popular for its walleyes and northern pike.

One early visitor into the lower valley, a true Midwestern "poet lariat," was unable to contain his enthusiasm. His resultant exultation only makes one wish, unlike Mark Twain and his feeling about his *Quaker City* companion, that he could have stayed around to celebrate in verse other events and local wonders:

> Green be thy waters,
>   Green as bottle glass;
> The fish that's caught in this here lake
>   Is mostly pickerel and bass:
> Here once the red aborigines
>   Fisht, fit and bled;
> But now the inhabitants is mostly white,
>   With nary a red.

The reputation of the St. Croix as one of the country's great fishing streams has had its ups and downs. It survived the excessive lumber practices of the nineteenth century when massive log jams not only destroyed both fish and their food, but also began the sanding in and speeded the deterioration of the river's bottom. The St. Croix has also come through the killing dangers of poisonous wastes from sawmills and from the cut and burned-over

northern regions. The struggle continues for waterways free from
the refuse of an ever-increasing population. Yet the city dump at
Spooner still borders the bank of the Yellow River and pollutes its
waters as it did more than thirty years ago when an ardent valley
fisherman complained in his diary: "Why such things are permitted is most astonishing. One would think a town like Spooner
would have some pride in a beautiful little river and not do their
best to ruin it."

All these desecrations of man have at one time or another en-
dangered the fish and consequently the recreation of thousands.
During the years since the lumbering era, sand deposited along
the river bottom has covered submerged logs and the rubble necessary for fish protection and food production. Conditions are still
not what sportsmen would like them to be, and the St. Croix continues to have its good and bad years. Recently the quality of
fishing has tended somewhat to deteriorate. But periodic fluctua-
tions in fish population are directly related to climatic conditions,
and these unpredictable results must be expected. Fish life in the
St. Croix River, nonetheless, continues generally abundant, and
the angler is happy because this river and its tributaries, in spite
of occasional yearly changes, is still one of the best for the fight-
ingest of fish, the smallmouthed bass.

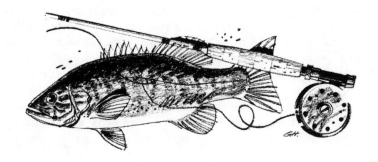

Chapter Eighteen

River Rats and Village Folk

O N THE long stretch of the St. Croix from its source near Solon Springs to Prescott where it gently mingles with the Mississippi, there are countless thousands of valley residents and summerfolk who have lived most of their years close upon its banks. Within each dwells a possessive devotion to his river which a Minnesota novelist and critic once said is "among the St. Croix's most interesting attributes."

Along the northern reaches of this stream, in the region of Upper St. Croix Lake, live several present-day residents who share this feeling. There's eighty-two-year-old Nick Limpach whose parents migrated from Belvaux (or Belès) in the southern part of Luxembourg when Nick was five years old. As he recalls his early life at White Birch (later named Solon Springs), and reminiscences about the Musser-Sauntry Land, Logging and Manufacturing Company for whom he and his father worked, he will proudly and carefully show you a decorated white porcelain pipe which hangs on the wall of his neat two-room cabin up near the Soo tracks. The words painted across the base of the bowl, "Nick Limpach—Belès—1883," commemorate the year of his birth. Reil Prevost, operator of a local bar, restaurant, and filling station, is also imbued with an outdoorsman's knowledge of the area, as are Frank Lucius and Frank Waterbury, for they and their families have lived through a good part of this region's modern history—a history that did not really begin until the coming of the railroad in the early 1880s.

Among the sandy, pine-clad hills bordering the eastern shore of the lake are others whose parents were also early settlers. Glenn Hankins' handsome, cultivated fields are almost unique on this land of sand and jack pine. He is one of the few farmers who have stuck it out and apparently made a living off the soil. Up the road some distance live Andy and Joe Lord, grandsons of Charles Lord, a fur trader whose marriage to the daughter of an Indian chief was the first wedding in the settlement of Superior. Later, the original Lord settled in the region of Upper St. Croix Lake. At one time he owned a good share of Solon Springs when it was still called White Birch. Andy Lord is a veritable merchandiser of unwanted material. He collects and keeps in several sheds, garages, and miscellaneous outbuildings clustered about his home things that other people throw out—from nuts and bolts and screws to jukeboxes, crystal set radios, and clocks. These he sorts, cleans, and repairs, and local residents often end up at Andy's when they can't find what they want elsewhere. From time to time he has to build additions to house his accumulations and his workshop. "Some people call it junk," he says with a twinkle, knowing full well that even museums come to him for help.

Farther downstream, at Riverside, where Highway 35 crosses the St. Croix, Frank G. Goldschmidt is a familiar figure, and can often be found fishing from the bridge for the ever-present redhorse and occasional hog-nosed suckers ("stonerollers," he calls them). He has lived in this area for all his more than seventy years and still guides fishermen to his favorite holes and deep pools on the St. Croix and the nearby Namekagon, Yellow, and Clam rivers. Frank lives on the site his parents first homesteaded in 1899, high on the bank among a beautiful stand of white pine overlooking Rollie Trudeau's new Riverside Resort and the highway leading north to Superior and Duluth. The Namekagon, Frank will tell you, is famous for its walleyed pike, and he always uses an artificial lure to catch them. Smallmouthed bass and northern pike fishing is also good there as well as around his home base. He is a genial, pleasant riverman, his broad-smiling face seamed and weathered by sun and wind. And he will stop anywhere, any time, to talk at any length about the St. Croix River. He is but one in a long line of rivermen. Each generation of St. Croix *aficionados* will remember its own favorite character—like Einar Nelson of Grantsburg or the late Sheridan Greig of Danbury or his son George of Hinckley who knows every turn and rapid in the river.

Nick Limpach, Reil Prevost, the Lords, Frank Goldschmidt, Einar Nelson, and George Greig are but a few of today's river rats and villagefolk along the upper valley. The lower river has its share, too; among them are Mayor Stanley Folsom of Taylors Falls, leisurely Charlie Brown, real estate agent at Marine, Stillwater newspaper editor Ed Roney, and a host of others. There are many more from out of the past—picturesque characters of a bygone day. After the turn of the century, for example, Peter J. Cottor was perhaps the best-loved riverman in the lower valley. A delightful companion and fascinating storyteller, Pete had a knowledge of the out-of-doors, inherited from his French-Canadian father, that made him perhaps the most skilled of all St. Croix fishermen and guides. He could handle a cumbersome flat-bottom like a canoe and often, while night fishing, would patiently and quietly paddle for hours along the shore without seeing a fish. Then suddenly there would be a whisper, "Look out, now, we are coming to some,"—and sure enough, the fish were always there.

Henry F. Otis, son of Benjamin, was another of a now-vanished breed. He logged the river, and during the summer months lived in a tarpaper shack on an isolated island opposite Copas. "There does not seem to be anyone to take the place of these old rivermen," John W. G. Dunn of Marine wrote in 1921 in his diary when Otis was in his seventy-seventh year. "They are a class by themselves and are mostly ex-lumbermen, river drivers, and trappers, and since their regular occupations have gone, they still follow the river; it seems to have a fascination they can't break away from."

Paul DeLong, on the other hand, was no river rat. Nor did he mingle much with the village folk. He was, so to speak, of a different kind. During the early 1920s he owned two forties of farmland in Somerset Township, on the edge of the Wisconsin river bluff directly across from the village of Marine on St. Croix. He had lived there since long before the turn of the century, and villagers around Marine knew only that he was a native of Switzerland who had come into the valley as a young man to clear his acres and farm the land. A bachelor, he lived alone in a two-room shack of questionable stability, high on this windswept hill. A nearby white pine, locally called the "umbrella pine," because of its unusual height and shape, was a century-old landmark distinguishable for miles around.

Paul's tenement, patched and partially tarpapered, with a leaking roof and broken windows, stood in the middle of a yard cluttered with old lumber, boxes, broken wagons, and miscellaneous junk. The inside of the building was equally disreputable, and Paul himself matched his surroundings. Full-bearded, clothed in shabby, patched, and dirty garments, he despised both soap and water and was forever actively scratching the vermin which must have infested him. In fact, many valley residents knew Paul De-Long by no other name than "Lousy Paul." Always eccentric, always poor, he would from time to time cross the ferry and drive to Marine in his wagon pulled by a horse and a cow, with a frayed rope or clothesline for reins. At Strand's, the old company store of lumbering days, he would gather with others to pass the time of day and, scratching as he spoke, would spin yarns which no one disputed—in his presence, at least. Paul DeLong collapsed in his field one stormy June morning in 1922, and lay there for three days before being found. His only obituary was penned by the Diarist Dunn: "Paul died about two weeks ago, and the umbrella pine is also dead—two landmarks gone."

From out of the past there are still more. . . .

A Big Thing on Ice

Martin Mower of Arcola was known as eccentric, stubborn, "sot in his ways," according to local historians, and forever spoiling for a lawsuit or a business fight, which he quite often won. "He is 'loaded for bear' and says someone is liable to get hurt," the *Messenger* reported during his successful struggle for control of the St. Croix Boom Company at Stillwater. Mower's opponents not only found him a vigorous fighter, but also a remarkable stayer. Stillwater attorney Gold T. Curtis was impressed by Mower's accomplishments and thought this Maine lumberman a person of "good character, habits and business capacity."

In short, Martin Mower was a successful man!

Although the area around Arcola never developed into much of a settlement, the sawmill he and his older brother John Edward started in 1847 prospered. Still more important to the Mowers' status in the valley were Martin's investments in strategic river frontage north of Stillwater, land holdings which, abetted by his business acumen, were soon to give him control of the profitable log boom and ascendancy over his rival, Ike Staples.

As part of the boom company business, Mower started building steamboats in the mid-1870s and during a ten-year period two pile drivers and two passenger steamers were launched from the shipyard at Arcola. The winter of 1876-77 was perhaps the busiest for Mower's boatbuilder, John Irish, and his crew. Not only were they hard at work on the *Ada B.*, a 105-foot stern-wheel packet, but they were also busy transferring from drawing board to finished product Martin Mower's pet project—an ice steamboat and its attendant passenger coach.

During October, 1876, a barge of oak timber from Franconia went downriver past Osceola, and when the editor of the *Polk County Press* noted this event in his newspaper, valley residents for the first time read about the upcoming construction of Mower's intriguing invention. From then until January, 1877, occasional items on the carpenters' progress at Arcola kept the curious informed. For example, early in December the *Taylors Falls Journal* stated that the iceboat itself would carry only the crew and necessary fuel—that freight and passengers would ride in attached covered sleighs or cars. On January 19, editor John H. McCourt visited Arcola to see this "ice steamboat or steam iceboat" everyone was talking about. He found that the completed superstructure measured about thirty feet by seven, under which, his fellow townsman, Irish, explained, were four ordinary sled runners. Two small engines which provided power for the miniature craft were connected with two iron-spiked wheels four feet in diameter located on each side opposite the rear runners and outside the hull. The wheels' spurs were about three inches long and dug into the ice as they revolved, pushing the vehicle forward. A screw arrangement raised and lowered the driving wheels and to steer the boat a wire tiller rope extended from the pilot's wheel to the front runners. Irish informed editor McCourt that four days after the arrival of the expected boiler from Dubuque, Mower's brainchild would be ready for its trial trip.

The greatly anticipated dry run, however, was a fizzle. On Sunday, January 28, in the presence of over two hundred curious spectators, brave attempts were made to get the vessel underway. With the accumulated power of 110 pounds of steam, four horses, and all the men in Arcola with crowbars to help, they were still unable to budge the craft. "Engines need to be five times as large," was Osceola editor Charles E. Means's succinct comment. Pending the completion of adjustments that were needed to get the boat moving, the *Stillwater Gazette* on January 31 printed a lyrical description of Captain Mower's steam iceboat, a story that was widely quoted.

By this time the iceboat had a name—the *Queen Piajuk,* after Polly, daughter of a Cross Lake Chippewa chieftain who, as a friend of the Americans, was said to have participated in the War of 1812. "She has a single smoke stack," continued the *Gazette* in reporting on the boat, "a handsome jack staff ornaments the bow, while perched jauntily on the pilot house is the figure of a swan with its wings outstretched as if eager to regain the graceful position on the bosom of the lake." Small wonder citizens of the St. Croix and elsewhere were on the *qui vive* to see Mower's amphibious invention which would, according to the *Mississippi Valley Lumberman,* "run over the ice, and in case of necessity . . . navigate the waters as buoyantly and gracefully as a swan in its native element."

But it was about the elegant Pullman car that the *Gazette* reporter became truly rhapsodic. Giving the drab gentlemen's smoker only cursory treatment, he described the remainder of the car in great detail. The walls of the ladies' sitting room, for instance, were handsomely paneled with rich yellow ash, black and French walnut, and bird's-eye maple; the windows reminded him

of "the new style now in use on Wagner's . . . silver palace cars."
A third room in this twenty-eight-foot car, the ladies' retiring
chamber, was "a perfect model of its kind." In fact its elegance
even eclipsed what he called "Pullman's cultivated taste in that
direction." The floor was carpeted wall-to-wall in the finest grade
of Axminster, its colors and design matching the crimson brocatel
upholstery of the high-backed, two-seated divans. A pair of large
mirrors were focal points in this tasteful room which could have
been no larger than a good-sized pillbox. What especially impressed the *Gazette* man about the looking glasses was that they
once hung in almost regal splendor—a part of the bridal chamber
in a Fulton City, Illinois, hotel. The over-all effect of this room
reminded him of the Egyptian Parlor at Chicago's Palmer House.

"During the past week," concluded the *Polk County Press*, "a
good number of our citizens have visited this propeller, and after
carefully looking it over, on seeing how simple and feasible the
application of steam is . . . wondered that ice-boats are not as
common as boats for open water." McCourt was hopeful that the
Queen Piajuk would be a success, for he, too, admired Mower.
"With the well known energy of the inventor," he concluded, "he
will have it perfected in time."

Excitement ran high in Stillwater on the expected big day, Sunday, February 4. Everyone knew that the shrill, repeated steam
whistles which early that afternoon echoed through the St. Croix
hills signaled nothing less than the arrival of Martin Mower's nau-
tical creation, and crowds quickly gathered at the elevator docks
as well as on the ice along the waterfront. "Sure enough," reported
the *St. Paul Pioneer Press*, there it came, "clawing along the river
at the rate of seven miles an hour." The boat and crowded "palace
car" were followed closely by proprietor Mower himself, driving a
team of horses that was obviously there to take over in any emergency. "His face beamed with satisfaction," added the paper, and
the inventor perhaps sighed with relief when he saw the craft
safely moored at the landing. The correspondent for the capital
city newspaper, on the other hand, was far from impressed. He
claimed that the passenger car was built with pine siding and tamarack fittings. He feared, too, that it might collapse at any mo-

ment, and he pronounced it "not palatial by any means." Chances are this reporter saw only the gentlemen's smoking room, and was not allowed access into the sanctum of that model of beauty, the female retiring chamber. Pilot Jack Kent felt that the boat was a "big thing on ice."

Martin Mower, however, could not get the kinks out of the *Queen Piajuk* in 1877, although some partisans felt he was partially successful. Nor during the following year could his inventive powers cope with some of the mechanical problems. He tried out the iceboat at Arcola early in February, 1878, and apparently everything worked to his satisfaction. But thin ice postponed a scheduled trip to Stillwater and Mower planned no additional excursions for the *Queen* that season. Late in December, with the coming of another winter, the *Stillwater Lumberman* announced that "As soon as the ice becomes strong enough, Capt. Mower . . . will start up his steam iceboat and run the same as a regular 'packet' between Stillwater and Taylors Falls."

During 1879 the Arcola lumberman fulfilled this promise—but only once. That was during the second week in January when Mower brought his boat down to Stillwater in what the newspaper called "fine style, whistling a lively tune and scaring the wood-teams to fits." By the end of the month, the owner was at last ready to hazard a longer trip. In four hours, at an average speed of ten miles per hour, he made the twenty-six-mile run from Arcola to Taylors Falls. This included stops at Marine Mills, Osceola, and Franconia where eager spectators lined the levees to catch a glimpse of the puffing, jumping *Queen Piajuk*, which local wags jocularly dubbed the "St. Croix Grasshopper." The *Polk County Press* envisioned water stations along the road but the iceboat was never to become a regular packet, as predicted. And Mower himself had doubts about his pet project. As he became more and more occupied with bcom company business, he perhaps found little opportunity for such a time-consuming winter hobby. Furthermore, there was the problem of how the *Queen* would be used. He must have realized that there was little future for such a vehicle except as a temporary freak and sideshow attraction. On February 5, 1879, the ice steamboat made its final departure from the Stillwater levee. "The iceboat is billed for the upper country," reported the *Gazette,* "and will leave . . . today, much to the regret of the curiosity hunters."

It is doubtful, however, that the *Queen* did much more traveling in the upper country, since on the following day the weather turned warm and the frozen river became dangerous. Undoubtedly the St. Croix's unique ice steamer safely reached its home port at Arcola. And it may be that the boat's oak timbers were eventually used in the construction of Martin Mower's next steamboat-building project, the pile driver *Arcola.* What became of the graceful swan is not known. At any rate, lumberman Mower presumably concluded that ice on the river forms a very treacherous platform on which to risk human life. In the annals of the St. Croix Valley, the *Queen Piajuk* then disappeared from sight and is today all but forgotten, along with the name of its crotchety, eccentric inventor.

"They Buried Him with a Great Parade"

"Lawyers are wanted in Minnesota," reported the *St. Anthony Express* in 1851, "men of education, character and refinement. Our Territory is large, but there is no room for miserable pettifoggers who gain a wretched subsistence by stirring up quarrels in the community."

Coroner Harley Curtis of Stillwater undoubtedly also noted the dearth of accredited disciples of Blackstone in that village. Morton Wilkinson and Henry L. Moss, the two earliest lawyers in the St. Croix Valley, had by mid-century already left for more lucrative fields in St. Paul. By 1852 Stillwater apparently had only three practicing attorneys: Michael E. Ames, who was curtailing his legal work preparatory to moving to the capital city, and Theodore E. Parker and Levi E. Thompson, whose partnership seemingly held a monopoly on the village's legal business.

Although lawyers were in short supply throughout the new West, back East there was a plethora. Harley Curtis' nephew, for example—Gold Tompkins Curtis—had been stuck since 1843 in a small, upstate New York village, trying to raise a family on a meager practice, and faced with little hope of future advancement.

Young Curtis had always been a good student. At the age of fourteen he was ready to enter college, and when Yale turned him down because of his youth, he decided on Hamilton College at Clinton, New York. He was graduated from that institution in 1839, ranking second in his class and with a Phi Beta Kappa Key attached to his watch chain. According to Simeon North, professor of classical languages and soon to become president of Hamilton, Curtis was distinguished "for rare scholarly habits, superior linguistic talents and fine oratorical powers, and attractive, genial social qualities."

In the early 1840s, Gold Curtis' Uncle Harley was still living at Greene, New York, not far from the young graduate's home town in Madison County. It was therefore to Greene and the locally celebrated law office of Judge Robert Monell that the aspiring attorney went to begin his studies for a legal career. He later concluded them at Utica under Horatio Seymour, who was to become governor of New York. Early in 1843 Curtis started the practice of law at Belleville close by Lake Ontario in northern New York, and during mid-May, he took into his office Orsamus Cole as a "Student at Law." Cole was later to gain prominence in Wisconsin's legal history, becoming chief justice of that state's Supreme Court. During the late 1840s Curtis had his office in Canastota, and from there in 1849 he returned to Belleville to marry a local girl. It is logical to assume that sometime about 1852 the younger Curtis perhaps learned from his uncle (who had been a resident of Stillwater for eight years) about the lack of lawyers in the new Minnesota Territory, especially along the St. Croix River.

Impatient of small-town life, certainly seeking better opportunities for himself and his family, and preferring to be identified with Western interests and progress, Gold Curtis started on May 5, 1853, for the Wisconsin-Minnesota border country. Leaving Sacketts Harbor, some ten miles north of Belleville, on the Chicago-bound steamboat *Northern Indiana*, he reached that Midwestern city two days later, after stops at Buffalo (to see Niagara Falls),

Cleveland, and Toledo. From Chicago, Curtis traveled by railroad to Rockford, Illinois, and then proceeded by stagecoach (he called it a "covered wagon") eighty-five miles to the busy Mississippi River port of Galena where he took in the celebrated lead mines. The remainder of the upriver trip to St. Paul aboard the side-wheeler *Ben Campbell* lasted two days. A short coach ride of eighteen miles finally brought the newcomer to his destination— Harley Curtis' home at Stillwater. Summing up the cost of this trip, the younger Curtis noted that the fare from Sacketts Harbor to Chicago was $15.00, with the rest of the trip coming to $15.75, including the $6.00 he had paid out for the two-day boat ride up the Mississippi.

Gold Curtis evidently liked what he found in the St. Croix Valley, since eleven days after his arrival he took over the Stillwater office of Lawyer Ames and on June 6 obtained the necessary license to practice law in Minnesota. During August, eight boxes of his household furniture, four barrels of china, and ten chairs reached the Stillwater levee from the East. Then early in October Curtis began the long trip "back East" to bring his family to the valley. Exactly one month later they reached Stillwater and immediately set up housekeeping.

The thirty-two-year-old lawyer soon began to make a name for himself in the bustling, fast-growing community. Many settlers in this frontier village had come West to make money, and business was carried on with a rush. Curtis was a hard worker, and his law practice prospered. During the early years, he also served as prosecuting attorney of Washington County, district attorney, and judge of probate, but he resigned these positions when they interfered with his private practice. His forensic abilities were considered exceptional both in and out of the courtroom. The *Hudson North Star* in May, 1855, reported that his handling of a Wisconsin murder trial showed that Curtis possessed a "mind ingenious." It was generally conceded, too, that he was without a rival in the conduct of a lawsuit and as a pleader in open court—never losing his self-possession or forgetting the one objective that he would win the case.

From the earliest days of his residence in Stillwater, Curtis also busied himself in social activities, especially with the Masons and, while it lasted, in the local lyceum. The Reverend Mr. Nichols attended one of Curtis' 1856 lectures before this group. The subject was "The Almighty Dollar," and Nichols praised the talk as "pithy, graphic and true." The *St. Croix Union* called it "instructive and highly entertaining."

The lawyer's temperament, ready wit, and untiring energy appear to have brought him considerable success outside the courtroom. In 1857 Curtis was a member of the convention charged with framing a constitution for the future state of Minnesota. A more important appointment came late in the same year—one that was to bring him considerable financial remuneration. He became agent number 12064 for the Mercantile Agency of Chicago (predecessor of today's Dun and Bradstreet). He agreed to collect debts and to submit faithful reports to this firm (organized "For the Promotion and Protection of Trade") on the financial standing of Minnesota tradesmen along the St. Croix River from Point Douglas to Taylors Falls. He was to use the code number, not his name, in submitting the appraisals, and, to avoid detection, the agency especially advised him to disguise his handwriting. Gold Curtis gained the confidence of local businessmen and made his reports to the Chicago firm regularly from 1857 until his departure from Stillwater in 1862. They are contained in two brown leather pocket notebooks which have fortunately survived, along with many of his legal papers and correspondence, to furnish a gold mine of information on the financial (and moral) standings of many important pre-Civil War St. Croix Valley businessmen. One of the most interesting of these appraisals is Curtis' report of his own abilities: "Is an efficient, reliable, & successful lawyer. Has some reputation also as a Criminal lawyer. Pays over monies promptly when collected which is not always the case with Western lawyers. His success is somewhat due to the fact that he attends to his business personally. Of good character & habits & a man of some considerable ability. Worth clear $15 to 20,000." Although he said it of himself, he told the truth.

During his nine short years in Minnesota, Gold Curtis built an enviable reputation for himself. Nor did several financial and pro-

fessional setbacks slow him down. Attempts to establish his two
brothers in Stillwater, one as a lawyer and the other as a book-
seller, both ended in failures. For a short time in the early 1860s
he also had considerable difficulties with a fellow member of the
bar. William M. Burt, who settled in Stillwater sometime in 1856,
was apparently the type of pettifogger the *St. Anthony Express* so
execrated in 1851. "Possessed of a most violent temper," reminisced
a local lawyer some years later, "he was savage in denunciations of
anybody or anything which ran counter to his views." Burt was at
odds with most of the legal fraternity, but it was Curtis who faced
him in a complex legal hassle of importance only to the two con-
tenders. During the short-lived flare-up, each accused the other of
being a damned sneak and a contemptible ass. A $15,000 lawsuit
for defamation of character instituted by Burt was decided by a
jury in favor of Curtis, and the *Stillwater Democrat* summed up
the whole affair by calling it "a rich joke." At any rate, it resulted
in Burt's indictment for perjury and the temporary suspension of
Curtis from practice. The litigants soon became too involved in
the Union cause to continue their personal vendetta.

"Slavery must fall," the Stillwater lawyer told his minister, the
Reverend R. C. Bull. "I want a hand in it. I want it said when I
am gone that I aided and participated in this great struggle." Late
in December, 1861, Curtis abandoned his legal practice and at
great personal expense opened a recruiting office. He was eminently successful in assembling a full company of area men for the
Fifth Regiment of Minnesota Infantry. Captain Gold Curtis, with
his adjutant and former law partner, Lieutenant John P. Houston,
on May 24 left Fort Snelling with their Company K and other
companies of the Fifth Minnesota to join General Henry W. Hal-
leck's Union forces. Arriving in the South, they became a part of
General John Pope's Army of the Mississippi near Corinth and on
May 28 engaged in their first battle at Farmington.

During the summer of 1862, the men of the Fifth Minnesota did
picket duty at the unhealthy Camp Clear Creek, Mississippi, and
the regiment suffered greatly from typhoid, malaria, and kindred
diseases. Among the many taken ill was Captain Curtis, who early

in July was furloughed and started for home. At St. Louis he became dangerously ill with dysentery and died on July 24, in his forty-first year.

Nine days later the *Fred Lorenz,* the largest and finest sternwheel packet on the upper river, docked at the Stillwater levee, and Mary Curtis, following her husband's flag-draped coffin, disembarked to face two days of the most impressive and solemn funeral ceremonies ever witnessed in the St. Croix Valley. Met at the landing by a concourse of citizens, the body was taken to the Curtis home. On the following day, Sunday, after the religious services at the Myrtle Street Presbyterian Church, the cortege (led by the Great Western Band from St. Paul) slowly wound its way to Fairview Cemetery, high in the hills above Stillwater. "We have seldom witnessed a more solemn or impressive scene," reported the *Messenger.* "The mournful dirges of the band, the slow and measured tread of the s.\ldiery with reversed arms and bayonets, the deep sorrow which every one in the immense procession felt and expressed—all conspired to render the occasion deeply impressive."

Ada Cornman was also touched by the spectacle, and wrote to her soldier friend, Corporal Sam Bloomer, who was stationed with the First Minnesota at Harrison's Landing on the James River: "They buried him with a great parade. First the Great Western Band, then the Hearse and mourners, then the old Stillwater Guards, & Masons, Citizens in Carriages, Citizens on foot. It was the largest funeral I ever witnessed. The Masons took charge of the ceremonies at the grave and after they got through the Guards fired over the grave. It was a very solemn scene." And young Ada was only one of the 1,500 to witness the burial who would long remember the eulogy: "No man could have been taken from our midst [and] as much missed as Gold T. Curtis; missed on the street; missed in his office; missed in the courtroom; missed in the sanctuary, missed everywhere."

Gold Curtis' widow, his son and daughter lived on in Stillwater. In 1869 Mrs. Curtis, trying to supplement her meager annual pension of $240, sought the appointment of postmaster. Considerable excitement and controversy, both personal and political, were stirred up over the affair, but in the end Governor Ramsey saw to it that H. Dwight Cutler was renamed to the position.

It was not long, however, before these difficult years were over. The Curtis daughter, Jennie Olive, married Henry White Cannon, a young banker from Delhi, New York, who came to Stillwater in 1871 to help form the Lumberman's National Bank. In 1877 he branched out to organize a match factory in the city. Cannon left the St. Croix Valley in 1884 to accept the appointment as United States comptroller of currency offered him by President Chester A. Arthur, and in 1886 he was chosen to head the great Chase National Bank in New York City. Mary Abigail Anderson Curtis ended her years in ease and comfort, dying at Delhi on October 10, 1909, at the age of eighty-five.

On the back of a business letter from St. Louis received at Stillwater on January 11, 1861, Gold Curtis jotted down the oath he took at the time of his enlistment. He kept it handy for reference when he in turn told each man about to join his regiment to raise his right hand: "You do solemnly swear that you will bear true allegiance to the United States and that you will serve them against all enemies whomsoever and that you will be a true and faithful soldier of the United States in the Fifth Regiment of Minnesota Volunteers."

Captain Curtis kept his pledge.

Sam, Duke of Somerset

In the valley of the St. Croix, Samuel Harriman had as great a reputation as Horace Greeley's *New York Tribune*. In Somerset, on the south bank of Wisconsin's winding Apple River, he was farmer, merchant, miller, lumberman, hotelkeeper, and Civil War hero—the alpha and omega, the village's chief attraction, the "Duke of Somerset."

At the age of twenty-two Harriman had ventured west to California's gold fields along a route that took him through the Wisconsin country. On returning to his home state of Maine, his glowing enthusiasm for Midwestern America so impressed his brother Hudson that in the mid-1850s they left the East together, bound for the St. Croix Valley. A few miles above the busy and growing village of Stillwater, the two ascended the Apple to a French-Canadian settlement then called Pont de la Pomme Rivière—or Apple River Bridge—where they immediately began making plans and putting them into action. In May, 1856, Sam Harriman renamed the site Somerset, and shortly built a dam to furnish power for his flour and sawmills. He proceeded to construct houses and business blocks and in general to superintend the development of his new home town. Under the Harriman aegis, Somerset prospered. And the French-Canadians called the place St. Morrissette.

Approximately one year after the beginning of the Civil War, this new Wisconsin duke left his little empire to join a Wisconsin volunteer infantry. During the next three years he gained many honors for meritorious services in the Union Army. From the rank of captain to that of brevet brigadier general in the Ninth Army, he participated bravely in the southern campaign and on May 24, 1865, marched proudly at the head of his brigade in the grand review before President Andrew Johnson and other government officials in Washington.

"Good-by, general," were the parting words of his army comrades when the parade was over and Harriman left Washington for the St. Croix Valley. "How are you, colonel?" were the salutations he received at Chicago. Friends in St. Paul hailed him with a "How d'ye do, captain." But when he came among the boys at home his exalted rank was forgotten. "Hallo, Sam," young and old greeted him, "got back again?" Somerset was glad that the general had returned, and so was Sam.

By mid-1865 Somerset's foremost citizen had resumed his multiple prewar occupations. "He is now simply Sam Harriman," boasted an area newspaper, "a true soldier, an intelligent and genial gentleman, an intensely loyal man, and such a one as loyal citizens like." In the village his business enterprises gave employment to many. Other activities benefited the entire region—the sawmill, the flour mill, and after 1869 a large warehouse for wheat that he built on the St. Croix at what is still called Harriman's Landing, in Kelly's Slough about four miles above Stillwater and

just below the bridge piers of the old Wisconsin Central Railroad.
A three-mile road led from Somerset to the elevator which stood
on a bluff overlooking the St. Croix. Grain brought in from the
Star Prairie wheat region was siphoned through spouts, some of
them ninety feet long, being cleaned as it descended from one
story of the warehouse to another. Then it was shot through
wooden conductors to the barges waiting below, moored to the
river's bank. The *Hudson Star and Times* called it the most con-
venient grain handler along the upper waterways, and added that
"the warehouse is going to be of great benefit to the northern tier
of towns."

Sam Fifield of Osceola visited Somerset one fine summer day
toward the end of July, 1869, and reported his trip. Harriman was
"emphatically a businessman," wrote editor Sam, "and while
many know him, or of him . . . few are aware of the breadth of
his domain, or of the amount of hard work he performs in running
his extensive business. Sam, as he is familiarly called by his friends
and neighbors, is a farmer, merchant, miller, lumberman and pub-

lic official combined, and like Wood's Combined Reaper, works well in all branches. Go ahead is written in every feature of his good humored countenance, and go ahead he does, in everything he undertakes. . . . He runs a saw mill that cuts 800,000 feet of lumber yearly, a custom grist mill, that turns out some of the finest flour manufactured in the West, and sells fifteen to twenty-five thousand dollars' worth of merchandise per annum. His farm consists of six hundred acres, one hundred in wheat and oats, and he has just finished breaking another hundred, and will fence his whole farm this season. His stable contains as fine a lot of horses as are to be found in the St. Croix region. . . . He raises his own pork, having a piggery and twenty-five pigs. His cows are blooded and his oxen are of the best."

But Sam Harriman was not only Somerset's entrepreneur and number one citizen, he was also a public-spirited man, interested in everything that pertained to the welfare of his community and country. He worked hard to push the first railroad through from Hudson to Superior. He also was instrumental in bringing the Wisconsin Central Railroad through the Harriman Landing pass in 1884.

Jovial Sam, however, was perhaps even better known and admired for his geniality and ability as a public speaker. The *Messenger* on December 16, 1881, called him the "best liked man on either side of the St. Croix valley. At wedding, husking bee, funeral, church festival, Republican caucus, he is equally at home. He has a story suitable for every occasion and finds an occasion for every story."

For years valley residents recalled Harriman's tongue-in-cheek discussion on how he started raising hogs. A friend, it seems, sent him three different breeds. After several months of what he called doubtful success, he gave these breeds the following classifications: *Borers*—hogs which had snouts of such formation that if the animal was placed headfirst on the ground, it would immediately disappear from sight. He tried this interesting experiment as long as the pigs lasted. *Third Row Hogs*—this breed could with ease reach over the fence and eat all the ears off the third row of corn in the next field. *Self Sustainers*—here, Sam said, was the only breed he succeeded in raising. At first he couldn't figure out why it was that the more they were fed, the poorer they grew and the louder they squealed. The general, always equal to an emergency, solved the dilemma by stopping their feed. Very soon they were unable to squeal and so immediately fattened themselves and became good porkers. As for the sheep he raised, they were able to shed their own coats and all he had to do was rake up the wool. They were even-tempered, too—never too fat to kill nor too poor to die.

Among his many duties, Harriman occasionally had to act as guide when out-of-towners came to visit and see both Sam and the sights of this "place with such a romantic name." One summer's day, while he was doing his best to entertain a group of tourists, a French-Canadian *gosse* crossed their path, sporting his first pair of pants. They were made from old flour sacks and the mother, who could not read English, had unknowingly placed the printing right side out on the broadest part of the trousers. There the boy was, parading the streets of Somerset and advertising Harriman's best flour in a manner which, they say, caused much merriment on the part of his guests. The advertisement read "Manufactured by Sam Harriman, Somerset, Wis." And the visiting ladies declared that the kid looked like Sam, too.

Ill-health in the 1890s forced the general to seek the therapeutic advantages of Hot Springs, Arkansas, and there he died in August, 1897. Sam then made his final trip into the St. Croix Valley, but not to the Somerset he had loved. He was laid to rest in the cemetery plot of his wife's family, the Fannings, at Cottage Grove not far from the river's Minnesota bank.

Sam Harriman is now long gone from the valley, but Somerset has continued to have its varied attractions. In the days of the lumberjack, the present generation boasts, everyone knew that the four toughest places on earth were Somerset, Hayward, Hurley, and Hell. Gareth Hiebert, in his book *Once Upon a Towne*, written under the pseudonym of Oliver Towne, quotes an old-timer as saying that elsewhere you had to insult a man to get into a fight, but in Somerset "just say *bonjour, mon vieux*, and you were in the most beautiful scrap this side of the Revolutionary War." For a while there was "Doc" Till whose salves and poultices drew the sick and lame, halt and blind to Somerset by the thousands in the early 1900s. During Prohibition years it was a wide-open village. Well known is the experience of a man from St. Paul who stopped a native on a Somerset street and asked where he could buy a gallon of moonshine. Getting into the car, the local resident directed the driver across the Apple River and up the hill to St. Anne's Catholic Church where he pointed out the priest's house. "That is the only place in Somerset," he said, "where you *can't* buy a gallon of moonshine."

Life is now quite different in this little French-Canadian village. Today it has gained widespread fame for its eating places specializing in frogs' legs and for restaurateurs who supply all dimensions of inflated inner tubes—from child size to blimp proportions—for cool and sometimes rump-scraping cruises down a stretch of the Apple.

Jovial Sam Harriman would certainly enjoy Somerset as it is today.

The Fisher of Corpses

"There ain't nothing wonderful about it," said John Jeremy of Stillwater concerning his unusual avocation. Yet many insisted his success as a raiser of drowned bodies came from magical, occult powers; others were equally certain Sioux blood gave this man they called "Indian John" the uncanny ability to find the corpse. It was also widely reported that he carried trained muskrats in a gunnysack; that he followed friendly fish as they gathered over the cadaver; that in some mysterious way he used bread loaves impregnated with mercury. Or did a seventh sense make him aware of the body? Could he see through the water? Did he use a "body compass" of secret invention? John Jeremy, being "as talkative as the Sphinx," would say nothing. With his motorboat the *Singing Swan* and the puzzling wet gunnysack, he would quietly bring in the body and then return to his regular occupation as commercial fisherman on the St. Croix. The newspapers, however, maintained "there's some black art . . . somewhere. He's too good."

Red-haired, full-bearded, eccentric John Jeremy's origin was as mysterious as his avocation. Even his original name, given variously as John Germain and John Jeremiah, is unknown. It is believed he was born in St. Paul between the years 1840 and 1848, probably on the latter date, and his French-Canadian father, Israel, was said at one time to have been employed as a fur trader by the Hudson's Bay Company. In spite of a report that his mother was a half-breed Sioux, both Jeremy and his son disclaimed any aboriginal blood. Another unverified account, written many years later, states that he began the body-hunting business in 1876, and that for many years he was also a steamboat pilot on the St. Croix and Mississippi rivers. During the 1880s, and on until 1892, there was a John Jeremy ("teamster and contractor") living on St. Paul's west side only a few blocks from the river. This may or may not have been the same person.

At any rate, it is certain John Jeremy, his wife, and four children left St. Paul for Stillwater during the mid-1890s. In the St. Croix Valley he soon became known as "Fisherman John" and also continued building his reputation as a fisher of corpses. "He has been in every corner of this country upon such missions," reported the *Stillwater Messenger,* "and has even had two calls from distant British Columbia." As to the number of bodies he located "from the Florida swamps to the lakes of Michigan and Illinois," no two accounts seem to agree. The total varies from 104 to more than 300, with very few failures. The public kept wondering how he did it, paying no attention to Jeremy's statement that there was "nothing to it but hard work and a good bit of common sense." As many as twenty hours would sometimes be spent retrieving a corpse, and the most Jeremy ever received in payment was $500. His service charge was usually whatever he thought he could get. Time and the forces of nature, however, worked against him in one instance. After the successful outcome of a case, relatives of the deceased refused to pay the $50.00 fee. Jeremy, to force the issue, hid the body. When payment was still not forthcoming, he held out as long as he could, but soon found it imperative to give it up. In spite of his success in locating the drowned, Stillwater's newspaper concluded that "he is modest and retiring and shuns publicity. He is a pleasant and affable man."

As a resident of Stillwater, Fisherman John had occasional scrapes with the law, mostly when under the influence of liquor. It is perhaps for this reason that his wife left him sometime shortly after the turn of the century. One drunkenness charge was reduced to begging, and at another time he pled guilty to taking part in a saloon brawl. When Hyman Levin, a St. Paul fishbuyer, brought Jeremy to court for assault, the Stillwater fisherman readily admitted pummeling the man, but stated that Levin had begun it by poking an umbrella in his belly.

On Saturday, July 20, 1918, John Jeremy visited the store of Charles E. Mosier. Saying he was going on a trip and did not expect to return, he had the Stillwater hardware merchant draw up a will leaving everything, including the unexplained gunnysack, to his only son. He then took the trolley to St. Paul where, under the pretext of hunting big game, he had his shotgun repaired and purchased buckshot shells. On returning from the capital city, Jeremy went to Ignatz Ziegler's haberdashery and purchased a white shirt. It would be his last, he said, and he wanted a good one. After getting a shoeshine he proceeded to the farmhouse of Joseph Bienner in nearby Oak Park. Since the departure of Jeremy's wife for St. Paul, Bienner's daughter had served as his housekeeper. She was about to be married, however, and had recently quit the position. When the Oak Park farmer refused to send his daughter back to Jeremy and ordered the intruder off his property, the Stillwater eccentric let loose with a blast from his shotgun, killing Bienner instantly. Police Chief McNaughton later stated the case to be one of unrequited love, and that the buckshot was intended for the daughter. Shortly after the murder, in a nearby woods close by the railroad tracks, John Jeremy blew out his brains.

Commenting on Fisherman John's sudden death, the *Messenger* expressed the opinion of many when it said, "The Northwest has lost an institution." Reassurance, however, came immediately. John Jeremy, Jr., announced he would carry on his father's work as a body hunter. Ever since he had been big enough to sit in a boat, young John had been schooled in the art of using whatever was in the gunnysack. He frequently accompanied his father on expeditions to recover the drowned, and at his side also studied the trade of commercial fishing. "I learned much from him," the son said in 1924, "and much, too, from my own observation."

Born in 1885 in St. Paul, the second Fisherman John, tall, broad-shouldered, olive-skinned, and clean-shaven, was less colorful and eccentric than his father. He was also more articulate and voluble. When questioned about his unusual side line he had no compunctions about telling everything. During October, 1921, a reporter on the *St. Paul Dispatch* interviewed young Jeremy. "I am a fisherman," the thirty-six-year-old riverman told Donald Hough, "just as my father was; I find the bodies of drowned people, as my father did also." Jeremy went on to censure those who suggested the use of trained muskrats, quicksilver, and supernatural powers. "When a man learns to do something better than anyone else, whether it's finding dead bodies or building bridges, people are always ready to say that he has some special line of bunk, that he 'gets away with it,' and are never willing to give him credit for honest, horny-handed work."

The legend, however, was slow in dying. To many the wet gunnysack was still a mystery, and only a few would believe a Stillwater neighbor when he saw what was in the burlap bag. "There weren't no trained muskrats or anything like that. It was a bunch of lead pipes with three-pronged hooks at the end. When he attached 'em to a line he covered every inch of the ground that way. His secret was patience."

Whenever either of the Jeremys was on a cadaver-seeking mission, detailed questions would first be asked about the accident. Then everyone was banished from the scene, and floating markers were set out. Tongues immediately began wagging about the gunnysack, its contents, and what the floats were for. John, Jr., insisted he sent spectators away not because of muskrats, but for the simple reason that if the water were crowded with boats he would lose sight of his floats and be unable to concentrate. He had to study the shore line, the currents and how they worked on the river bottom, and be able to anticipate drop-offs and unexpected sand bars. On a lake the problem changed with the depth and purity of the water. "Nobody makes a business of it as I do," he frankly stated, "or perhaps they could do as well." Jeremy tried to show the public the truth of his father's statement, "There ain't nothing wonderful about it." But no one would be convinced, and the myth continued.

The second John Jeremy died suddenly in November, 1926, after returning from Washington State where he had recovered two bodies. Newspapers reported that his total of nearly five hundred far exceeded the father's record. For a few years the so-called "weird secret" seemed to be general knowledge. R. Emmett McLeer, another Stillwater fisherman, said he had the family's permission to work under the name Fisherman John. Local resident Frank Runk, who on occasion assisted the second Jeremy, also claimed ownership of the mysterious body-finding invention which, he said cryptically, "was small enough to carry in a wet gunnysack." The *Minneapolis Journal* reported Joe Reuter, a Jeremy cousin, would be handed the secrets. George P. Thompson, a grandson of the original Fisherman John, was fourteen when his uncle John died. In a few years, young Thompson became the recognized successor, and except for cousin Joe, who continued as an assistant, the other claimants quickly passed from the scene.

Thompson was a full-time employee in a Stillwater shoe factory when he inherited the lead pipes and grappling hooks. He therefore was able to accept only the most important jobs of corpse raising. Service in the army during World War II also interrupted his work, but the successful outcome of the few cases he did undertake continued the dynasty and the legend. As late as 1941, the *Daily Sentinel* of Fairmount in south-central Minnesota bannered across its front page: INDIAN JOHN IN MYSTERY HUNT FOR GALLAGHER BOY. Apparently the puzzle of the wet gunnysack was still going strong. Thompson kept at his side line from the 1930s through 1951 when, as his last and most important mission, he recovered the body of Iowa's amateur woman golf champion and socialite, Mary Louise Cordingly. "The system we use has been in the family three generations," the wiry, muscular Thompson told newspaper reporters. "It is not patented, but we just don't talk about it."

There is no longer a Fisherman John, an Indian John, nor a professional bodyfinder in the lower St. Croix region. George P. Thompson has left the valley, but some people remember his enigmatic reply to questions about supernatural powers and mysterious processes: "You'll have to say for yourself whether that's true. Just say it's a different method." Still today there are valley residents who think of muskrats, mercury, friendly fish, and a wet gunnysack when they recall the exploits of Stillwater's three fishers of corpses.

Chapter Nineteen

Quacks and Quackery

THE ST. CROIX Valley has had its share of medical quacks and vendors of magic nostrums for the remedy of untold ailments and afflictions. Itinerant barkers for bottled cure-alls sold quantities of their Chinese Magic Geese Extraction and Royal Balm, according to an 1870 issue of the *Stillwater Republican*, to the "boys, ninnies, and suckers" of villages up and down the river. The barkers claimed much, but cured little. Their interest was in the pocketbook, not in the patient.

A Dr. McBride, the self-styled great King of Pain, was one of many. He appeared on the sidewalks of Stillwater one day in September, 1869, distributing handbills and hawking drugs. His street-length overcoat, wide-brimmed hat, and curled locks which fell gracefully in long ringlets down his back startled the local residents. They gazed, admired, wondered, and purchased his miraculous all-purpose elixir which was guaranteed to wipe out any pain the sufferer might have in exactly seventeen and one-half minutes. The public's capacity for being swindled by phony medical experts has always been unlimited. McBride's method was to "shower and shampoo the apex of the pericranium with some fiery liquid, till the smarting so exceeded the ache that the patient was glad to escape by acknowledging that he didn't ache any more." As will be seen, this was the same psychology used by a later valley practitioner, Dr. John Till.

When brought before the village mayor by local policemen and ordered to pay three dollars a day for a vending license, McBride gathered up his traps, paid his bill at the Sawyer House, and quickly departed toward the west. The local newspaper, however, kept track of the eccentric doctor, and in September, 1871, announced that this quack who had once harangued valley residents in the "most mellifluous tones" was dead. "The noted 'King of Pain,'" the *Gazette* reported, in a short, succinct obituary, "led a dissipated life, lost several fortunes by gambling and made several by Faro and quackery. He was a man of generous impulses, but lacked judgment."

Of all the nostrum-vending medicine shows to travel the valley, perhaps the most widely known were the Kickapoo Indians who successfully promoted their remedy of herbs and alcohol—Kickapoo Indian Sagwa. Hamlin's Wizard Oil troupe, running a close second in popularity, stumped the length and breadth of the Midwest entertaining the residents of main streets from a specially constructed wagon drawn by a team of four "elegantly equipped" bays. In October, 1869, one such group pulled up at Stillwater's main corner, opened the portable stage, and by the light of naphtha oil lamps amused the natives with a lecture and songs rendered by a male quartet of "five manly young fellows." At intervals throughout the program they pitched for their product ("There is no sore it will not heal, no pain it will not subdue") and when the "blowoff" came—the climax of the sales talk—free applications of the Wizard Oil were dispensed to "painful persons" in the audience.

Valley residents, by consulting the advertisements in their local papers, had a wide choice of these health-restoring patent medicine bracers, most of them intoxicating. During the 1870s, for example, a stimulant good for both man and boy was Warner's *Vinum Vitae*, a blood purifier which produced a "free flow of lively spirits" and was plugged as "far superior to brandy, whisky, wine, bitters, or any other article." There was also Dr. Wells' Extract of Jurubeba with its stimulating South American herb that had "wonderful curative power," and Dr. J. Walker's nonalcoholic California Vinegar Bitters, one of the few professing and actually toeing the temperance line.

A decade later the names were different, but the inspiring results were the same. Perry Davis' Pain-Killer could be used both

internally and externally, and Allen's Lung Balsam was graphically illustrated, in best television style, by a cross section engrav-
ing of the lungs in their "healthy state"—a condition presumably
brought about after indulging in a few shots of his patent concoction. Most famous of all the medicines, however, was Asa T.
Soule's Hop Bitters, The Invalid's Friend and Hope, which St.
Croix residents learned would completely revitalize all gay young
bucks suffering from any indescretion or dissipation. It was also a
welcome restorative for men of letters who toiled too long over
their midnight work. Businessmen, too, would benefit greatly
from its thaumaturgic power by drinking Hop Bitters, as would
the weak and low-spirited. Many local residents were seldom
without their three-a-day dosage.

These were only a few of the plethora of cure-alls peddled in
the valley by the King of Pain and others of his coterie during the
mid and late 1800s.

The method used by another charlatan, Captain Ammi Cutter,
consisted of a complexity of wires, bands, caps, and batteries. He
was a magnetic healer, and like Doc McBride, promised to cure
all man's ills. The captain first appeared in St. Paul during 1880 as
a sawmill operator, but when unsuccessful in this endeavor, he
turned healer and soon was visiting localities along the St. Croix
to bring his pitch for harmonious brain and body vibrations to the
river folk. For three weeks he was in Stillwater, receiving the ailing at his rooms in the Sawyer House. It is not known whether
Captain Cutter made any return visits to the valley during his few
remaining years in St. Paul. He did, nonetheless, continue his
practice in the capital city as a magnetic *physician,* and for a short
time before his departure for regions unknown he was the proprietor of a bathhouse. Perhaps healing was not the money-maker
he thought it would be.

The far-traveled Kickapoo Indian Medicine shows, in addition
to selling their bottled wares, provided entertainment of sorts to
draw the crowds. When they stayed in villages the size of Sandstone and Marine Mills for an entire week, as happened in 1895
and 1896, the attendance must certainly have been good enough
to make the liniment and medicine business profitable. As late as

May, 1922, long after the horse-and-buggy era, similar troupes were still touring the valley. Some present-day residents may remember one group which played at the Marine village hall to a small audience: "Down to the village," recorded a local diarist, "for the patent medicine show . . . not much medicine sold. Three kids played quite well, rest of the show rather punk." Up near Rush City, Minnesota, a faith healer's sign is still posted at the entrance to a Chisago County farmhouse. It is said, though, that this practitioner has gone back to barbering.

But of all the healers and quack doctors to come to the valley, none had the phenomenal success of John Till. Even Boyd T. Williams, the controversial cancer specialist from Minneapolis who after much litigation was forced out of Minnesota and established a clinic in his home town of Hudson during the 1930s, could in no way measure up to this backwoods lumberjack, who for almost two decades practiced with little hindrance his own particular brand of medicine.

During the fall of 1905, people around Somerset, Wisconsin, talked of little else but the "miracle cure" of Meline Cloutier, the wife of a nearby farmer. Mrs. Cloutier had suffered an infected cheek which many villagers feared might threaten her life, and it was suggested that a woodsman who worked in a logging camp not far from Turtle Lake and who practiced medicine on the side could save the suffering woman. The medicine used, husband Octave Cloutier learned, was a healing oil which had already performed miracles. The amazing career of John Till, the "Plaster Doctor of Somerset," was launched when he successfully treated Mrs. Cloutier with his secret salve.

After Mrs. Cloutier's quick recovery, the services of John Till, the "Wonder Healer," were much in demand. With Cloutier as his manager, Till first traveled from Turtle Lake to Somerset once every three weeks for a short visit. At the Cloutier farmhouse about a mile south of Somerset, he treated all comers with his secret ointment and a burning plaster. The salve, said to contain a mysterious ingredient known as "4X," was applied to open wounds; and the plaster, composed largely of croton oil and kerosene, was used for every other variety of affliction. Such was the demand for these heady concoctions that within a few months Till abandoned Turtle Lake and moved in with the Cloutiers.

From Hudson, New Richmond, and other villages in Wisconsin, and from such Minnesota towns as Marine Mills, Taylors Falls, and Stillwater, strings of teams were constantly Somerset-bound, bringing customers by the thousands to what a reporter on the *Stillwater Messenger* in August, 1907, called "that Eldorado of supposed health." From other points in the two states, railroads carried patients who hoped that perhaps this wonder doctor could cure them. On and on came the believers, suffering from palsy, paralysis, rheumatism, locomotor ataxia, cancer, appendicitis, dyspepsia, blindness, varicose veins, in fact "all the diseases not contagious that man is heir to."

Tall stories glorifying the effectiveness of Till's concoction circulated throughout the Somerset area. Some said that the plaster was used to cement back a dog's severed tail and that in ten days the appendage was healed and its wag restored. Another hound's tail was chopped off, so a second story went, but when the animal ran off yelping, the owner took the remaining piece to Till who used double-strength plaster and grew on a brand-new dog.

Postcard portraits of the plaster doctor, with an accompanying rallying cry for all believers, were hawked on the streets:

> John Till—to him we drink, for him we pray,
> Our voices silent never;
> For him we'll fight, come what may—
> John Till and his plasters forever.

From Somerset Till moved on to Almena and in 1909 to New Richmond where he operated at various locations until 1916. "He sure has put New Richmond on the map, all right," the clerk at Beebe's drugstore told St. Paul magazine editor Samuel A. Phillips.

Throughout the post-Somerset years, the plaster king was constantly plagued by lawsuits and damage claims, varying in amount from $100 to $120,600. The state authorities continued to pursue him. There were numerous private suits by people like Pat Sullivan of Milwaukee who claimed to have lost the sight of one eye because of the plaster treatment. Most of the time, however, the newspapers would merely state, as did the *Stillwater Daily Gazette* in September, 1907: "There have been so many cases of horrible suffering occasioned by visits to Till that we are ashamed to chronicle them." So far as is known, no death was ever legally found to have come about as a result of Till's treatments. Being hauled into court became a common occurrence and he soon regarded it as a part of the day's work.

The State Medical Board, long hindered by the fact that Till never posed as a doctor nor charged for prescriptions, finally made an old conviction stick. Till, in November, 1920, was taken from Hudson where he was then practicing and placed behind bars at the Barron County jail. A condition for his release ten months later was that he, his family, and what money he had left should go back to Europe. The *Star-Times* predicted that Till would soon be sponging the spine of the Khedive of Egypt, or "sewing cotton batting on the undergarments of the Sultan of Turkey. . . . Perhaps he goes to cleanse his one and ever ready sponge in the waters of the river Jordan." The Tills sailed on March 12, 1922, apparently unwept and completely unnoticed by all the St. Croix Valley newspapers that had given him so much free advertising during the palmy years of his plaster doctoring. "Till has promised to leave the country," the *Hudson Star-Observer* had reported on November 25, 1921, "which is something to be grateful for."

What were the reasons for John Till's popularity? Why did so many thousands storm the onetime lumberjack's door demanding the magic plaster and salve? Why do stories of miraculous cures effected by this wonder healer still circulate in the St. Croix Valley? Perhaps the explanation lies in the relative isolation of the farming community and its lack of competent medical assistance. In their overwhelming desire for freedom from pain, these people were easy prey for all the quacks and charlatans who made their fortunes from patent medicine panaceas, sure-fire cancer cures, and bottled nostrums.

Dr. Justus Ohage, a former St. Paul health commissioner, testified at one of Till's 1912 trials. He gave the same logical explanation which years before had been voiced about Doc McBride, the King of Pain: "If a man suffering from stomach trouble applied to Till for treatment, he became absorbed in the condition of his blistered back and so forgot, by simple psychological process, all about his stomach disturbance. There is just where the success of this man Till lies. When people go over there, as so many thousands do, they can't *all* be fools!"

Twenty-four years later, having lost most of his possessions first to the Nazis and then the Communists during and after World War II, Till quietly returned to the United States which had granted him American citizenship at Hudson in March, 1910. While visiting friends at Kiel, Wisconsin, he died of a heart attack on July 14, 1947.

Over the years, the salve and plaster which the Octave Cloutiers once brewed in the Apple River Valley have not been forgotten. Meline Cloutier—until her death in 1963 at the age of 96—continued the tradition by occasionally cooking up a batch of the 4X formula when asked to by Somerset old-timers. For it is still a fact that many in the country bordering the St. Croix have faith in this wonder medicine and in the miraculous cures of Wisconsin's controversial wilderness Paracelsus.

Chapter Twenty

Pinery Ballads and Valley Saws

THE VALLEY of the St. Croix was a land of noble pines. And the men who swung their axes along the Snake and Kettle rivers, the Clam and Namekagon, rivaled in strength the tall, straight trees they cut. Working in the deep woods from the first frost until spring's thaw, these lumberjacks had to be a hardy, rugged, rough and tough lot. But at the camp, after a long and arduous day's work in the pineries and with a hearty meal under their belts, they made the log rafters and thatched roof shake with their stories and songs and laughter.

In the center of the lumbermen's bunkhouse shanty, about thirty-four feet long and twenty-four wide, was a sheet-iron heater above which a frame of poles, hanging from the ceiling, supported steaming and odorous stockings, moccasins, and shirts. Two rows of bunks were built against the walls. In front of them ranged the long, crudely constructed log benches called deacon seats. At the far end of the room were tables, placed transversely, which divided the living quarters from the kitchen. Around the cheerful fire, crowded on these deacon seats, the lusty lumbermen relaxed, played cards and other games, swapped stories and jokes, sang, and dozed until their nine o'clock bedtime.

Many were the songs the 'jacks sang; most of them epic in theme, poorly rhymed and monotonously droned with little skill and no method. The tunes mattered little, and were often just about any singsong half-melody that crossed the singer's mind. The words, however, did not often measure up even to the haphazard tune, as in four execrable lines from a belabored six-verse ditty detailing work at a St. Croix Valley lumber camp:

> On the banks of Kettle River, among swamps and bogs,
> We've been busy all winter getting out logs.
> To stay all winter is our design,
> And the firm we work for is called O'Brien.

This undoubtedly was the operation on the Kettle, a few miles below Sandstone, run by Joseph O'Brien. It was in Pine County, too, that Joe's brother William O'Brien of St. Paul is said to have made his first million at lumbering.

"The Last Clam Falls Sensation," on the other hand, is one of the better songs to come out of the St. Croix Valley. In 1872 the former Wisconsin River and St. Croix Falls lumberman Daniel F. Smith founded the village of Clam Falls, Polk County, along the south fork of Wisconsin's Clam River, and two years later he there engaged in a celebrated fight with one Pease Jackman. At least it was famous among the lumberjack balladeers, who seemed to take to the idea of a victorious Uncle Dan's "shelling the Pease,'" since the same theme recurs in several other ballads. Although the encounter is referred to in "The Last Clam Falls Sensation," this song is primarily about another battle which followed the Smith-Jackman affair. Unfortunately it leaves blank the names of the participants. The Bashaw and Court Oreilles mentioned are two lakes located northeast of Clam Falls in the area of the Namekagon River. "The Last Clam Falls Sensation" could have been sung to the tune of the most popular of all lumbermen's ballads from Maine to Oregon, "The Jam on Gerry's Rock."

> I got on board a tote team, at the town of Taylors Falls,
> Rigged out in bran new overshirt, and snow white overalls;
> I started up the river o'er the crisp and frozen snow,
> Toward the far off pineries, where the stormy winds do blow.
>
> I bade adieu to Mike, and I bade adieu to Joe,
> Saying, you'll have to trust me three months more, or so,
> For that little bill of sundries, whisky, punch and beer;
> But I'll pay you when the logs come down; you never need to
>   fear.

Then our tedious way we wended, past Chippewas and Danes,
Over heights and hollows, and out through wooded lanes;
Till we reached the Clam Falls Station, some forty miles or
more,
Where Uncle Daniel shelled the Pease in eighteen seventy-
four.

Here again the elements of strife were gathering into form,
And the low and smothered mutterings foretold the coming
storm.
The bull pups trotted up and down, and sniffed the tainted
breeze;
Too eager for the coming storm to step and scratch for fleas.

Old ——, he of Bashaw and Court Oreilles renown,
On his way to Namekagon, had just arrived in town;
While —— from a logging camp, with courage bold and free,
Swore that e'er another day should dawn, old —— a corpse
should be.

You have trifled with the ladies; you have broken sacred ties;
So Old Boy stand on your guard, for I'm bound to black your
eyes.
Then such a row as there began, I never saw before,
While the bull pups barked in chorus, to swell the grand up-
roar.

Dan's numerous bull pups stood guard at every door,
While —— cried for quarter, as he struggled on the floor;
Oaths, curses and bad language resounded far and wide,
While a lot of men stood ready to pile the stiff outside.

But fortune favors age as she sometimes does the brave,
For the lady she came just in time, the Old Man's life to save;
Now run, old boy, a widow cried, nor tarry by the way,
Until you find yourself safe back again, with friends of Court
Oreilles.

Now all you old gray headed boys, wherever you may be,
Always be very careful and never make too free

With any nice lady you may pick up by the way,
Or the same misfortune may be yours, of —— from Court
Oreilles.

The ballad of "Mickey Free" blazons in song the exploits of Ed
Hart, a well-known cruiser along the valley, whose job was to
scout out good stands of pine for the lumber companies. In 1868
he kept a stopping place on Potato Creek near Veazie's, the Marine lumbering firm's camp on the Namekagon. The modern traveler is near the site when he passes over (on Highway 35) a creek
close by the Bill-Mar Motel just south of Trego, Wisconsin. As in
so many lumberjack songs, this one enumerates many names once
familiar along the St. Croix River. Among them are several Stillwater lumbermen still remembered in the valley, including Frederick Schulenburg, Robert Malloy, the partners Louis E. Torinus
(one of the few Russians to settle in the valley) and William
Chalmers ("New Brunswick Bill"), the pioneer Elam Greeley,
Thomas Dunn, Patrick Whalen, and lumber baron Isaac Staples.
And "ould Dan" Smith is up to his tricks again, shelling "the
Pease." The song of "Mickey Free" made its first known appearance at Taylors Falls early in 1878 and was widely repeated up
and down the valley:

> I'm from the town of Bangor
>   Down in the state of Maine,
> A native American Irishman,
>   That spakes the English plain;
> I landed in Stillwater town
>   In the year of fifty-three,
> Me arm was strong, me heart was warm,
>   And me courage bould and free.
>
> It's on the Boom I sarved me time—
>   Wid corporation fare,
> Plenty to eat sich as it was,
>   And something I had to wear;
> And I've worked on the Namekagon

In ould Schulenburg's employ,
And on Clam and Yellow rivers
For the valiant Bob Malloy.

And I've camped among the wigwams,
    On Totogatic's shore
Where I held me own with Whalen,
    Jim Crotty and George Moore;
And I worked wid Pease and Jackman
    In the year of seventy-four,
And when ould Dan, he shelled the Pease,
    I heard the cannons roar.

And on the Namekagon drive
    With Tom Mackey I have been,
Where I fought the great Tom Haggerty—
    While Bill Hanson stood between;
And I fought with big John Mealey—
    And might have won the day,
If bould Jake Resser had been there
    And seen I had fair play.

And I've been at stoppin' places
    When travellin' on my way,
Where gray backs big as June bugs
    Were thick as flowers in May;
And I've been with ould man Greeley
    Upon the St. Croix drive;
Where misketeys big as hummin' birds—
    Used to ate the min alive.

And I might have been a partner
    With Ike Staples in the mill,
Or at least a boss for Louie
    Or ould New Brunswick Bill;
But I'm always weak with wimmin—
    Let them be wives or maids,
They may be fair and pretty
    Or black as the ace of spades.

And they've broke me heart entirely—
    Nary a cint's forninst me name,
I may work for Dunn or Crotty
    It's always just the same,
But I'm thinkin' to turn farmer
    And forget me early days,
Take "homestead" up in Bashaw
    Where I'm sure to mend me ways.

National events, when they touched directly the lives of valley residents, also found local expression. The financial collapse of 1873 was brought on by the overextension of railroads, by the flagrant abuse of credit, and by excess borrowing. During the depression and hard times that followed, another St. Croix balladeer fulminated against the "bummers," or political hangers-on. Taxes, the high cost of railroad transportation, and governmental corruption in general made him equally vituperative:

It is pretty hard times for the farmer,
Who lives by the sweat of his brow,
Who to pay his delinquent taxes
Has to sell the old brindle cow,
His store account has run over a year,
It's close work to pay the whole bill,
While Railroad Bummers have lots of cash
To spend at the Old State Mill.

It is pretty hard times for the Farmer's wife,
A mendin her old man's clothes,
A patchin his old blue overalls,
And a darning up of his hose,
Blue drilling is forty cents a yard,
And jeans they are dearer still,
But the politicians all wear good clothes
Who attend at the old State Mill.

It is very hard times with the river man,
Who worked last spring on the drive,
He has sacked on the St. Croix and waded in Clam,
But with poverty still he must strive,

State agents took most of the profits,
The Boss couldn't pay all the bill,
For Pine logs have always to pay a big toll,
When they run through the old State Mill.

It is pretty hard times for the every day man,
Who is working around by the day,
For the harder the times they are getting,
The smaller is getting his pay.
The worst kind of Whisky is a dollar a quart,
While Tobacco is taxed to kill,
Still Bummers keep smoking the best of Cigars,
And Old Bourbon are drinking at will.

It is pretty tough work for the tote teamsters,
A hauling their big heavy loads,
A follering deer trails and bear tracks,
Which is all you can make of their roads,
But there is no use in trying for a road,
Or even for a State road Bill,
For there is always some big corporation Grist
To be ground at the old State Mill.

The Swedes, working in lumber camps or on the farm, could always sing jokingly about themselves. It was around 1912 that Ludwig Rydquist, shoemaker at Marine Mills, copied into the back of a small notebook his version of what is perhaps the best-known song to come from any immigrant group, one which has long been a part of that nation's colorful folk idiom. Called "Swede from North Dakota" and sung to the tune "Reuben, Reuben," it was also taken into the north woods by Swedish lumbermen. In his book *Lore of the Lumber Camp*, Earl C. Beck quotes a dialect version which begins:

Ay ban a Svede from Minnesota;
Vork in de Nortvoods 'bout two yare,
Tank ay go to Sainta Paula
An Minneapolis to see vat's dare.

From the Rydquist notebook comes the following version which was once so familiar in the valley of the St. Croix. When sung, the

J's, of course, became Y's and the W's, V's—and no spot was more popular among Swedesmen than the old Stockholm cafe in Minneapolis.

> Great big Swede from North Dakota
> Worked on a farm for about a year,
> Think he go to Minnesota,
> To take a look at the Big State Fair.
>
> Got my ticket and got my bottle;
> All dressed up, looked out of sight;
> Jumping Jimminy, I feel so funny
> Felt just like I'd want to fight.
>
> Jump on Jim Hill's great big wagon,
> Had me along mine alcohol,
> Woke up early the very next morning
> In the city they call St. Paul.
>
> Walking along the streets of St. Paul,
> Couldn't find any Swedesmen there;
> Jump a street car go to Minneapolis,
> Bet your life there's Swedesmen there.
>
> Walking along the streets of Minneapolis,
> Go to Stockholm just for fun,
> Great big Swede girl slapped me on shoulder
> And she says, "God dagar, Swan."
>
> I turned around and feeled so funny.
> Never seen this girl, I think,
> I ban foxy, say, "Hello Tille,
> Wouldn't you like to have a drink?"
>
> We began to feel so funny,
> We began to laugh and sing,
> And I says to all Swede fellers
> I shall pay for the whole damn thing.

Then there were the tales told by lumberjacks (though not a trace of Paul Bunyan has been found in the St. Croix Valley) and jokes played on the greenhorns! It is said that a yarn, begun at one end of the bunkhouse, would grow so big by the time it reached the other that it had to be shoveled out. The stories of great and awesome creatures which inhabited the north woods and were met with on the tote roads were naturals to bait the new arrival in camp. Perhaps the most fearsome of all along this border stream was the agropelter (*Anthrocephalus craniofractens*) who, hidden in a hollow trunk, would let fall a tree limb on anyone approaching too close. And invariably such a blow was fatal. It was the rugged St. Croix timber cruiser, Big Ole Kittleson, who alone survived a meeting with the terrible agropelter, but only because the limb that hit him was punky.

A savage catamount was also reported roaming the wilderness of the upper St. Croix, around the headwaters and along the Totogatic River. Many were the tales of unearthly screams which shook the forests as the vicious beast's cruel fangs slashed the throats of oxen and sucked out their blood. The dark body of this colossal lynx was twelve feet long, with a tail measuring ten, and no lumberjack dared meet up with it even for Ike Staples' generous $250 reward. The monster, they said, would toss a mere man just as a cat would play with a mouse before the kill. There was also the mysterious and elusive wild auger handle of the St. Croix Valley, known only by the single track it left in the snow.

Most numerous of all were the jokes on unsuspecting, gullible novices. Early in 1886 Sam Lull went from Stillwater to the Snake River and then to Staples' Groundhouse River camp.

"Any game around here?" he asked.

"Oh yes, yesterday I saw a lot of Sledbunks."

Said Sam, "Sledbunks? I never heard of 'em. What are they like?"

"Well, they ain't very big, but sometimes they're awfully lively and give a heap of trouble. At night they are often found in groups about the camp or near the landing; they ain't fir to eat 'cause they're 'bout as tough as oak timber, but if you can kill one you'll do what no fellow has been able to do this winter."

"By giminy," Sam said, "I'll try the blamed critters anyway. I'd like to take one home; which way had I better strike out?"

"Well, take down the logging road and circle 'round to camp; you'll see some."

At camp that evening, while Sam's frame lay heavily on the deacon seat, exhausted from fruitless Sledbunk hunting, not all the chorus of stories about the creature's ferocity aroused one particle of interest in Sam's saddened soul.

Long-time lumberman Peter Jourdain of Stillwater, widely known in the Wisconsin pineries as "Namekagon Pete," liked to tell the story of one of the bullcooks (chore boys) in his camp who was a French-Canadian with dim eyesight and an unbounded curiosity. He came into the cookhouse on a winter's evening and sauntered over to the caboose (stove) where the hashslinger was boiling up his red underwear. "By Gar," he exclaimed to the cook as he tasted the contents of the pot, "zee cranberree, she need more sug-gaire."

And there was the one about the two Stillwater lumberjacks driving their oxen to Staples' camp. Coming to a fork in the road and a sign which neither of them could read, one said, "Say, Bill, how would it do to show it to the bulls; they'd be a damned sight more liable to read it than us."

To an outsider, the lumberman's jargon was for the most part unintelligible. He had a pungent, colorful vocabulary all his own, born out of the deep and isolated wilderness. A 'jack, whose dangerous job was that of top man in loading logs (skyhooker), met with an accident which broke his leg. He explained that, since they were short of help, the boss foreman (or push) had to hire a stranger to work on the ground sending logs to the top of the load. This novice did everything the wrong way. Instead of using the cant hook over the log (sag), he placed it on the underside (St. Croix). The log went up endways and landed on the skyhooker's leg.

"You see," complained the log loader, "I am a skyhooker. Well, we was shy a grounder that morning, when a gazaboo blew up the tote road from somewhere and the push hired him, he representing that impersonating a grounder was his long suit. Well, the first thing he sent up to me was a blue butt. I yelled at him to throw a sag in her, but instead of that he gave her a St. Croix and gunned her, and she came up and broke my stem. He must have been bughouse or juggeroed."

For a farmer in the highlands of the lower St. Croix Valley, there was no subject of greater interest, no topic which more directly concerned him than the weather. He tried constantly to outguess it, and had to rely on signs to guide his activities. In the spring, after March had gone out "like a blue ribbon mule," he would eagerly watch the southern skies for the first sight of wild geese, the certain sign of an early ice breakup on the river. Peter J. Cottor of Marine, onetime hunter, fisherman, trapper, and constant source for valley lore, years ago said that if on Good Friday the wind was out of the north, then for forty days it would blow from that direction; that the crow of the cuckoo meant rain— hence its other name, "rain bird." The farmers around Marine, too, would listen for the whistle of the evening train crossing the distant Soo Line bridge near Arcola. When it sounded up the valley loud and clear, they knew there would be a south wind and rain in the morning. Weather prophets also claimed that when crows flew toward the north, instead of east into the Wisconsin hills, a warm spell was expected; and if at sunrise many fine-laced cobwebs were spun across the ground, a fair day was to come.

For a bountiful harvest, spring rains are of course needed. A wet April speaks well for fruit, said the valley farmer, and,

> When April weather is fine and clear,
> So much more savage will May appear.
> When April weather is wet and cold,
> 'Twill fill the cellar as full as 'twill hold.

Anyone who kept bees claimed that if they swarmed in midsummer, they would make only enough honey for themselves. There would be none for a family table:

> A swarm in May is worth a load of hay;
> A swarm in June is worth a silver spoon;
> But a swarm in July isn't worth a fly.

There were prognostications for every season of the year. Throughout the autumn months, portents were just as eagerly sought to predict the winter's weather, for

> When the days begin to lengthen,
> The cold begins to strengthen.

Pete Cottor used to say that if he wanted to know what was in store, he would "look to the trees." Thin bark meant a mild winter. This was also true if the muskrats built their houses along the banks instead of on the lowlands. But when their homes were large and numerous, then watch out for cold months and a rugged winter ahead. In 1855 a Marine resident was hopeful that the muskrat houses high on the banks would mean the early arrival of a steamer in spring. Sure enough, ice left the river earlier than usual that year, and a boat reached the village at the beginning of April.

Just as important as the breakup of ice in spring was the question, when will the river freeze over? Experienced steamboatmen believed that this could not happen on Lake St. Croix until the last full moon of the year—as one Taylors Falls resident put it, "The river closes up at the full of the moon." And at the year's end, to herald in the new, many would first check their calendars and then quote the pessimistic saw: "If New Years falls on a Friday, expect a stormy winter and no pleasant summer, an indifferent harvest, and small store of fruit." Friday, of course, is the devil's day.

These proverbs and sayings of St. Croix Valley residents were once a natural part of everyday speech. In some localities they continue to be, even today. Here are a few more of what should be a vast treasury of folksay still a part of the St. Croix Valley:

As poor as Job's cats. (1853)
Money makes the mare go. (1855)
He is like his shirt collar—Smooth, Dry, and Stiff, and just out of the Bureau. (About a Taylors Falls minister in 1855.)
Human nature can't stand everything, as Aunt Suzen said when she fell into the hog pen. (1855)
Cold enough to freeze a Negro white. (1862)
You can't make a whistle of a pig's tail. (1871)
As neat and tasty as a schoolmarm's apron. (1881)
As fretful as a full grown snap bug. (1888)

Never trust a bull, a stallion, an old rope, an egotistical man, or chance.
   (1888)

It cannot be said, however, that a proverb, a song, or a folk fancy is typical of this particular valley, or even of the Midwest, because folklore and folksay are universal. Historian-folklorist John T. Flanagan, a summer resident in the St. Croix Valley, has stated that "folklore is neither rural nor fixed, but rather a living, flexible, colorful tradition preserved wherever people congregate." Ballads and saws like these found along this river traveled westward with the early settlers from New York and Maine, from French-Canada, Sweden, and Germany, and although much has been handed down to the present generations, no one along this Midwestern river has up to now made any attempt to collect or record what might turn out to be an important addition to the area's history. Someday it ought to be done, and soon!

Chapter Twenty-one

Down the Two Valleys

SPRING is beautiful in the valley of the St. Croix. The pink-stemmed dogwood is in blossom close by the highways, the bird-foot violets and gill-over-the-ground carpet damp shades, and brilliant orange-yellow marsh marigolds border cool-running brooks. In moist woods, fresh with the light greens of spring, nodding trillium unfold their shy white flowers. The stirrings of spring in the upper valley are usually a sun-drenched week behind those in the lower portion. They were already in evidence as a friend and I traveled north in mid-May toward the source of the river and the beginning of a long-planned canoe trip down the full 115-mile stretch of the upper St. Croix from Solon Springs, Wisconsin, to Taylors Falls, Minnesota.

My fellow *voyageur* was tall, rangy Donald C. Holmquist, who during the workaday week makes his living as a St. Paul piano tuner and rebuilder. On weekends, however, he is first and foremost an outdoorsman who for a greater part of his life has followed Midwestern wilderness canoe trails—in more recent years with his wife June. At the age of fifteen Don jerked sodas to save enough money for his first canoe and in it, twenty-five years ago, he made this same St. Croix trip for the first time. My father, too, was a frequent visitor in these upper reaches, and faithfully recorded his fishing expeditions in carefully kept diaries. Some thirty years earlier I had fished with him on the upper river near Riverside (a name then recently changed from Swiss) as well as along the Namekagon and Tamarack rivers, but this was to be my

264

first real camping expedition down the whole upper country of the wild, adventurous St. Croix River.

The May morning was windy and cool when Don and I reached Solon Springs and the headwaters of the St. Croix thirty-two miles south of Superior, Wisconsin. We warmed ourselves with a cup of hot coffee at Reil Prevost's combined restaurant, bar, and gas station, and admired several mighty sturgeon through the glass front of his freezer. Then we headed down the main street of this attractive Wisconsin summer resort village to the boat landing adjoining Lucius Woods State Park.

It was back in 1896, local residents told us, that the name Solon Springs was given to a small lumbering community and sportsmen's resort formerly known as White Birch. A few years earlier, Thomas F. Solon, postmaster at West Superior, came to White Birch, where he developed a spring-water bottling works. Undoubtedly as a reward for bringing a new industry into the region, Tom Solon's name was given to the community. The water-bottling enterprise did not long survive, but the Solon family remained to spend many summers on Upper St. Croix Lake. Today a son, Lorin Solon, onetime All American football player at the University of Minnesota, continues the family's St. Croix tradition, but he now lives along the Minnesota shore of lower Lake St. Croix. Lumbering, on the other hand, continued at Solon Springs, and today reforestation and pulpwood cutting and shipping are important sources of local employment, thanks to the Douglas County Forestry Department, the Penta Wood Products, Inc., at Siren, and the Mosinee Paper Mills Company.

At the Solon Springs landing, we loaded the canoe, a seventeen-foot aluminum Grumman, and a half hour later Don and I were speeding at five miles per hour on our way through Upper St. Croix Lake, propelled by a one-and-a-quarter horsepower motor. Getting down the length of the lake would have taken energetic paddling, and we were grateful for the small motor, a welcome compromise for anyone in the so-called "middle" years. Passing many cottages along the lake's west shore, and circling Crowhart Island, once the site of an Indian village and graveyard, we soon entered the narrows where the St. Croix River begins. This stream is per-

G.HAZZARD

haps unique among American rivers since it starts and ends in a lake—Upper St. Croix Lake at Solon Springs and Lake St. Croix below Stillwater.

The St. Croix River at its beginning is a shallow, winding, slow-moving, wild-rice-bordered stream. It is a veritable wildlife refuge, and in this stretch its black spruce are reminiscent of Canada's north country. We followed the stream's tortuous course, passing under the Soo and Omaha railroad bridges (where the Eau Claire or Clearwater River meets the St. Croix) and beneath the old and new highway bridges which lead into the nearby village of Gordon. Near here, some eight miles from the Solon Springs boat landing, the river's character changes, and it becomes a large swampy lake with sedgy shores.

This area, which some maps label the St. Croix Flowage and others call the Gordon Flowage, was originally created by a natural obstruction the Indians knew as *Namai Kowagon*—Sturgeon Fish Dam. Early explorers named the sizable lake or flowage Whitefish, and Henry Rowe Schoolcraft, when he traveled up the St. Croix in 1832, wrote in his journal of Chippewa chief Kabamappa's flourishing village along the lake's east bank with its fine gardens of corn, potatoes, and pumpkins. The long expanse of lazy water was made even more extensive when lumbermen fortified the natural obstruction by installing what was known as Sauntry Dam. In 1936 with WPA funds it was replaced by a concrete structure, usually referred to as the Gordon Dam. In 1965 this dam is to be raised yet another foot to increase the level of water in the flowage and in Upper St. Croix Lake. We are assured by Wisconsin officials that this operation will not change the flow conditions downstream from the dam where the St. Croix becomes a quick-flowing wild river.

The high head wind made it necessary for us to hug the lake's more protected north shore. We stopped to eat lunch and absorb a little warm sun on the dock of a not-yet-occupied summer cabin. Sizable waves and the crisp, cold air made this part of the trip wet and uncomfortable, and it seemed an interminable time before we covered the fifteen miles or so and reached the Gordon Dam at about 3 P.M. Five jolly Negroes from Chicago, on a fishing vacation, helped us carry the almost feather-light canoe over the fifty-foot "portage" around the upper St. Croix's only major man-made obstruction. Our canoe weighed about seventy-five pounds and its aluminum construction made it sturdy enough to withstand the bumps and scrapes of the rocky, shallow, upper St. Croix.

We reloaded and headed down what was now a clear, fast-flowing stream looking for a good campsite for the night. The first one we tried was well covered by a healthy growth of fresh young poison ivy, so we moved on a short distance and found an ideal spot only a mile below the dam. Here the river divides and its two narrow channels ripple over ledge rock, tumbling musically past a small island about fifty feet long by twenty-five wide. Shaded by six large white pines, by smaller cedars and spruce, this spot (locally called Elizabeth's Island) is a scenic gem with the added comforts of a picnic table, rock fireplace, and for us a glossy green carpet of Canadian Mayflower under the pines.

Unlike most of them on the trip, our first campsite was snug and clean, for other users had thrown their beer cans and bottles over to the mainland. "The mess left by former campers," my father wrote in the early 1930s of other camping spots along the Namekagon, the Yellow, the Clam, and the St. Croix, "is enough to disgust one. Rags, old clothes & shoes, tin cans, bottles and paper of all kinds scattered everywhere. This is the condition of every campground. By the time half a dozen have camped in one place," he concluded sadly, "it is a nasty mess." Time has only worsened this casual, let-the-next-fellow-clean-it-up attitude until now, in the words of Secretary of the Interior Stewart L. Udall, "Americans have become the litter champions of the world."

Don and I waded across to swampland on the shore to cut five eight-foot ash poles for our tent. We carried these with us in the bottom of the canoe for the rest of the trip. As we made camp, the rapids on both sides of the lovely little island were turbulent with red horse suckers feeding off the shallow bottom. They made quite a racket as they thrashed about, half in and half out of the water. As evening fell there were a few mosquitoes and many gnats, but they disappeared when the sun went down and the chill air descended. After we had eaten supper and warmed our second cup of coffee over the fire, Don, with a strong flashlight, lay on a log and watched the suckers and a four-foot-long sturgeon feeding among the rocks along the shore. The light did not disturb the red horse, but the sturgeon splashed noisily and disappeared.

The night was cold and damp, a heavy mist filled the valley, and the temperature plummeted to the low thirties. My air mattress developed a leak, sleep was slow in coming, and by morning the ground felt rock hard. I was awake several times during the night, and each time I thought it was raining until I remembered the still unfamiliar sound of water tumbling over the rapids.

The morning dawned sunny and somewhat warmer, with a light north wind sifting downriver. When we broke camp and left Elizabeth's Island, we ran our first rapids—the beginning of an eventful day of rock dodging. Our introduction to the fast water of the St. Croix was smooth and easy. The first rapids are short, albeit shallow. The difficulties gradually increase as one travels downstream. The upper reaches of the St. Croix are seldom monotonous, for the canoe slides and bounces along from the rapids to deep water, and from easy paddling to rapids again. Although they are numerous, the rapids in this river need not be dangerous. Of course, one can drown in any water, and carelessness in even simple rapids can lead to spills and accidents. But with care and a little skill, most of the rough water on the St. Croix can be safely negotiated when the stream is high. In low water the upper river is something else again, and Don tells me it is really a long, wet walk in many stretches. By the day's end I felt myself quite an "expert" bowman. At least in an aluminum canoe one need not worry about ripping a canvas bottom. With fragile birchbark craft, it is little wonder that Lieutenant James Allen, the leader of Schoolcraft's military contingent, complained so frequently about the low water, the river's many difficult rapids, and what they did to his canoes!

A short distance below our first campsite we passed two large log houses, the mouth of the Moose River, and a new highway bridge (Scott's Bridge). After leaving the Moose we noted that boulders replace the ledge rock, and several smaller streams (like

Crotty Creek) enter from the right. Almost five miles below our camp, we reached the Coppermine Dam of lumbering days. We looked over the four broken sluiceways to determine whether to run the plummeting water. Prominent spikes in the apron's timbers make this a dangerous sport even in an aluminum canoe, and the dam should be negotiated only when the river is high. Don selected the second sluice from the right as having the most water, and as I poised with camera below, he came swiftly over the brink.

Immediately below the dam we passed through two sets of rapids (Coppermine Rapids) and then stopped for lunch on the left bank. Refreshed, we paddled on to one of the most beautiful parts of the St. Croix River. The channel is divided by an island. To the right for a distance of almost a quarter mile the river cuts through a mass of red rock. The low russet cliffs bordering both sides of this channel are topped by pines, and the shallow rapids descend over numerous rock shelves which create choppy, turbulent water and a fast, smooth ride—almost like an otter slide. On August 3, 1832, Lieutenant Allen passed through this region on his way upstream. "The river has become so low," he complained, "that we have to wade over all the rapids, *which seem to be interminable.* Many of them to-day," Allen continued, "were over shelving sandstone rock; the fragments of which, broken and strewed in the channel, have cut up my men's feet, and the bottoms of the canoes, horribly." There was no reference to these rapids on the maps we carried, nor do they today seem to have any name. Explorer Joseph N. Nicollet, when he ascended the St. Croix in 1837, called them the Sheldrake Rapids, perhaps because the colorful cliffs suggested to him the plumage of the sheldrake duck. He wrote that in ascending they offered no danger, only hard work. Future maps of the river might well revive the name Nicollet gave to these scenic rapids.

About a mile farther on we successfully negotiated the fast water just above the Highway T crossing, but below that bridge we encountered the St. Croix's most frustrating white water—the extensive Fish Trap Rapids. Explorer Nicollet claimed these *rapides aux galets,* or cobblestone rapids, were the hardest and longest on the river. They consist of at least eight sets, each separated by a deep and sometimes extended pool. In spite of the comparatively high water we could run only two or three of them. On all the others we ran afoul and had to pull, drag, and rock the canoe over and around numerous large, obstructing boulders which were well scarred by aluminum scrapings from other canoes. When we attempted to shoot the last set, which had ample water, the sun blinded us as we rounded a bend, and we ground to an abrupt halt on top of two sizable rocks.

My fellow *voyageur* told me that often the best way to study a set of rapids is from below and after we were through these Don looked back. After careful study he said that he could see no possible way to run most of the Fish Trap—even at the present water level. Later we learned that only three days earlier, when a United States Fish and Wildlife study team came through, the river at this point was about two feet higher, enough to enable them to get through the rapids with greater ease. On the other hand, in 1934 when my father and George Greig hit the Fish Trap with a canvas canoe, they thought it wiser to portage several miles around some of them. Early travelers in their birchbark craft also carried over here so frequently that the portage has a name— *Portage des Femmes,* Women's Portage.

At about 6 P.M. we picked a campsite on the left bank where a gravel road, a south spur off Highway T, comes close to the water's edge. Here there were no rapids to awaken me, for the river flows gently between marshy, mud-banked shores. Even so, the place had its night noises, of deer and rabbits grazing close by, of whippoorwills calling throughout the long evening. Thirty years earlier, my father commented on the whippoorwills: They were so noisy, he said, that they kept him awake "even after the mosquitoes quit." In 1850 the young English traveler Edward Sullivan also commented on the song of this "small brown bird, with the very pleasing note."

It was a quiet, windless, star-studded evening, much warmer than the previous night's almost freezing temperature. The waxing moon approached the full and the tall trees waved darkly across the horizon. Here was solitude and peace. As we sat around the flickering light of the campfire stretching tired muscles and sorting out the events of the day, we could only agree with Schoolcraft who wrote of the fast water we had descended, that rapids succeeded each other "with such short intervals that it would be impracticable . . . to speak of this part of the stream, in any other light than a continued series of rapids."

Another unsatisfactory night for sleep. Why are the noises of after dark seemingly amplified tenfold? For some time, even the snapping of the dying fire kept me awake. Although my air mattress had been repaired, it soon sprang another leak and quickly deflated, leaving only the relentless ground to paralyze hipbones and legs. Got up at six thirty, the tent getting too hot and uncomfortable inside.

The day again was sunny, with a southeast wind and thunderclouds forming in the west. These, however, soon disappeared, and it promised to be very hot indeed. We had more fast water to look forward to, for only a short distance below our camp were the so-called Little Fish Trap Rapids. The white water began at a small island with four white pines—a nice picnicking place, but no room for a tent—and extended downriver about a half mile. Two sharp turns, one to the left and the other right, choppy water and a fast drop make Little Fish Trap Rapids especially exciting, and a sharp test of the stern man's ability. We ran them well and had to push off rocks only twice. The Little Fish Trap continues under and past the CCC Bridge.

About twenty-eight miles below its source at the mouth of the lake, the St. Croix River picks up its first large tributary, the Namekagon. This handsome stream is quite developed at its mouth where the shore is lined with a number of summer cabins—a rarity in our traveling to this point. The Namekagon (enlarged by the flow of the Totogatic—locally pronounced the "Tógatic") is here larger than the St. Croix and adds vast quantities of water to it. This tributary is also good canoeing water and excellent fishing. It is a white-water stream, flowing through hilly, wild, and scenic country. After receiving the Namekagon at a spot once known as

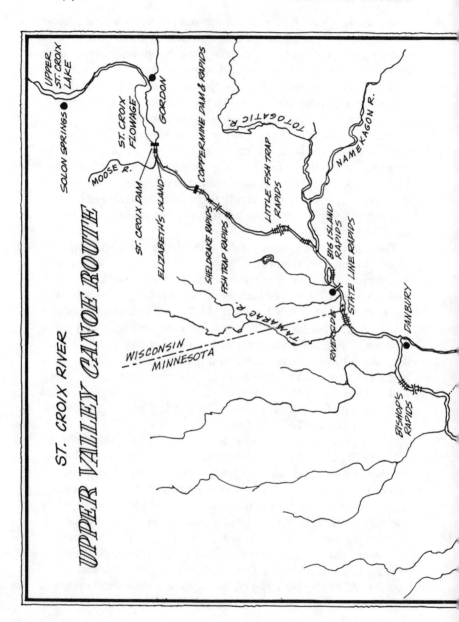

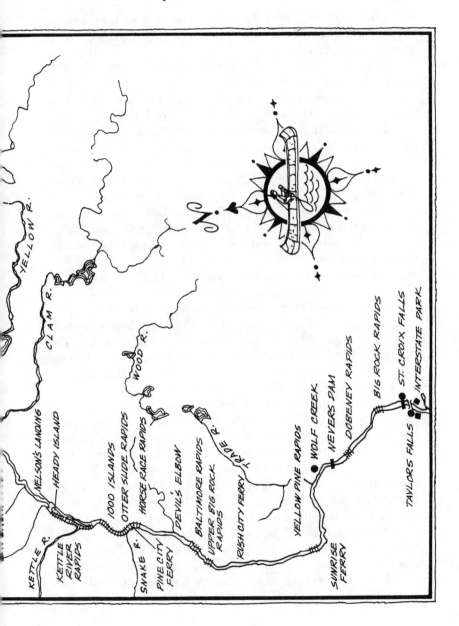

the Forks of the St. Croix, the main stream widens considerably
and for a good number of miles it is relatively straight and varies
from 190 to 500 feet across.

We ran with no trouble the last bit of white water (the Big
Island Rapids) before reaching Riverside, the Highway 35 crossing, and civilization in the form of a resort. Bernie Palmer, then
the owner of the rebuilt Riverside Resort, greeted us pleasantly,
refreshed us with beer, and pointed out Frank Goldschmidt's
spring on the opposite bank where we could fill our canteens.
Fisherman and guide Goldschmidt, who has lived on this land
since 1899, has for years tended a stream-flow measuring station
at the bridge. As we left Riverside, proprietor Palmer serenaded
us over an amplifying system with "Floating Down the River" and
"Down by the Riverside"! To preserve our image as "voyageurs,"
we paddled energetically until we were out of sight and sound.
Only then did we put the motor back on the canoe, prop our feet
up, and continue our southwest course. (Three months later,
when my wife Mária and I drove back into the valley, we found
that Rollie Trudeau of Hudson had purchased the resort.)

A relentless head wind whipped up swelling whitecaps which
completely drenched me from waist to toe as we proceeded. The
strong wind and rough water persisted throughout the day. Two
miles below Riverside we ran the last rapids for that day, the
State Line Rapids—a little ripple with a big name. Up to this
point the St. Croix lies entirely within Wisconsin. Below the appropriately named State Line Rapids, the St. Croix becomes a
border stream. To our right was Minnesota; to our left Wisconsin
—a state of affairs that continues throughout the entire remaining
course of the St. Croix until it joins the Mississippi at Prescott.
From State Line Rapids, sloughs become more common. We got
to know a number of them as we sought their shelter to avoid the
wind and waves of the main channel.

Just above the mouth of the Yellow River near the village of
Danbury, Wisconsin, we passed the hutments of the Indian settlement discussed in an earlier chapter. Farther down, below the
mouth of the Lower Tamarack River on the Minnesota side there
is what my father would have called a "rather pretentious cabin,"

and then as if in contrast there are a number of Indian tarpaper huts. A Chippewa father and his small son cheerily waved to us as we passed. Don said that this little-known Minnesota Indian settlement had had a mission when he made the trip twenty-five years ago, and my father's diaries of the early 1930s record Jim Saugetay and other Chippewa Indians living there. An old fur traders' trail known as Sioux Portage, which led from the St. Croix to Wisconsin's Yellow Lake and River, is also in this area.

One of the maps we carried locates Bishop's Rapids below the mouth of the Lower Tamarack near the northern boundary of Minnesota's St. Croix State Park, but the river was still rather high, at least below the Namekagon; and we "ran" them with the outboard. When we reached St. John's Landing, twenty miles below Riverside, we were completely bushed—and burned to a crisp by the unending wind and glaring sun. We decided to camp at this spot (named for the onetime Marine lumberman Ed St. John) where during logging days there had been a boardinghouse or "stopping place" which was extensively used by lumber crews and toters on their way to and from upriver logging camps. St. John's Landing was once also the site of a busy ferry leading into the Wisconsin pineries, but evidences of all these activities have long since vanished. Only the clearing remains, and this area within St. Croix State Park is now a children's summer camp.

As we unloaded the canoe we discovered that the hot weather had brought out the scourges of the north country—mosquitoes and gnats. By June the mosquitoes would be fully hatched, and would combine forces with black flies to make the canoeist's life almost unbearable without a stiff breeze. This is one of the reasons why early spring is desirable for a trip down the St. Croix. The water is up and the mosquitoes aren't. After the first frost in the fall the insects are not numerous, but then the level of the river may be quite low. On the shallow upper reaches of the St. Croix, water is all important, for it can make the difference between a pleasant canoe trip and a long, tedious walk.

After supper we gratefully crawled into the tent, where safely protected by mosquito netting we reviewed our trip thus far. En route down the river we had seen so many white-tailed deer in the

area between Gordon and Riverside that we had lost count. Usually we saw them in pairs, and sometimes as we rounded a bend
we came upon them swimming in the water. Birds, too, were
plentiful, for in May the spring migration reaches its peak along
the St. Croix. We saw mallards and blue-winged teal, black terns,
the inevitable blackbirds, belted kingfishers, osprey, loons, yellow-
leg snipe, grebes, warblers, purple martins, swallows, great blue
and green herons, and we heard the spring call of the woodcock.
Only a partial listing of the birds we saw during four days on the
river includes at least sixty-four varieties. One of the highlights for
us were two whistling swans which we spotted in the widest part
of the flowage above the Gordon Dam. The graceful white birds,
who were perhaps late travelers to the arctic, flew majestically off
as we approached.

My companion had said it would take three nights to get used
to out-of-doors living, and he was right. On our third night out we
had our first really good sleep, from 9 P.M. to 6 A.M. My repatched
air mattress held up soft and comfortable until I was no longer
conscious. During the night it slowly deflated, but by then I didn't
care.

Starting out bright and early from St. John's Landing on a hot
morning, we found the St. Croix more placid, wider, and less exciting but no less beautiful. In search of shade, we tried to go
through Proctor Slough at the Little Yellow Banks on the Minnesota side below where the Clam River enters from Wisconsin.
There was plenty of water, but a half mile from the entrance a
large soft maple had fallen across the channel, completely obstructing our passage.

By nine thirty we had covered the almost six miles to the main
St. Croix Park landing at the Big Yellow Banks. This spot in lumbering days was the terminus of the old Fleming logging railroad
which hauled vast quantities of timber from the backwoods to the
river's edge and spilled it over the sandy bluff into the water for
its trip to southern sawmills. We stopped at the landing to stretch
our legs, and noted a collection of square-stern aluminum canoes
as well as boats, apparently for rent.

At ten twenty we passed under a high cable from which was

suspended a small boatswain's chair. It crosses the river near a public access road at longtime river guide Einar Nelson's landing on the Wisconsin side. The apparatus is used by the U.S. Geological Survey to measure the quantity and swiftness of the water.

Still within St. Croix State Park, we made our second stop at a beautiful little island nine-and-a-half miles below St. John's Landing which others had told me was "an ideal spot and the prettiest on the river." Scarred by centuries of campfires, this pine-studded isle and Elizabeth's Island—our first camp—stand out in my mind as the loveliest scenic gems of the upper St. Croix. Like Elizabeth's Island, this one divides the swift-flowing water into a tumbling stretch of rapids. It was, however, laid out by nature on a grander scale—statelier pines, wider vistas, and more white water bordering it. Unlike the smaller island, this one was a mess of human refuse. Its name and that of the adjoining rapids did not appear on the maps we consulted, and both seem to be steeped in confusion. One old-timer told us that the only name he knew for this beautiful place was Head of the Rapids Island, which he said was frequently shortened to Heady Island. My father and his guide always referred to the area as the Big Eddy. Some rivermen say that this name belongs to another rapids farther south near the mouth of Wood River, while others firmly maintain that the only Big Eddy they know is on the Kettle River, a nearby tributary of the St. Croix.

Leaving Heady Island, we made sure our duffel was secured in the canoe, for now we would face the seven-mile-long St. Croix-Kettle River Rapids. At this spot begins an extensive, beautiful, and potentially tricky set of rapids—the largest we would encounter. We turned to the right and followed the Minnesota shore line through what is known as the Kettle River Slough. The river's main flow, which runs to the left, is easier to navigate and therefore considerably less exciting. No matter which channel the canoeist chooses, however, here the long rapids begin. Schoolcraft considered them a "most formidable obstacle" but he encountered them in unusually low water. *Iscutta, iscutta*—exhausted—the Chippewa told him.

We negotiated the first part of the white water with ease and stopped for lunch just below the mouth of the rocky Kettle River on one of the three large islands which divide the stream. These islands which extend through the seven miles of rapids, are high-banked and crowned with magnificent century-old pines. Taking up our paddles again we skimmed along at breath-taking speed. Almost before I knew it, Don called, "Last set ahead, dig in!"

That last set, just above the point where Kettle River Slough meets the main channel, temporarily terrified me. Our paddles churning, we pitched over a wide ledge which created what for a moment (from my bow position, at least) took on all the appearance of a small Niagara. I braced myself for the worst. Immediately beyond the "waterfall," large, white-capped, wind-blown waves rolled menacingly toward us. I kept a firm hold, but all we did was ship a few buckets of water.

There is a real thrill, a keen sense of danger in racing through boiling rapids. It cannot be adequately captured either in words or in pictures. It is an exhilarating experience, and I would go back for a repeat performance any time. In this instance. I was glad that my companion was an expert canoeman. He needed to be, for it was necessary to think quickly, interpret or "read" the white water to locate submerged rocks, and to use good judgment in selecting the correct channel. In these rapids and on other occasions, Don Holmquist followed the common practice which Calvin Rutstrum of Marine in his excellent book *The New Way of the Wilderness* calls running rapids at as high a speed as possible to gain steerage on the turns. At other times, we approached white water more cautiously with Don standing or kneeling in the stern to get a better look before making the plunge. Then he would yell out the right order to me in the bow. Immediate co-operation between paddlers is absolutely essential in fast water.

About two miles below the Kettle Rapids we passed the upper and lower mouths of the Snake River—the Chippewa Kinábic and the fur traders' Rivière au Serpent. Little has changed along the magnificent stretch of the St. Croix from Heady Island and the Kettle Rapids, past the Thousand Islands to the Snake River since my father recorded in his diary early in September, 1932, that "one could not imagine a more beautiful river, high banks covered with large hard wood, with scattering pine, mostly white pine. Islands, large & small without number & these also covered with big trees. A good many of these islands are high and rocky on the shore line. No end of springs and spring creeks coming in mostly on the Wisconsin side." He expressed the fear that the Northern States Power Company (which still owns most of this shore line) might soon build dams that would, as he put it, "ruin the beauty of this river as well as its value for recreation purposes. . . . This river," he concluded, "from Snake river up to the mouth of the Tamarack river should be made a state park by Minnesota & Wisconsin, and should forever be preserved in its present state for the people of both states."

Three years later, in 1935, Minnesota took the first step which eventually led to the formation of St. Croix State Park and the Chengwatana State Forest, thereby safeguarding a good share of this stretch along the river's western bank. And now there is a good possibility that the entire upper St. Croix Valley (as well as a portion of the Namekagon) will soon become a part of our great chain of wild rivers stretching across the length and breadth of America.

The St. Croix merits preservation. Its rapids, springs, islands, and wild shores so impressed explorer Nicollet in 1837 that he described this area as *l'endroit fort agréable*. History, too, makes the St. Croix important. On the small peninsula at the Snake, a mile south of the Thousand Islands, Schoolcraft was welcomed by Chief Pizhickee, the Buffalo, and his band of Chippewa. "They fired a salute," the region's first native American explorer recorded in his account of that early St. Croix trip, "and crowded down to the shore, to welcome us." It was some miles up the Snake that Tom Connor constructed his important North West Company fur trading post during the winter of 1804-05.

Below the Snake River, many cabins line the Wisconsin shore. Upstream and downstream from the site of Sodabeck's once busy "Riverdale Ferry" east of Pine City, we passed several sets of rapids (the Otter Slide and the half-mile Horse Race). So high was

the water that we went through them with the motor going full
speed ahead, and by one fifty the Grantsburg bridge and its pine-
forested camping spot on the Wisconsin shore were behind us.

The weather had fulfilled its early morning promise. It was just
plain hot. Later we learned that the temperature set an all-time
record high of 92 degrees for that date. To add to our discomfort,
a strong wind was blowing upstream at more than twenty-five
miles an hour. It pushed the water toward us in white-capped
waves which easily measured three feet in height. In a vain effort
to avoid the wind, we hugged the shore. Each time we cut across
the stream, the whitecaps threatened to swamp us. Again we were
grateful for the small motor, for paddling into such a head wind
even going downstream is brute work. So strong was the gale
that we would have had to paddle with all our strength merely to
keep from being swept upstream.

We passed the Devil's Elbow, where Wood River enters from
Wisconsin, and reached the old Rush City ferry landing four miles
from the Grantsburg crossing, and twenty-nine miles above Taylors Falls at 3:40 P.M. There we came across four fisherman in a
boat and a canoe out for a few days of camping and angling.
Largely because we made the trip at midweek, we saw on the
entire expedition only some half-dozen Izaak Waltons, white and
Indian, trying their luck along the river's banks. Had we traveled
downriver on a Saturday or Sunday, the situation would have
been quite different, for the St. Croix is the weekend playground
for many residents in and near the valley. From its mouth at Prescott as far north as the mouth of the Sunrise, boats and campers
line its banks.

As we traveled southward from the Rush City landing, we saw
more deciduous trees and fewer pines. We also noted considerable stretches of well-grazed pastures and fields which reached
down to the river's edge. Here and there a farmer's house and
barn stood only a few hundred feet back from a badly eroded
shore line. Such pastoral scenes are unusual along the St. Croix.
The banks of both the upper and lower valleys are for the most
part heavily wooded, and on the lower river steep, tree-topped
bluffs are characteristic.

We passed the mouth of the Sunrise River and the site of the old cable ferry at five fifteen. Here some twenty miles above the Dalles, the effects of the large power dam there can be perceived. The river becomes wider, the water runs more slowly, large sand bars are numerous, and the shore line is muddy and lacking in variety. Elm, soft maple, birch, and ash are the predominant trees, and lofty pines no longer grace the hills until one reaches the Dalles.

From Riverside down, I was impressed by the possibilities of this upper river for a canoe-rental business similar to those of the lower valley. The stretch from the Grantsburg bridge to the twin villages of St. Croix Falls and Taylors Falls offers an easy and very pretty trip for the less venturesome or the inexperienced. The frequent sand bars make fine picnicking spots and good swimming beaches. One week after our return I observed with interest that the *St. Croix Falls Standard-Press* reported the establishment of a canoe-outfitting service (called the Voyageur) between Riverside and the falls.

In the Sunrise area the river makes a large gradual bend, and for a time the stream flows in an east-west rather than a north-south direction. In this wide-running portion of the St. Croix we saw the only bald eagle of the trip. With two crows, it was feeding on some dead fish on a sand bar. We got a good look at this magnificent specimen of our rather rare national bird, for although the bald eagle is protected, his numbers are not great. With his vast wingspread, he makes far too tempting a target for those who like to shoot at anything that moves. As we passed the feeding birds, the crows flew off, but the eagle moved only to a nearby tree where he sat undisturbed as we passed.

Sleepy porcupines, high in the treetops, and wonder-eyed cattle in pastures edging the river banks placidly watched us glide by. Deer remained numerous, an occasional great blue heron erupted languorously into flight, and the staccato hammering and fierce cries of the pileated woodpecker echoed through the evening. By six thirty we had reached the spot where the platted twin ghost villages of Amador and Sebatana were once to be built—Nevers Dam.

At one time this considerable structure, built in 1890, was of great importance to the lumbermen of the valley. It is now gone and the St. Croix River again flows unobstructed past Wolf Creek. Only the icebreaker cribs and a few wooden pilings of the dam remain to tell us that here, for sixty-five years, was what is said to have been the largest pile-driven dam in the world. Today at Nevers Dam there is a noticeable drop in the river's flow when the water is low.

Although we were tired and hungry, we were now so close to Taylors Falls and the end of our journey that it seemed foolish to make camp. So we pushed on. At 7:00 P.M. we passed the once difficult but now imperceptible Dobeney Rapids. Today submerged, the rapids some eight miles above Taylors Falls are a favorite local fishing hole for smallmouthed bass.

Twilight descended, and beautiful, though temporary, thunderheads billowed pink and white to the south. Just as the sky was darkening we saw the lights of St. Croix Falls and the power dam in the distance, and we passed the former Lower Big Rock Rapids —an extensive area along both banks of the sluggish, impounded river. The large and widely scattered boulders were eerie, almost ghostly in the crepescule. These, too, must have been quite an impressive obstruction before the building of today's Northern States dam at St. Croix Falls.

As we ended our journey, the river was sparkling and beautiful by the shimmering light of a full moon and a star-filled sky. Regretfully we paddled in to shore at Taylors Falls convinced that of all the fair things in the Northwest, few can compare with the St. Croix and its magnificent valley. For a white-water canoe trip the St. Croix can certainly hold its own with the Midwest's best— Wisconsin's Flambeau River. Our weary bodies were also convinced that to make the trip in only four days was both too fast and too tiring. It would have been wiser, we decided, to camp somewhere between St. John's Landing and Taylors Falls, thereby breaking into two days the final, exhausting twelve hours of travel. As we ate our belated meal in a local restaurant, we resolved to return to the upper St. Croix to see it again in a more leisurely fashion.

For canoeists and boaters, the lower valley of the St. Croix starts at Interstate Park, a short distance below the hydroelectric dam and highway bridge linking the villages of Taylors Falls and St. Croix Falls. Here towering granite cliffs line the foamy, turbulent river below the rapids, and the water runs deep and fast. Ambitious *voyageurs,* venturing the entire St. Croix trip, will occasionally portage their canoes around the dam and through the streets of Taylors Falls. The most popular of all canoe trips, however, starts at Muller's dock below the village.

At the Dalles, begins a picturesque cruise quite different from our journey down the exciting and less settled upper river. The lower portion of the St. Croix displays another mood; it is a lazy, floating river of relaxed bass and walleye fishing, of delightful scenery, of sloughs and inviting backwaters which make the St. Croix one of the Midwest's most popular recreation streams. Along this stretch of the river—and on the Minnesota side especially—the canoeist is frequently in sight of summer cabins and larger houses, of carefully tended lawns, screen gazebos, and a boat, canoe, or pontoon at many landings. The lower St. Croix is smooth-going, an easy two-day trip down the twenty-eight miles to Stillwater, with no rapids, dams, or major obstructions. But the excursionist may well find other hazards in the form of sand bars, a channel that changes, and during weekends armies of speedboaters and ever-increasing numbers of daredevil water skiers.

When Mária and I traveled the lower St. Croix, we also picked a midweek day. It was late August when we started by canoe from Muller's Landing to make our first lap—the sixteen-mile-trip to Marine. Our first stop was at the Lower Dalles, about three miles below Taylors Falls and a short distance above the placid remnant of Franconia village. There, hemmed in on either side by precipitous basalt cliffs, is Rocky Island (officially Rock Island), a small, mid-channel, tree-clad outcrop of rocks and sand. This is perhaps the best-known and certainly the most used single camping spot on the entire river. But times have changed since my father, brothers, and I—often with friends or a cousin—would travel upriver from our cabin at Marine several times during the summer months to set up housekeeping for a week and make our home at this peaceful, rock-bound spot. Because of the abuse of camping privileges, the owners today will tolerate only daytime picnicking and swimming. Overnight camping, we learned, is forbidden.

Just below Rocky Island, on the Wisconsin side south of Cushing's Cliffs, begins Close's Slough, the first of many shaded side channels which, when there is water enough, make exploring the long, quiet stretches of this lower valley such a delightful pastime. It is a different world in these winding bypasses—disturbed only by the distant, withdrawn hum of outboards. Up and down the St. Croix the tranquil sloughs are special haunts for the stately great blue heron. Here they, too, can temporarily escape the inroads of civilization. On this trip, because of low water, Mária and I had to forgo these diversions and follow the main flow.

Close's Slough ends about a mile above the village of Osceola at the long, narrow Boom Island of early lumbering days. About the same distance below the bridge, which carries Highway 243 into that Wisconsin village, is the beginning of West Slough. This extensive backwater is two miles long, reaching south to Cedar Bend—the Standing Cedars of the 1825 Chippewa-Sioux boundary line. In the main channel, which follows the Wisconsin shore line, we passed first a high and prominent bluff—Eagle Rock—where once stood the popular Riverside Hotel, then to the old limekiln chimney, Buttermilk Falls, and finally past the gravelly expanse of Sweezie's Landing. At Cedar Bend in recent years extensive trout pools have been developed by the land's owners and the character of the region has greatly changed. A few paddle strokes downstream and we beached for our sandwich lunch among the mossy, cool shades of overhanging, tree-topped cliffs where rock formations and water trickling down soft strands of lichen give the location the only name it could possibly have— Harp Spring.

Just beyond the Soo Line railroad crossing, the river's channel has in recent years cut a new path. Because of indiscriminate farming, poor highway planning at Taylors Falls, and badly located gravel pits in the nearby Minnesota hills, the once deep waters at Cedar Bend are now filled with tons of gravel and rocks.

Over the years this dross has washed past the bridge where the river, narrowing into a trough, is confined and turbulent, and a short distance below it has piled up to form an immense bar which effectually dams the main channel and sends the river rushing through narrow McLeod's Slough. The St. Croix, therefore, instead of favoring the Wisconsin side, now hugs the spring-saturated Minnesota shore line. This fast-flowing, deep channel has somewhat widened McLeod's, an area with boulder-lined banks that are pleasantly reminiscent of portions of the wilder, more remote upper valley. When the two of us last saw it on that pleasant day in August, its darkened edges were solidly covered with masses of delicate, pale blue forget-me-nots and ruddy-stemmed gold-flowered jewelweed. After a delightful, but too short one-mile paddle past a number of rustic cabins tucked back in the fern-carpeted forest, we emerged again into the St. Croix's main channel where the river's banks at Otisville and Copas are also lined with larger, more elaborate dwellings. These continue along the Minnesota side well beyond the village landing at Marine.

Also at Otisville is Loghouse Landing, once an exciting destination for many a Sunday School outing in the days of paddle-wheel excursions. A short distance beyond the northern boundary of Minnesota's William O'Brien State Park, the river traveler may head toward the Wisconsin shore and seek the solitude of Towhead Slough. On this trip, however, Mária and I chose to follow the main channel, and were almost immediately at a mile-and-a-half long island which is also a part of the state park. Recently named Greenberg Island, local residents insist on their right to resist change and continue to refer to it as Berkey or Pine Island, as they have for the past hundred years. To the right is Pine Slough which runs past low cliffs to the main picnic grounds of O'Brien Park, its new swimming pool, fishing ponds, and small marina.

Immediately below, and away from the busy park area, we suddenly stopped paddling. In the still early evening air we could hear what sounded like the soft, unintelligible chattering of small children before they learn to talk. A quick glance along the swampy shore line revealed a family of beaver at play. But in less than three seconds we were spotted. Slapping their broad, flat tails on the water's surface as a warning signal, they quickly dove out of sight and into the safety of their nearby house.

Along Pine Slough are also evergreen-clad sandstone cliffs, the Iron Spring, and two rustic cabins. Back in the hills is the old farm now operated by my contemporary, Franklin Bruette, a grandson of the original settler. This is the land which instilled in me a childhood love of the St. Croix and which continues to draw my wife and me from the hurly-burly of everyday city apartment living. We rested for the night in one of the cabins there before continuing our downriver journey.

In waning summertime the islands of this lower valley are asplash with the blaze of the cardinal flower or red lobelia. When Mária and I left our boat landing early on the following morning, we marveled at the showiness of these late wild blossoms, so unequaled is the beauty of their spiked pillars of flame which burst forth among waving grass blades or reflect in the water as they stand erect amid the rocks and boulders of the river's edge.

Out into the main channel, after rounding the tip of Berkey Island, we were on our way down the remaining twelve miles to Stillwater. Several fishermen, with cane poles, were lazily waiting for a strike from the deep pools in this wide stretch of river. We passed the old Marine ferry landing where for exactly ninety-eight years traffic flowed between Marine and the Wisconsin farmlands. Since 1954, however, the ferry has no longer operated and the spot now offers refreshments, gas, and canoe rentals. Hidden behind a small island just to the south are the ruined remnants of the third successor (1873) to Minnesota's first commercial sawmill, and here the village landing, now also a put-in spot for boats, leads uphill a block to the historic, sleepy settlement of Marine.

From this point, the river traveler has a choice of several routes. Directly across from the Marine Landing is the entrance to Deadman's Slough which hugs the Wisconsin shore line into Rice Lake and then, via any of several meandering exits of the Apple River,

returns again to the main stream. There is also the nominal channel (never used in times of low water) and paralleling these two,
on the Minnesota side, flows Page's Slough. From the beginning
of the valley's story this has been the traditional water highway
for river traffic and we followed it past numerous summer cabins
and winter residences to the handsome homestead at Arcola where
crotchety Martin Mower ruled the river and built his steamboat.

Beyond the long, lacy span of the Soo Line high bridge at
Arcola, river traffic became heavier since it was Friday afternoon
and the beginning of a busy weekend. To avoid the wash from
speedboats, we headed toward the Wisconsin shore line and at
the piers of the old railroad bridge we entered the lower end of
Kelly Slough at Sam Harriman's once bustling Somerset landing.
From here to Stillwater the main channel was not for us. We explored, instead, the sylvan, shaded wonders of Little Venice
Canal—one of the many catfish trails of the lower river—and
rested for a while under the sheer sandstone cliffs around the
Twin Springs. Out of sight, on the other side of numerous midstream islands, the main flow of the river passes the St. Croix
boomsite park and its several long, narrow islands which were of
such importance for the collecting and holding of logs during the
heyday of lumbering. These are the "drowned lands" of the early
explorers and here the river begins to widen to form Lake St.
Croix.

A quarter of a mile below the steep lift leading to the bluff-top
home of our friends, the Wallace Thextons, we cut across river to
Wolf's marina, past Dutch Town in Stillwater, and on to Muller's
boat landing where we returned our rented canoe. We had come
to the end of our two-day floating trip down the lower valley of
the St. Croix. From here the river quickly widens to the beautiful
expanse of lake which, with its Catfish Bar and estuary at the
mouth of the Kinnickinnic River, has often been compared with
the Hudson and Rhine rivers. This Lake St. Croix is frequently the
destination of boaters seeking uncommercialized, clean, and
barge-free waters for numerous "sail aways" from nearby harbors
along the Minnesota and Mississippi rivers. It is a lake for sail-
boats and small craft, too, and for those not owning a boat, a trip

on the diminutive *Miss Prescott* which harbors at that village, is a perfect climax to anyone's personal exploration of the evanescent St. Croix. And may it ever remain thus.

Wherever an American river runs, there are always those who love it. Over the years, the St. Croix River has especially attracted the proprietary affection and unswerving loyalty of all who have come under its influence. In the late 1920s Ruth Lusk Ramsey summed up her feelings about the St. Croix acres she and her doctor husband shared at Copas—and she spoke for all of us:

> I bring you beauty from the river,
> Shadowy hills in a rising mist,
> Pine trees standing high
> And a river flowing, flowing,
> Flows forever by.
>
> I bring you beauty from the river
> Where leaves a golden carpet lie.
> There are no smoky buildings here
> To shut away the morning sky—
> Just shadowy hills in a rising mist
> And pine trees standing high.

A Word of Thanks

For their assistance and constant vigilance I wish to thank my colleagues on the staff of the Minnesota Historical Society: the late Evan A. Hart, whose untimely death took from us a talented historian and illustrator; Russell W. Fridley, director; Lucile M. Kane, Mrs. Rhoda R. Gilman, and Bertha L. Heilbron who have alerted me to many choice items; my secretary Mrs. Margaret E. Nelson (how valiantly she has struggled to decipher the hen tracks I make when putting pen to paper!). But my greatest indebtedness goes to Mrs. June Drenning Holmquist who abetted and guided me through the difficult years of organization and writing. Her suggested alterations and corrections did much to shape the finished product. Grateful thanks also go to editors Carl Carmer and Jean Crawford of Holt, Rinehart and Winston. Whatever faults now remain can only be blamed on the author.

I have also benefited from the helpfulness of Robert C. Toole, Hanover College, Franklin, Indiana; of Alice E. Smith, Madison, Wisconsin; of Donald L. Empson and my brother Montfort Dunn of Marine on St. Croix and of Thomas Bonde of Arcola for reading all or parts of the manuscript and making valued suggestions. Many residents both in and out of the valley also contributed to the original research, and most are mentioned in the book; but I want to signal out Ray Orner of Solon Springs, Roy E. Strand and Frank McDonald of Marine, E. L. Roney and Robert A. Uppgren of Stillwater, and Donald C. Holmquist of St. Paul, who led me down trails I might otherwise have missed.

Most of all, however, I owe an abiding debt to my wife Mária, for without her encouragement, patience, forbearance, and levelheaded criticism (all attributes of her Luxembourg heritage) I would never have survived this fifteen-year task.

St. Croix Sources

THE FOLLOWING can no more be considered a complete bibliography of the St. Croix River than this book pretends to be a work of scholarship. Call this chapter, rather, a guidepost to reading. These are the more important sources culled from many hundreds of books, pamphlets, articles, newspapers, and manuscripts read and carefully noted over the past fifteen years. It is hoped that such an informal listing will lead the reader to dig more deeply into the fascinating history of this valley. There is much yet to tell.

BOOKS

Only one book has been written about the St. Croix River which encompasses the entire valley. And fortunately it is a useful one. *Fifty Years in the Northwest,* by the Taylors Falls lumberman William H. C. Folsom, was published in 1888 and is the keystone for any collection of books about the valley. The second most helpful volume which also covers both sides of the St. Croix (but only the lower river counties) is *History of Washington County and the St. Croix Valley* edited in 1881 by George E. Warner and Charles M. Foote. This is frequently and erroneously attributed to the authorship of the Reverend Edward D. Neill. The third compilation, in two volumes, was edited in 1909 by Augustus B. Easton, Stillwater newspaper publisher. The counties included in his *History of the St. Croix Valley* go as far north as Burnett County, Wisconsin.

These are the three secondary sources which give the essential facts concerning the St. Croix up to their dates of publication, although they frequently err in the details of that history. No adequate books have yet been written about the neglected northwestern Wisconsin counties, so there is need for good reference material on Douglas, Burnett, Washburn, and Sawyer counties. The *History of Northern Wisconsin* (1881) is hardly adequate.

One more publication of general valley interest should be mentioned. Albert M. Marshall, former Wisconsin journalist, now of Red Wing, Minnesota, has authored the most useful of all histories concerning the source area of the St. Croix. His thorough, well-written story called *Brule Country* is an indispensable volume, all the more useful because of its recent publication—1954. Also recommended is a pamphlet *The Brule River of Wisconsin* (1956) by Leigh P. Jerrard. The maps are especially good.

Of all the explorers who journeyed up the valley, the only ones to leave extended accounts of a trip were those on the Schoolcraft expedition of 1832. The 1834 first edition of Schoolcraft's own *Narrative of an Expedition* is useful for the map made by Lieutenant James Allen and published as a part of the chapters on the "St. Croix and Burntwood Rivers." Far better for today's reader interested in this Minnesota and Wisconsin region, however, is the 1958 edition published by the Michigan State University Press and extremely well edited and annotated by Philip P. Mason. Entitled *Schoolcraft's Expedition to Lake Itasca* it contains not only the St. Croix journal mentioned above (without the map), but also reprints the scarce and fascinating Allen diary first published as a government document. In this modern edition are also pertinent materials written by the Reverend William T. Boutwell and Dr. Douglass Houghton.

As for Du Luth, Le Sueur, Carver, and other explorers into the valley, these and many additional references to the river's history can easily be located through the text and footnotes of the one standard history, William Watts Folwell's *A History of Minnesota*. The first two volumes, which should never be out of reach, have been revised and reprinted by the Minnesota Historical Society (1956 and 1961). There is little need to refer to the last two volumes of the set. Theodore C. Blegen's excellent *Minnesota, A History of the State* (1963) should also be constantly within reach, and its bibliography, "For Further Reading," must not be neglected by any reader seeking background material.

Two specialized books of great usefulness have been written by Louise Phelps Kellogg: *The French Régime in Wisconsin and the Northwest* (1925) and *The British Régime in Wisconsin and the Northwest* (1935). The three fur traders' accounts of life along the upper river in Wisconsin have all been published. George Nelson's *A*

Winter in the St. Croix Valley, edited by Richard Bardon and Grace Lee Nute, was issued in 1948 by the Minnesota Historical Society. The Michel Curot story appears in the State Historical Society of Wisconsin, *Collections* (vol. 20, 1911), and Charles M. Gates edited the Thomas Connor diary in *Five Fur Traders of the Northwest*, (1933), a book republished in 1965 by the Minnesota Historical Society.

The first tourist-travelers to ascend and/or descend the St. Croix and set down entertaining accounts of their Midwestern experiences were Ephraim S. Seymour in his *Sketches of Minnesota* (1850), Edward Sullivan, *Rambles and Scrambles in North and South America* (1852), and Mrs. Elizabeth F. Ellet in *Summer Rambles in the West* (1853). Like Schoolcraft and Allen, they include lengthy, revealing chapters about the St. Croix.

There are also three scarce publications, not of great research value but much sought after by those who collect St. Croixana. The first is a little forty-six page illustrated hard-cover booklet called *Captain Jolly on the Picturesque St. Croix*. It was written by William H. Dunne and printed in St. Paul in 1880. Fortunately for those unable to secure a copy of the first edition, it was reprinted in 1953 by the St. Croix County Historical Society, Hudson, under the editorship of local newspaper publisher Willis H. Miller who has done so much to further the cause of history in the valley. The second collector's item, a large pictorial volume issued at Neenah, Wisconsin, in 1888, is entitled *The Valley of the St. Croix. Picturesque and Descriptive*. It was first sold in parts, by subscription only, and later released in attractive bound form. By far the best early map of the entire valley was done in the 1870s by Ezekiel Warren McClure, Stillwater surveyor, land agent, and explorer. Its detail of tributary streams, lumbering dams, and rapids is unusually accurate and complete. This map is the scarcest of the three items.

Finally, several other volumes stand in the front rank, and will continue to be used by anyone interested in Midwestern history. Two of these books, already classics in their fields, are *History of the White Pine Industry in Minnesota*, by Agnes M. Larson, recently retired from the faculty at St. Olaf College, Northfield, and Merrill E. Jarchow's very fine study on agriculture in Minnesota to 1885, *The Earth Brought Forth*. Both were published in 1949. Also useful are *Log Transportation in the Lake States Lumber Industry* (1953), by William G. Rector, and *From Canoe to Steel Barge in the Upper Mississippi* (1934), by Mildred L. Hartsough.

PAMPHLETS AND ARTICLES

Numerous articles concerning one phase or another of St. Croix Valley history have been printed over the years in *Minnesota History* and *Wisconsin Magazine of History* as well as in the multi-volumed *Collections* of both state societies. Only a few can be given special mention. A felicitous introduction to the newspapers and manuscripts of the region is "Some Sources for St. Croix Valley History." This entertaining essay written by the eminent Minnesota historian Theodore C. Blegen can be found in *Minnesota History* for December, 1936. The same magazine for June, 1937, and March, 1950, contains outstanding articles on lumbering.

In the *Collections* of the Minnesota Historical Society are two especially useful pieces: "History of Lumbering in the St. Croix Valley, with Biographic Sketches" by William H. C. Folsom (vol. 9, 1901) and "Lumbering and Steamboating on the St. Croix River" by Edward W. Durant (vol. 10, pt. 2, 1905). These were later issued as separates. Edward D. Neill's "The Beginning of Organized Society in the Saint Croix Valley, Minnesota" is a pamphlet published in 1890 as number three of the *Macalester College Contributions*. Perhaps the most valuable single booklet on the Swedish settlements along the St. Croix is Robert Gronberger's *Svenskarne i St. Croix-dalen, Minnesota* published in Minneapolis in 1879. A translation of the "Historical Account of the Swedish Settlement Marine in Washington County, Minnesota" later appeared in the 1924-25 *Year-Book* of the Swedish Historical Society of America. Also in the December, 1936, issue of *Minnesota History* is George M. Stephenson's "Sidelights on the History of the Swedes in the St. Croix Valley."

Swedish novelist Vilhelm Moberg has written a popular trilogy on the migration of his people into the St. Croix Valley. The setting for the last two volumes, *Unto a Good Land* (1954), and *Last Letter Home* (1961), is in the area of the Chisago chain of lakes—the *Kitchisasega sagaigan*, large and lovely inland lake.

The chronological story of the settlement which grew up around the St. Croix Valley's first operational sawmill is told in the 1963 booklet, *Marine Mills, Lumber Village: 1838-1888*, by James Taylor Dunn. Other recent pamphlets about river villages are: *This was Hudson* (1955), edited by Willis H. Miller; *Hudson in the Early Days* (revised edition, 1963), by Genevieve Cline Day; *Triple Centennial Jubilee Somerset, Wisconsin* (1956), by the Reverend John T. Rivard; *The History of Franconia* (1958), by Judith J. Wahlquist; *Pioneer Traces in and Near Chisago Lakes Area* (revised edition, 1962), by Theodore A. Norelius. Some vary in degrees of accuracy, but all are useful additions to the local story. Needed are similar publications for the river towns of Prescott, Stillwater, Osceola, St. Croix and Taylors Falls, Danbury, and Solon Springs, as well as for other valley settlements like River Falls, Pine City, Grantsburg, Spooner, etc.

NEWSPAPERS

Because of the dearth of published histories about the St. Croix Valley, great use has to be made of all available primary sources. Newspapers, which furnish the only complete history of a man's generation that can be obtained, must therefore be relied upon for that large segment of the river's story nowhere else recorded. These and manuscript diaries and letters are the many and varied treasures without which it would be impossible to reconstruct the diverse activities of the valley. All the newspapers of Taylors Falls, St. Croix Falls, Osceola, Marine Mills, Stillwater, Hudson, and Prescott must be carefully gleaned, as well as selected papers published in such localities as Prairie du Chien, Sandstone, St. Paul, St. Anthony (which later became Minneapolis), etc. In the research work on this book the Osceola and Hudson papers were read at the publishers' offices; the Prairie du Chien weekly was consulted at the State Historical Society of Wisconsin; the remaining are in the collection of the Minnesota Historical Society. Of special value is the lengthy series from the *Saturday Evening Post* (Burlington, Iowa) on "Steamboats and Steamboatmen of the Upper Mississippi" (1913-1919), by George B. Merrick. This amazing compilation has recently been made available as a micropublication of the Minnesota Historical Society.

MANUSCRIPTS

The manuscripts studied must also bulk large. The Henry H. Sibley papers, the Edmund F. Ely diaries (typescript), the Lawrence Taliaferro journals, and the Nicollet journal (microfilm) are all-important in telling the early story of the valley. There are also the extensive and unusually fine William H. C. Folsom papers and the account books spanning many years of the Marine lumbering concern and its successors. The Sam Bloomer letters, the Ignatius Donnelly and Levi W. Stratton papers, the Henry M. Nicols diaries, the Caleb Cushing collection (microfilm), the Hersey, Staples and Company papers are only a few of the many that are extremely useful. All these and numerous other miscellaneous manuscripts are housed in the Manuscripts Division, Minnesota Historical Society. The original Ely diaries are owned by the St. Louis County Historical Society, Duluth, and the Nicollet and Cushing manuscripts are at the Library of Congress, Washington. Several letters from the private collection of Floyd E. Risvold, Minneapolis, also proved useful.

The Minnesota State Archives own the Land Office Records, the Governors' Papers, and the Territorial and State Prison Record Books. The State Historical Society of Wisconsin holds a number of useful items including material on Caleb Cushing and his lawsuits with William S. Hungerford. But the greatest cache of documents on that supercomplicated case is in the vaults of the Rock County Courthouse, Janesville, Wisconsin, and the Crawford County Courthouse at Prairie du Chien. Files number 150, 151, and 152 at Janesville are especially productive of an amazing amount of hitherto unused information concerning the history of St. Croix Falls. A master's thesis written at the University of Wisconsin by Mrs. Sara Hughes (borrowed from Alice E. Smith of Madison) is a good guidepost in telling the story of that hexed village. The files of the Washington County courthouse, Stillwater, also house pertinent valley material including a great deal on the history of Osceola; Stillwater material is at the Public Library and the Washington County Historical Society.

Three useful collections at present in the author's possession are the Gold T. Curtis correspondence, legal manuscripts, notebooks, and ledgers (1853-1862), the Margaret Miller diary (1854), and the illustrated river diaries kept from 1914 through 1936 by the author's father, John W. G. Dunn.

Index

299

Haskell, Joseph, 54
Hastings (Minn.), 30, 195
Hay Lake, 161
Hayward (Wis.), 21, 24, 25, 106
Hazzard, George H., 207
Healers, 245
Health, 37, 40, 200–204
Heilbron, Bertha L., viii
Hennepin, Father Louis, 27, 29
Hersey, Staples and Co., 103, 104, 107
Heywood, Joseph L., 127
Hiebert, Gareth, 236
Highland Mary, steamboat, 175
Hinckley (Minn.), 207
Hoaxes, 134, 259
Holbrook, Stewart H., 106
Holcombe, William, 61, 80, 153, 155.
Hole-in-the-Day (elder), Chippewa chief, 14
Hole-in-theDay (younger), Chippewa chief, 19
Holidays, 139; Fourth of July, 61, 133, 139–141, 144
Holmes, Joe, 24
Holmquist, Donald C., xiii, 264–284
Holmquist, June D., 264
Homestead Act of *1862*, 57
Hone, David, 69, 70
Hone, Mrs. David, 70, 71
Hough, Donald, 240
Houghton, Dr. Douglass, 37–40
Houlton (Wis.), 106, 107
Houston, Lieut. John P., 230
Hoyt, Dr. Otis, 204
Hubbell, Judge Levi, 87, 89, 91
Hubbell, Lucius F., 124
Hudson (Wis.), 51, 53, 58, 72, 132, 198, 201, 211; social life, 134, 136, 138, 141, 143, 181, 204, 246; rivalry, 145–150, 176; mail service, 151, 152, 154, 155, 158
Hudson Literary Society, 131
Hultgren, Gustaf P., xii
Humboldt, steamboat, 175
Humphries, Ray, viii
Hungerford, William S., 80–94, 98
Hunting, 211–213
Hutchinson family, 129, 130

ICEBOATS, 221–226
Ida Fulton, steamboat, 182
Immigration, 161–170, 189, 192, 218
Imperial, steamboat, 147
Indian agents. *See* Taliaferro, Schoolcraft
Indians, living conditions, viii, xiv, 22, 24; attitude toward, viii, 17, 20–22, 25, 30, 49; prehistoric, 11; mode of warfare, 16; effect of liquor on, 17, 33, 47; rehabilitation of, 22–25. *See also* Annuities, Chippewa, Fox, Sioux, Treaties
Interstate Park, xii, xiii, 98, 182, 207, 209, 285
Irish, John, 222
Itasca, steamboat, 140
Izatys, *see* Kathio

JACKMAN, HENRY A., 122
Jackman, Pease, 251
Jackson, Mitchell Y., 194
James Means, steamboat, 179
James Raymond, showboat, 134
Jenks, Capt. Austin T., 148
Jeremy, John, 237–240
Jeremy, John, Jr., 239–241
Johnson, Abraham, 160
Johnston, George, 37
Jourdain, Peter, 260
Judd, Albert H., 52, 69, 70, 73
Judd, Elizur, 69
Judd, George B., 52, 69, 72, 73, 101
Judd, Lewis S., 69, 70, 73
Judd, Samuel B., 73, 112
Judd, Walker and Co., 73, 101, 172, 187–189. *See also* Walker, Judd & Veazie

KABAMAPPA (Wetmouth), Chippewa chief, 42, 45, 54, 268
Kanabec County (Minn.), 167
Kate Cassel, steamboat, 132
Kathio (Izatys), Sioux village, 11, 26
Keep, Judge John M., 91
Kent, Jack, 225
Kent, William, 72, 101
Kettle River, 6, 9, 33, 82, 207, 208,